~ A ~
CATHOLIC PRIEST
MEETS
SAI BABA

Don Mario Mazzoleni

~

Translated by Christian Moevs

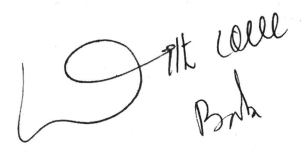

LEELA **INC.**
PRESS
A Non-Profit Corporation
Faber, VA

English edition first published in 1994 by
Leela Press Inc.
4026 River Road
Faber, Virginia 22938
Ph: (804) 361-1132 Fax: (804) 361-9199 email: jscher@leelapress.com

Translated from the Italian by Christian Moevs
Un Sacerdote Incontra Sai Baba by Don Mario Mazzoleni
© 1991 Armenia Editore, Milan, Italy

English Edition, First Printing, 1994
© 1993 *Leela Press Inc.*
Third printing, November, 1999

Library of Congress Catalog No. 93-086227
A Catholic Priest Meets Sai Baba

Cover Photo: Kekie Mistry

ISBN 0-9629835-1-9

Typeset in 11 point Times Roman

To my Mother,
the Catholic Church,
because I continue to love her
despite the misunderstandings,
and in order that she might not be jealous
of a Spouse
such as Sathya - the Truth -
to Whom no one can ever deny
the possibility
of becoming flesh
for the Eternal Wedding
of whoever falls in love with It.

TABLE OF CONTENTS

Foreword

Part I: A Journey in Search of God

Chapters:

Part II: The Teachings of Sai Baba

Chapters:

Part III: Coming to Sai Baba

Chapters:

Special Note: *Almost all the biblical quotations come from the Jerusalem Bible: the few that do not come from the New American Bible.*

Foreword

Many of my friends were alarmed when they learned of my intention to write a book about Sai Baba. They were aware of my convictions about this Being, who is human only in body. With brotherly concern, they variously advised, begged, or beseeched me to publish it under a pseudonym, imagining the unhappy consequences I might encounter from the ecclesiastical hierarchy.

I asked myself what I should have to fear in saying what my own eyes have seen. Why should I be afraid to make known what this poor heart of mine experiences before an extraordinary presence? Should I feel guilty for what I have discovered during these years, and be afraid to announce it? Certainly not! On the contrary, I feel quite fortunate. *Necessitas enim mihi incumbit*: it is not possible to resist the impulse of Truth, and woe to me if I should remain silent!

I write this book dedicating it above all to the Church precisely because I could not let pass, without pointing it out to Her who is my Mother, a piece of news which can no longer remain unknown, hidden by indifference, fear, or by general confusion. This work is an undertaking which has made use of me, I would say, only as hired manual labor: I consider its contents the work of Another. It has been written above all for my bishop, the Pope; and then for all my fellow brethren, for my superiors, and for all those who through the centuries try to work in the service of, and in the search for, Truth.

Contrary to what those friends of mine fear, I hope - and my heart is certain of it - that these reflections will sound like a call and a warning for a great spiritual re-awakening.

This era - the era of Sathya, the era of Truth - is, in my opinion, a unique moment, which will change the historical and religious order of nations. Certainly the most extraordinary characteristic of this study, in an age in which there is so much talk about sects and religious factions, is that in all the things I have discovered in these years, I have found nothing which would prompt an aversion to our religion, nothing which would obstruct our faith. On the contrary! Everything I have meditated on has brought me that much closer to the mysteries I had been celebrating, often without knowing them thoroughly. And it is precisely to Sathya Sai Baba that I owe the renewal of my life as a priest!

In short, my hope is this: that the same thing might happen for many of my fellow brethren, whom I have found tired, strained, and disappointed.

I am grateful to all those who have offered me precious suggestions, in particular to Professor Pierantonio Di Coste, who encouraged and supported the drafting of this book.

I place this book at the Feet of Him who inspired it -- the Only-begotten Son of yesterday, of today, and of always, the immutable Truth -- in the hope that this fruit which He alone has the right to gather will be pleasing to Him and that He will accept it as an offering for His greater glory.

November 23, 1990   Don Mario Mazzoleni

"Every Avatar is an amazing phenomenon, but it is also amazing not to recognize Him."

Sai Baba

Part I: A Journey in Search of God

CHAPTER ONE

The Search Begins

*The desire for Wisdom
leads to the Kingdom.*

Wisdom 6.20

When I began writing this book, I had two ideas that were fixed in my head. The first was that anyone who writes is like an expectant mother: that writing requires extreme concentration, many sacrifices, almost all of one's energy and a great desire to bring the creation into the light. The process is always accompanied by the anxiety for the health and wholeness of the offspring, as well as an excessive attachment to it once it is born.

It's not that I didn't like the idea of writing, but I saw it as a threat to my humility and an obstacle to the destruction of my ego, both basic virtues for my spiritual development. My motives for writing required that I accept the idea that this was a mission for the good of humanity. This thought seemed like the subtly diabolical and alluring little voice of the serpent of Eden, dragging me to consume the forbidden fruit. The ambition to consider oneself useful to the human race is even stronger than the instinct of self-preservation.

The second idea, which I have not completely overcome, is that everything that anyone wants to say has already been said again and again. Over the millennia, rivers of words have been spoken, and since the invention of the printing press, reams of pages have been written. This conviction grows more solid in me every time I enter a bookstore, and discover that for every question, even the most banal, someone has laid out a treatise. This had a considerable part in inhibiting my inspiration and in reinforcing the laziness which kept me from dedicating myself to a work of this kind.

Although this book does not have autobiographical intentions, I shall have to touch on certain facts of my life. My sole purpose is to shed more light on the origins of the spiritual path, its impulses and obstacles. However, if I were beginning an autobiography, I would start out by saying that I began to live when I adopted the attitude of a seeker. I consider my life before then like the life of a dead man, or, if you think the image is too extreme, like the life of someone who is terminally ill with no hope of a cure.

It might seem strange to you that a priest should talk like this. You are used to seeing priests who seem so full of self-assurance that they inspire awe and timidity in you. Anyone who has come to believe that we have the power "to loose and bind" will be astonished to hear that a priest has put himself on a path of spiritual searching. "Poor soul!," you might say, "he compares part of his priestly life to that of a dying man."

Why on earth would a priest, who has been taught so many well-packaged and inviolable truths, need to be a seeker? Are there any existential questions which a priest has not answered? Can there still be problems awaiting solutions for a man charged with the exalted mission of guiding the human conscience? And - you might ask - what does a man of the church, who should already have perfected his education and knowledge, still need to investigate? You might conclude that if such a priest exists, he does not deserve to be included in the ranks of the people who through the centuries have been responsible for spiritual direction. If he is blind himself, how can he lead other blind people without bringing them to ruin?

Well, then, yes! I will say it again, without qualification. I was truly born when I stepped across the hallowed threshold of my interior laboratory. Here I began to conduct experiments, to lift the phials of absolute principles, to pour out the rigid schemes of a static education, the solemn and inaccessible alembics of a theology which has become a mere intellectual exercise.

In nature, everything undergoes change, and our reason is part of nature. The fundamental truths might not change, but the human approach to these truths does, and this amounts to admitting that it is necessary to review and correct the way sacred truths have been formulated in the past. The level of consciousness of a people gradually expands, and a formulation which seemed right centuries ago today appears honestly outdated. It is not the underlying truth which goes out of date, but the way in which it is expressed. The clothes change, but not the body dressed in them.

But why on earth did a young priest feel he had to put himself on the path of spiritual inquiry after just ten years of pastoral work?

To show you the reason for this change of course, I shall have to tell you some personal facts. Finally, for once, you will play the role of the one on the other side of the grate, hearing a priest say his confession!

In 1972, I was convinced that in order to exercise my ministry with greater wisdom, I had to have a specialization in theological studies. I persistently petitioned my bishop for permission to establish myself in Rome for a year or two. In Rome there was an academy which met my needs perfectly (it still exists today), where I could gain competence in the subject of Moral Theology. The bishop, Monsignor Clemente Gaddi, amiably consented to my wishes. We were talking about two or three years, and then I would return to my own diocese, Bergamo, to take up my activity again with new energy and new cultural tools.

But He who already was closely watching over everything I did changed my plans. Instead of three years, it took four. After receiving the certificate, I took my doctorate, and in the meantime the bond that had developed between me and the capital helped to keep me in that city indefinitely. Cardinal Ugo Poletti, who was then Vicar of the Diocese of Rome, made me the tempting proposition that I be incardinated[1] in the Diocese of the Eternal City and remain as associate pastor in the parish where I was performing my pastoral service, without income[2] but in exchange for room and board. In the

---

[1] A term of ecclesiastical jurisdiction which indicates that a priest becomes affiliated with a diocese.

[2] A diocesan (also called "secular") priest has to manage his own affairs economically, while "religious" priests, those who belong to a particular congregation or live in a monastery, are supported by that institution itself. At that time, the new agreement between the Holy See and the Italian State, through which 0.8% of the gross tax revenue paid by citizens is in part transferred to the support of the Church, had not been stipulated; and in any case, especially at that time the responsibility for his sustenance rested entirely on the priest himself or on the parish in which he performed his religious and pastoral service.

meantime, on the diocesan level I would work in the field of mass media applied to religious instruction.

I saw laid out before me a series of activities that would fill and fulfill my life. At that time, I did not yet know what "renunciation of the fruits of action" meant, even though I knew and preached the common evangelic phrase that "we are all unnecessary servants." And so everything that promised movement and action fit perfectly with the aspirations of that young priest who fell out of the Val Brembana into the lap of Rome, at the explosive age of 27.

Before long, the wind blew favorably and everything was proceeding under full sail: I was contributing to a broadcast of the Vatican Radio, I was giving lectures on the use of audiovisual aids in pastoral work, I was in touch with authorities of the Italian national radio and television system, I was writing articles, and I had easy access to high-placed persons in the ecclesiastical world. The benevolence toward me of certain eminent prelates seemed like an encouragement to continue on that active path. Some friends and colleagues predicted a brilliant career.

When I would go home for a few days of vacation, the people of my town would look at me with a certain admiration, and the priests would turn to me for information on trends in the Vatican and to find out details on the lives and thoughts of bishops and cardinals. They thought that just because I happened to be situated at the center of Christianity, I was acquainted with every rumor whispered in the corridors of the Vatican palaces.

All this greatly alleviated the suffering my parents went through for having been separated from me. A mother especially, if she has a son who is a priest, is moved to compassion by the life of emotional solitude to which he has devoted himself, and does not consider him "settled" until she sees him at the height of his career. One of my mother's friends, who was a bit of a sorceress, even put the amusing idea in her head that one day I would become Pope! And Mom, poor soul, would swell a little with pride when she could tell people, with the exaggeration typical of maternal love, that her son "was in the Vatican."

I thought that in this way I had quieted my conscience; indeed, I thought I was giving my all. In truth, I was out for myself in everything I did, but I didn't realize it. Those around me, sharing my illusion, either applauded my deeds or were jealous of them. Both responses amounted to confirming, both in my eyes and theirs, the validity of my choices.

Something, however, left me dissatisfied. At first it was something very indefinite, evanescent as a phantom that I couldn't lay my hands on. Then my analysis started gradually unravelling the skein. Even though there wasn't a soul around who could help me understand the problem or who would say to me bluntly, "Look, you're getting everything wrong, because you're aiming only at your own rewards," I knew, because of my own dissatisfaction, that I had to make a complete revision of my life. I was moved to reflect by the dedication that a doctor friend of mine penned on the first page of a book he was giving me: "To my dearest Don Mario, so that he may be ever more *Don*[3], and ever less *Mario*."

For many, dissatisfaction is surely the first teacher on the spiritual path. If one is attentive to its messages, it reveals the diagnosis of one's own mental state, and points the way toward therapeutic growth. Here it was a matter of my becoming conscious of my disillusionment and analyzing what caused it. This therapy couldn't happen if I persisted in examining my conscience only superficially, which is what I always had done in the past. In the course of the spiritual exercises that I would do every year at a retreat, the situation would come brutally to the surface again, and it was like coming upon a corpse in an advanced stage of putrefaction. The course of exercises would always come to a halt at the moment when it became necessary to find some remedy for that pitiful discovery. The silence of that week always guaranteed me excellent results as a part-time contemplative monk, because the corpse did not pollute the waters of my consciousness; still, it was necessary to get rid of that encumbrance. Unfortunately, my sudden re-entry into activity had the power to cancel any trace of that discovery. In fact, I saw activity with relief as the remedy for that disillusionment. In Western culture, we are accustomed to rejecting inaction as an ignoble excuse to avoid one's responsibilities. However, it is necessary to be still on occasion, or at least once in a lifetime, if you want to find yourself. A pause

---

[3]In Italy *don* is a title of respect given to priests [Translator's note].

reveals to us all the filth that has accumulated under the rug over the years.

To flee pain and pursue pleasure is part of the human instinct. Even when we do not pursue pleasure directly, either because of an ethic which imposes abstention on us or through our own choice, we still want to escape pain at any cost. To achieve this end, anything will do, and work activity presents an effective escape from self-analysis, a noble and motivated distraction. And yet, what makes us different from the busy beaver or the industrious bees is the fact that we can be conscious of this feeling: I am unhappy, but I don't know why. Work, when it is embraced as a lifesaver against the hoard of problems that want to surface in our consciousness, becomes a perverse remedy that transforms us from humans into robots.

Many human beings lead a superficial way of life. This is due to their fear of discovering who they are. I, too, in the fear of seeing myself in the mirror, would dive back into the vortex of an activity whose senselessness was becoming more and more apparent to me.

But the worst enemy of someone who is about to set foot on the path of inquiry is presuming to have understood the problem and conceptualizing it in simplistic terms. I would confide my mood to some other priest, but the answer was always: "Don't be complicated. These are fancies which pass through the mind. Don't you have some hobby? Amuse yourself a little and you're bound to recover your serenity." At times, even my reading helped compound the problem by stuffing my mind with concepts and ideas. Instead, there was only one thing to do: to empty my mind, to still the surface of the water, in order to see reflected in it without tremors the image of the sunlight...

But instead, if I didn't stir up the waters myself when they were about to grow calm, there was always some pious soul who thought that by stirring them up he was doing me a charitable service. The incipient awareness which was pushing me to demand an answer would always be inhibited by advice, by activity, and by mental laziness. And thus I drowned my questions in my irresponsibility.

Today I understand how fundamental it is to "love oneself." I am not talking about what most of humanity already knows how to do, but I mean to emphasize that someone who does not pay attention to his own life in order to improve it cannot say that he loves himself, nor will he be in a position to love others. In fact, how can one love one's neighbor as oneself if one doesn't know oneself well enough to love oneself? This limitation, already in itself quite sad in any person, is even sadder in someone who has dedicated his whole existence to the divine mysteries.

In that particular moment of my life, the first stage of an irreversible process was taking place, which would reach its culmination in the experience which induced me to write this book.

I knew that in order to have the exceptional and the revolutionary erupt in our inner life, the first step was to invoke it, as Solomon advises:

And so I prayed, and understanding was given to me;
I entreated, and the spirit of wisdom came to me.

Wisdom 7.7

Then came one of those days when it seems that the moment for great decisions has arrived. I went to my confessor, Father Henry, a dear Jesuit, who has a demeanor that is both imposing and sweet. He is full of the love of God, revolutionary but, at the same time, obedient to the dictates of Holy Mother Church. Even though I had not been going to him long, he knew my life well in every detail because with my spiritual directors I have always tried to be like an open book. One of the most frequently recurring sentences which he would repeat to me and which had become at that point a personal slogan of his was: "If you want to change, hurry up, because you'll only be able to do it before you're 35. After that, it will no longer be possible for you."

I don't know if this principle is really to be understood in such a peremptory manner, but I certainly understood it that way, because I believed intensely in the truth of that assertion. He had been repeating that refrain to me for some time, and now that I was about to turn 35, I felt the water at my throat. On the one hand, I desperately wanted something to change in my life; on the other hand, I didn't know where to begin.

"Father," I said to him that day, "today I am particularly distressed. I don't see a way out. I feel like I've arrived at a terminal in the suburbs where there are no connecting buses."

And he said: "If you want to turn your life upside down, immerse yourself in the love of God. Don't wait any longer; you know, after 35, there aren't many possibilities left."

To talk to me about immersing myself in the love of God was like reminding a condemned man about his sizeable bank account; at that moment the memorandum about the deadline for conversion irritated me. In reply, I objected: "But, Father, if my love toward God is not complete now, perhaps later on it will be. Perhaps the passing of years will grant me wisdom. Besides, growing older, my self-control will be greater and everything will be easier, don't you think?"

"Why wait for time to pass in order to offer to God a half-eaten apple?" he answered. "Give Him your best energies now, at once. Don't wait for tomorrow."

The analogy of the "half-eaten apple" re-awoke in me a sense of sacred pride. I had never heard a more efficacious expression.

"Help me, I beg you," I said to him. "Your words today, on such a grey day in my life, could not have been more to the point, though they upset me so much."

My agitation was profound. I turned my thought to God, and in those few moments of silence, I said to Him:

"O God, how far away You feel! But if it is true that You are so close to us in our moment of trial, reach out Your hand and free me. I don't know what to do, I'm confused, I don't understand. Intervene, I beg You. Find a remedy, whatever it may be: sacrifice whatever You wish. I shall accept anything from Your hands, even those cures which make me suffer. But, I beg You, don't leave me like this, alone in this affliction."

"You're pensive!" said Father Henry to me.

I spoke to him about the prayer I had just formulated in my heart. I had tears in my eyes, but I was ready for anything. He assured me that he would join with me in my invocation. Then he blessed me, embraced me, and accompanied me to the door with the usual parting wish: "Go in peace!"

CHAPTER TWO

A Cross to Smooth the Road

Bear hardship
along with me
as a good soldier
of Jesus Christ.

St. Paul to Timothy II, 2.3

When the mind is oppressed by an immeasurable sorrow, it loses the capacity and strength to turn toward the search for truth: its first concern is the elimination of that sorrow. This is why there are few sincere seekers of truth in the world; most people are involved in the urgent need to escape from their own suffering by pursuing ephemeral pleasures. Gratified and drunk with these short-lived satisfactions, people become dependent on them, they entangle themselves in them, and in the end they no longer feel the need to come out of that precarious situation, thinking that it is "natural." With their heads bent down over things, they cannot see That which lies beyond mere objects.

But when the sorrow is existential, when it claws you from every side and does not give you another chance, when all the remedies that you sought until then - mere surrogates - are themselves part and cause of that sorrow because they are laden with delusion and insufficient to fulfill the soul's need for happiness, then the stimulus to search is born.

I have met many people, often among the wealthy, who claimed they were fully satisfied with life and did not feel any need to follow a path of spiritual inquiry. "What's there to look for?" they say openly. "We have obtained everything we desired from life: a good spouse with an excellent social position, studious and healthy children, a perfect religion. It's hard to understand this torment of yours about the search for truth."

But if you try to shake their certainty with the question "Don't you think that all this good fortune could end at any moment? What would you do then?" -- at that point they will say that they don't think about it because it hasn't happened to them yet; or they'll knock on wood and become irritated.

It is much more likely that someone will change when he reaches the point where everything seems unimportant to him and the question arises in him: "What can I do to get out of this absurdity?" No particular caste grants access to this inquiry: both the rich and the poor can arrive at it, the rich person because he is nauseated by the excess he has always had, and the poor person, provided he never desired wealth, because he has kept himself from becoming corrupted by it.

When a person comes to feel that all is vanity (*Vanitas vanitatum*), he immediately gains a new sensibility which makes him receptive to all the possible solutions to the fundamental questions of life.

The summer of 1979 arrived: 35 years old! It was the ultimatum for a definitive solution or for spiritual sclerosis. But by now, after that heartfelt prayer on my confessor's kneeler, it was as if I had filed the question away. It was no longer within my jurisdiction, and I set myself to await further events with implicit confidence, as a patient waits his turn in the receiving room of a clinic.

I spent the month of August in the hot Roman summer. Even the temperature had reached, as if in insolent comment on my age, 35 degrees Centigrade (almost 100 degrees Fahrenheit). My body was giving some strange signals which should have sounded an alarm, but which I didn't interpret correctly: I had chills, an inability to bear the breeze which should have been a relief for anyone gasping in that heat, a general feeling of tiredness, and a cold sweat at each minimal effort.

The body too has its laws, and when it signals some damage, it should be listened to with attention and cared for. But, while it is easy to detect the damage when there is acute pain, it is not so easy when the damage insinuates itself treacherously, without the host being able to detect it. In a physiological sense, pain is a blessing, because it often signals the ailment in time for a cure. And it is a blessing also in a figurative sense, because in this world in which people do not want to listen to the silent voice which speaks from inside, it is precisely suffering, sometimes very intense, which wakes them from their torpor.

It took me a long time to understand that my body had some leaks, and I was offered the final warning when I realized that my clothes and shoes had suddenly become tight and that I had abnormal swelling, especially at my ankles. I finally realized that I had to go to the doctor, and so another search began, parallel to the one that was about to get underway in my spiritual life, but relegated to the physical level, which is also important, even though not essential.

In the course of my life, I have repeatedly sought the secret of distinguishing that which comes from God from that which is the fruit of our egotistical desires. I have discovered that when the Lord decides to take a creature to heart because that creature has invoked Him in his moment of need and has asked Him for spiritual blessings, everything proceeds as if by a magical and perfect plan. Even now I continue to have experiences of how protective this Divine Mother is who, in order to defend Her beloved children, turns all events to Her children's advantage in unfathomable ways - or I should say, to the advantage of their spiritual evolution. And I underline this last clarification, because what we believe to be good for us almost never is in the eyes of Him who guides our destiny and knows its most intimate turns. The son is not always able to detect benefits in the events by which he seems to be dragged, often without his even realizing it; but in the course of life, some time later - months or years - those events will reveal themselves to have been providential. Human logic is not compatible with divine logic.

A surgeon, a faithful parishioner, immediately offered to host me in his hospital ward, of which he was vice head physician. He secured a hospital bed for me, which was not always easy to get when needed, and he oversaw all my clinical tests with joviality and tended me more like a friend than a doctor. At the conclusion of fifteen days in the hospital, the diagnosis: membranous glomerule nephritis.

It was essential to stop my activity immediately because the disease was in an acute phase. There is no specific medicine for this infirmity, and spontaneous cures are very rare, so out of fear that it would get worse and lead to dialysis or even death, it became necessary to plan a life of absolute rest. There was never a measure more providential than this one. Finally, the frenetic physical activity had to cease.

I left Rome without regrets, like a blind man led by a trusted hand toward an unknown road. Moreover, since it was a departure that left room for hope of a return, there weren't any of the heart-rending farewells which are usually reserved for priests when they leave one place to go to another. My surgeon friend warmly advised me to reserve a place in the sleeping car. The evening of my departure, a lady of the parish looked at me with a melancholy air and said: "Don Mario, you are going away forever." This in effect was my discharge. I am glad that my departure did not have any sentimental trailings and that, in the end, I was able to go away on tiptoe, as it were.

The departure from Rome was the first step - even if compulsory - in a strenuous and deeper inquiry. It is said that not all ills come to harm us. And the sickness really turned up at the right moment, even if at the beginning it was no fun at all. Because of this, still today I continue to be grateful to the Lord for having programmed it at the right moment, and I consider my having gotten sick as one of the greatest blessings of my life.

A serious illness also has the merit of taking away every material security. Without the body, every one of our material projects goes up in smoke. This discovery is an advantage to anyone who is about to put himself on a spiritual path, especially when he has not yet acquired enough strength of will not to fall away from it.

To surrender to God in a moment when your material resources are on their way to depletion is certainly not an act of heroism. But would anyone who is sinking in quicksand be so proud as to refuse help, even if offered by a stranger? After all, however humiliating the experience of the prodigal son may have been, his return to his father was crowned by a triumphant reconciliation.

I should have been obligated, especially as a priest, to reflect on why suffering exists, but now that I think about it, in the moment in which I myself was struck with illness, I didn't pose the question. Instead I was prone to depression. I was really clumsily hiding my cowardly lack of will to live behind a declared acceptance of my fate.

People react to suffering in the most diverse ways. Weak people rant under the blows of misfortune and can even lose their equilibrium, abandoning themselves to desperation. Immature persons occupy themselves with several kinds of amusements: sensual, intellectual, even religious. There are those who, in order not to suffer, dive headfirst into the satisfaction of the senses, those who struggle in the maze of cerebral explanations, and those who take refuge in the practices of an exaggerated piety.

To understand pain, however, all that is needed is some innocence and a great deal of inner strength. I don't know if I had even a fraction of these two qualities, but one thing is certain: the usual set speech people trot out for the occasion - "Suffering assimilates you to Christ, who suffered for all" - didn't say much to me, and it was even less consoling when it was on the lips of people who didn't believe it. And so when I heard these phrases repeated to me, I understood to what degree we priests often trivialize elevated truths, making them seem insipid and vacuous, when we haven't directly experienced what we say.

You can tell instantly when someone says something that comes from the heart; you know right away when a word is pronounced as if it were said by a tape-recorder and not by the heart. Moreover I have noticed that people who are put to the test do not like to philosophize with words, but, if they are mature, they will offer an example of serenity and detachment from the body. The smile of someone sick with cancer is worth much more than an academic discourse on pain.

When Father Henry, my confessor, came to see me in the hospital, he gave me the same "stereotypical" speeches. Coming from his lips and his heart, however, they gained a superhuman power, to the point that they moved me profoundly. The words of a nun who I saw appear before me, apparently out of nowhere, when I was lying face downwards in an operating room after a renal biopsy, had a similar effect: "Offer your pain," she begged me, clasping my hands in hers. "There are souls who are waiting for this offering of yours."

A knot gripped my throat. At that moment I was not inclined to think about souls to rescue. But the infinite Goodness of Him, who never abandons us and who follows us as teacher in all circumstances and in the guise of persons, had come near me in the form of a nun to remind me that my priestly mission should not falter even in a crisis in which I was worried only about my body.

Since ancient times, sickness has always been considered the direct consequence of human sin. In this sense, the doctrine of *karma* propounded by Eastern religions does not differ at all from biblical thought. The Old Testament has innumerable passages which attribute the responsibility for suffering to man. Naturally, in biblical literature where the image of God as Person prevails, karma is translated in terms of the "punishment of God". If one admits, in fact, that God is immanent in each one of us, as well as transcending human nature, the perfect law which regulates the balance of give and take connected with human conduct can only come from that inherent Divinity. At times, understanding how close we are to our brothers of the East is only a "theographic" question: it is enough to place God in His proper dimension in order to recognize the same author of all. We shall speak of this in a chapter dedicated entirely to the question of karma.

If we do not create our own joys and sorrows in the world, why on earth would Jesus forgive the sins of the paralytic before granting him a healing? And why did prophets predict misfortunes for cities corrupted by vice and injustice? Babylon, Nineveh, Sodom, Gomorrah, and so on, were the settings for prophecies which were punctually fulfilled. Sometimes the predictions were woeful; other times they promised a remission of the sentence if one began following God's laws.

Unfortunately, today this wisdom and this knowledge - the fact of the interaction between sin and suffering, between bad conduct and misfortunes - have been lost right in the heart of Catholicism, even in the chairs of theological teaching. It is not hard to find scholars who laugh at the ingenuousness of those **who still** believe in these things. Today people prefer to seek scientific solutions. They look for the external causes: they talk about viruses, about DNA, about cellular proliferation. Theologians do not yet know how to give a serious explanation for suffering. Modern holistic medicine with its new view of mind and body as one, accepts more and more the hypothesis of psychosomatic illness. Today many doctors weigh the psychological conditions of the patient, and this new awareness is also changing the concept of hospitalization and therapy. In other words, even the world of science is on the verge of recognizing that our sufferings have much deeper origins than the physical ones.

What diagnosis can a doctor write when he certifies the death of a spouse who dies a few instants after his or her companion? Cardiac arrest? Cerebral ictus from severe circulatory imbalance? Myocardial infarction? What does he know of the extremely fine threads which bound those two lives in such a duet of love that the cessation of either one's melody would stop the other's also? And what caused the death of Argus, the dog of Ulysses, who before falling to the ground dead was the only one able to identify his master? And what is the medicine which heals a child who feels loved and surrounded by attention? Or what is the poison which brings a rapid end to a hospital patient who is filled with depression and fear, who is tired of life and lonely, and whose only impulse is to die?

From these scanty reflections, we can intuit how harmful it is to think negatively and what a remedy it is to think of the good. But at the time of my illness, I did not see it this way, not because I didn't think it was valid, but because no one had ever talked to me about it. Even if I knew that good thoughts are a principle of ancient and wise morality, I did not understand how broadly that principle applies, because I did not know about its enormous influence. Therefore, I treated my physical ills chemically and my moral ills by seeking consolations, gathered here and there in human company or in hobbies, which at that time were easy remedies for my depression.

"What about prayer?" you will ask. "Shouldn't you of all people have sought consolation in prayer?" It is not likely that prayer will raise the spirits of a human soul when the mind is oppressed and ill. First one must care for his mental condition, then prayer does its work. Can one who lacks faith in himself, who he knows exists, expect to have faith in a God whom he does not know and does not see?

The more one convinces himself that he is a wretch, that he is unfortunate and without hope, the more he becomes vulnerable to exhaustion, for he is constantly opening new breaches for the work of demolition. That is why cancer races through those who are sad, and slows down or even recedes in those who live with optimism. But, to paraphrase the faint-hearted Don Abbondio,[1] one could reply, "You can't give yourself optimism!" Certainly, someone who is optimistic must have some good reasons for being so.

Psychic life is only an aspect, subtler and therefore less immediately understood, of the complex machine which manufactures pain. In practice, it is not always possible to glean the mental state of a person and to establish a link between the illness and the cause. The person could be good, and the sickness might have no direct explanation. But the rhythms which govern the particular balance of give and take registered in the mind do not always have the same punctuality and regularity of those which can be recorded by the body.

In fact, being composed of dense matter, the body also follows a denser time sequence. This is why the effects of smoking, alcohol, stimulants, and drugs in an organism can be verified in the short term. Physical agents, no matter how slow their action, are always faster in causing damage than psychic agents. And people certainly are not doing their health a favor when, in order to anesthetize their moral suffering, they turn to the pleasures of the palate. If you think about it, the "solutions" attempted by most people in order to deflect suffering are even more baleful than the damages already incurred. In the last analysis, a psyche which wanders among its own sorrows brings on illness, but the attempt to escape pain with harmful distractions generates even more suffering. It's like opening a dike in order to put out a little fire.

There is no escape! Suffering demands to be understood, not avoided.

In the natural world one can distinguish three fundamental qualities. The first is inertia, which in humans manifests itself in the form of ignorance; the second is energy in action, which manifests itself in activities; and the third is intelligence, which culminates in wisdom. When these three qualities are in balance among themselves, man and nature live in a harmonious and optimal relationship. When

---

[1]A character in the famous novel by Alessandro Manzoni, *I promessi sposi (The Betrothed).* [Translator's note.]

one predominates over another, a state of imbalance and disharmony is generated at every level.

For example, these three qualities can be seen in the equilibrium of a plant. A tree knows when to flower and to manifest its colors and perfumes. That is its aspect of intelligence. In winter it falls asleep, and it is living as if in inertia. Then there is the moment in which it reproduces and makes fruits, and this is the moment of active and vital energy.

Human beings have these qualities in them, but, while in all other beings - mineral, vegetable and animal - the qualities operate in a perfectly harmonious equilibrium, in humans they follow the drift of one's predilections and idiosyncrasies. The intelligence is used in percentages vastly inferior to its real potential, and the little which remains is largely enslaved to perfecting war and disorders, to military projects and technologies. Humanity moans under sores like cancer and AIDS, but how many hospitals, institutes, and scientific studies could have been created with the funds employed in armaments for so-called defense?

Another sign of imbalance, of which only humans have been capable, is the fact of relegating a large part of human activity (including recreation) to periods in which the human organism requires rest, stasis, inertia. This imbalance is evident both within the span of the day and within the span of the year. In the day, the hours dedicated to work, eating, recreation, and sleep are in sharp disproportion to those dedicated to reflection. At night, when flowers close their petals and animals retire to their lairs, people hold meetings to decide important questions, or else they go to the movies, and so on. The best moment of the day, the purest, which is the early morning, is used by most people for sleeping or for reaching their work place, while at that hour birds dedicate to Nature their best symphonies. In the span of the year, work activity is greater during winter, when the natural tendency is to settle into lethargy, or at least to carry on a more moderate and interior activity. This is why people reach spring tired, and attributing the cause to the ills of the season, they take tonics to rouse bodies worn down by the excessive activity performed at the least appropriate moment.

Winter, in effect, is a season which calls people back to rest and reflection, but people place productivity before health. And it is because of this that when many people reach old age, the season of rest and reflection, they have a terror of being inactive, and will not leave their work unless required to by an age limit. Many people after retiring die from a crisis of inertia, while they should have gotten used to this inertia in advance, for inertia permits not only rest, but also the activity of a tranquil interior life.

The race and toil to gain greater material comfort and technological progress are exploiting the best qualities of mankind, depriving them of the mystic and contemplative moments which render them wise, balanced, and capable of solving the woes of the world.

The disequilibrium of the vital rhythms is, then, one of the major factors responsible for suffering, illness, and pain. But where did this imbalance come from? What reason can we find for the absurd inconsistency of humans, who even though possessed of a potentially high level of consciousness, do not act with ordered intelligence? Humanity has reached the point where it cannot compete with a plant, which surely has a significantly lower level of consciousness, but which possesses an interior intelligence which governs its entire life with extreme order.

If mankind did not squander energy in organizing destructive activities, human technology would be considerably more advanced than it currently is, and it would be applied to all the spheres of life. There would not be inequalities between rich and poor (or at least there would no longer be the poor); there would no longer be the disparities between those who squander resources on weapons and those who die of hunger. The Sahara could be a fertile garden, seawater could be desalted to irrigate the fields, the roads could be full of cars that run on clean energy, like solar energy. What on earth happened in humans to change this equilibrium, which could make our planet an authentic earthly paradise?

To say that it was original sin, even if that corresponds to a truth (to be explained!), does not at all clarify the question. When you abandon intellectual acrobatics to try to find explanations for the condition of humans and enter instead into your own heart to X-ray it, you discover a reality different from the one written in so many volumes of history and morality.

It is a fact that humans tend always, everywhere, and with whatever means necessary to obtain what they like, and in ever greater measure.

In itself, this is not negative. It is their right to seek what makes them feel well. It is not a crime to seek happiness. On this point, certain men of the Church have not done credit to Catholicism, reducing it to a religion that punishes those who stain themselves with the disgrace of seeking pleasure. The attraction toward joy is one of the few signs which demonstrate how the essence of man is divine: it is not a good idea to destroy such a precious clue. To renounce this right is equivalent to pushing a person to a suicidal masochism. Many people who are considered saints tortured themselves to give the body pain while it was calling for pleasure. But many more saints could have been born if people had asked themselves the reason for that urge toward pleasure, and whether there existed an objective which does not vanish so rapidly and disappointingly as the objectives usually sought in order to satisfy the yearning for happiness.

If I take away from a person the conviction that he is seeking joy in itself, and that his mistake is only an error of perspective, what do I have left to push him toward God? If a human being is on a desperate hunt for continual satisfactions and draws them from external objects, why should I jump on him, rather than showing him how he is drilling the ground horizontally? If I tell him that in order to find diamonds, he must dig deep, maybe he will be convinced to change his method. In any case, he can follow in his heart the truth of what I am saying, and as a consequence, experience the desire to escape incorrect choices.

To seek horizontally, that is to say, on the surface, is an out and out deception, and you can realize it from the fact that once you have pursued all the desired things, the happiness savored by mouthfuls never settles down as a stable quality of the heart. Furthermore, to reach all those objectives of ephemeral "joy" requires enormous efforts, gigantic sacrifices, the dispersion of mental energy and of money: an expense truly disproportionate to the result of the undertaking. How many people reach death in complete idiocy after a life spent in the spasmodic search for money, working day and night to that end, forgetting family and health and declaring that they never have time to reflect!

To go in the wrong direction using the wrong means is the source of the imbalance among the three human qualities.

CHAPTER THREE

From the Paranormal to the Supernatural

*I am going to speak to you in parables
and expound the mysteries of the past.*

Psalm 78:2

I retired to my native town. Along with the treatment based on rest which was supposed to restore me physically, I also began an interior treatment, based on reading, study and reflection, in order to satisfy my thirst for truth. There were too many questions which remained unsolved in the theology I had studied. More than once, the catechists and young people of my parish had tried to induce me to respond to such burning questions as the hereafter, the existence of angels, and life after death. My answers were always evasive because, even though I had faith, they were not based on personal experience.

I have always been rather rational in my investigations, yet even with the theological knowledge I acquired through my studies, I was not satisfied by my past inquiries into Truth. The answers offered by official doctrine left some serious unknowns for me to fill in. When I would put the same questions in turn to other priests, they would say, "It's faith that tells you that." This is one of the most senseless answers I have ever heard, because the power of faith is such that if I have it, I have already resolved all problems and all doubts. So what need would I have for religion and its pomp if I have already arrived at the destination of faith? On the other hand, if religion is a means which is supposed to lead me to faith, why does it answer me by referring me to precisely what I am looking for, and which it as a religion should offer me?

Faith is a word which needs to be understood in the right way, because one can also use it to kill, make war, commit violence.

I realized right away that in our Western philosophy, and as a consequence also in the theology of our time, there is a serious lacuna: all the esoteric aspects have been banished as an ignoble and degrading way of addressing spiritual questions. Esoterism and the entire world of the occult is identified with magic and confined to the narrow rooms of necromancy, thus becoming something to be condemned. During many dark years not only fanatics but also serious investigators of the occult were condemned as wizards and witches and burned alive in public squares. More recently there has been an attempt to eradicate indiscriminately even the memory of a field of study - parapsychology - which instead more and more deserves to be numbered in the album of the sciences and which has very little indeed in common with the world of sorceresses.

The Bible is crammed with paranormal events, which shade easily into the miraculous, and which cannot be understood without some preparation in the field of parapsychology.

The celebrated phenomenon of ideoplasty[1] of the kittens of Nice recalls an analogous biblical incident. When those kittens were born in Nice, the numerals of the year 1921, were impressed upon their abdomens. The numerals were printed on a sack the gestating mother had crouched in front of for several hours, her gaze fixed on it while she waited for a mouse who had taken refuge behind it. Genesis 30:37-43 recounts that Jacob placed some branches with the bark peeled off in strips in drinking troughs in order that the animals who came to drink, mating in sight of it, would give birth to "streaked, speckled and spotted kids."

It is a phenomenon which has nothing magical about it, but can be explained by the power of visual impressions, which play a determining role in all aspects of the life of a living being. Imagine how liable a living being is to such impressions when it is also endowed with mind.

The existence of giants is no longer so mythical, nor is it ingenuous to believe in it if we take what is written in the Book of Numbers seriously.[2] There we are told about a country populated by "men of high stature" (*gigantes* in the Vulgate[3]), in front of whom the explorers sent by Moses "seemed like locusts."

---

[1]Ideoplasty is a word created by Durand De Gros in 1860 and used in parapsychology. It derives from the Greek *eidas* (image, idea) and *plassein* (to model, shape). It indicates the impressing of an idea on a hypnotized or influenced subject.

[2]Cf. Numbers 13.32ff

[3]The Vulgate Bible is the Latin translation of the Bible made by St. Jerome.

What should we say about the spells worked by the sorcerers of Egypt, who when Moses turned a stick into a serpent, were able to do the same thing? And what should we say when Moses turned the waters of the Nile into blood and the sorcerers again repeated the same miracle?[4]

Surely one of the most curious paranormal phenomena of the Bible is that of the ass of Balaam, which, "seeing the angel of the Lord standing on the road with sword drawn, turned off the road and began to go through the fields" until "the Lord opened the mouth of the ass," and it spoke to Balaam, the severe master who beat her.[5]

In the Gospels, as in much of the Old Testament, an important place is given to the power of dreams to foretell the future. Joseph had some very significant dreams which he knew how to interpret and which came true punctually. But his brothers made fun of him as a dreamer and ended up selling him to a caravan of travellers.[6]

The other Joseph too, the spouse of Mary, Mother of God, took his dreams seriously. A dream revealed to him that he should accept becoming the putative father of the Messiah; a dream warned him that Herod was looking for the baby in order to kill it; a dream told him that now the baby's enemies were dead and that therefore he could return to Israel. Then there is the dream of Pilate's wife who, "while he was presiding on the bench, sent him a message: 'Have nothing to do with that just man. I had a dream about him today which has greatly upset me.'"[7]

What is most striking, however, is not so much the frequency with which dream-apparitions occur, but the fact that it is taken for granted that they are truthful, and that therefore it is necessary to make decisions with full deference to what is revealed through that unusual type of communication. All of this is found in the Gospels, but we priests, in our homilies, have never given any weight to the esoteric world which surrounded those facts of daily life. A nocturnal vision was enough to change the destiny of the carpenter of Nazareth, and he accepted it even though it complicated his life considerably. This does

---

[4]Cf. Exodus 7.11-22
[5]Numbers 22.23-30
[6]Genesis 37
[7]Matthew 1.20; 2.13,19; 27.19

not mean that the people were oppressed by old superstitions, but rather indicates that they knew well the value of interventions which transcend the coarsest level of sensory activity, a deeper level on which the Divine can play out its plan of salvation.

The ancient and by now forgotten rural society knew, even if in generic forms, the value of what does not lie directly before our senses. Religion itself in peasant times complied with the need to exorcise occult powers, whose influence was not entirely obvious and therefore was not to be underestimated.

The old Rite, the one which was practically eliminated under Paul VI, took into account innumerable situations in which people asked for divine help, feeling that they were impotent to handle these situations with their own powers alone. In those times one would often see the good country parish priest carrying the sacred book wrapped in a stole under his arm. The book contained special blessings to help deal with unpleasant circumstances. There was a *Benedictio deprecatoria contra mures, locustas, bruchos, vermes et alia animalia nociva* in order to avert the invasion of mice, locusts, caterpillars, worms, and other harmful animals.

Several years ago in front of my house a tree was felled. The huge tree stood three stories high and its only fault was that it had some moths which disturbed some of the neighbors. The innocence of the farmer has been lost, to be replaced by a superficial and destructive technology. Today people don't ask for the help of a priest in getting rid of an invasion of ants; instead they use the more practical and surer powder which exterminates them. In that old Rite there were also prayers and processions *ad petendam Pluviam* or *ad postulandam Serenitatem* or *ad repellendam Tempestatem*, in order to ask for rain, clear weather, or to keep away hailstorms.

What is most amazing is the efficacy and results of those prayers. When my grandparents, who were farmers, had a sick cow or a sow that had gone mad and was devouring her newborn, they would turn to the parish priest, who would come to impart the special blessing of the Rite, and everything would resolve itself. The film of E. Olmi *The Tree of the Wooden Clogs* records just such a moving episode.

I'll stop here with the list of benedictions, because they were extremely numerous and there was a blessing for every occasion. What I wish to underline, though, is the reality of the phenomenon. I don't even wish to inquire into the religious value of those practices, nor do I intend to assert that those times were better than ours. The man of that time was unaware that the divine power inherent in himself would have been sufficient to resolve whatever problem he had. Yet, with his attitude of faith tenderly rooted in the certainty that the prayers would not pass unobserved by the eyes of the good God, he was the other pole which, with the mediation of the priest, liberated the Omnipotent Divine Energy.

What happened was that materialistic philosophy, which had been so opposed by the men of the church, had already filtered into their own hearts to such a point that when the old Rite was dropped, no theologian had the courage to defend the validity of that ancient and superseded form of worship. Priests began gradually to curb the request for benedictions and sacramentals.[8] Those rites seemed a suitable ground for the sprouting of superstitions; to have a handkerchief blessed in order to place it on an ailing part of the body was considered paganizing fetishism; fewer and fewer women in labor asked for the *post partum* benediction; and, as a final blow, the new decrees of Paul VI eliminated from the sacresties the *Rituale Romanum* of another Pope, whose name was (what a coincidence!) Paul V. To compensate, the formularies *De exorcizandis obsessis a daemonio* were maintained (but only *ad usum delphini*). The interest in the power of the devil has never waned in the Church.

A few years ago, in certain country parishes, the celebration of the *Rogationes*, prayers and processions which served to bless the harvest, still continued. They corresponded to the sacrificial celebrations of Vedic origin, called *Yajña*, in use among the Hindu cultures. I know quite a few old farmers who would confirm what a beneficial power those celebrations exercised on the fields and on the people themselves. But in those fields cement buildings have sprung up, and the custom of traversing the paths among fields fragrant with spring has been lost. It would be excessive to attribute the current ecological

---

[8]"Sacramentals" are not to be confused with "sacraments." The latter are the seven rituals adopted by the Catholic Church as signs of salvation and are required of believers as indispensable milestones on the journey of faith toward God. Sacramentals, on the other hand, are all prayers, benedictions, and sacred ceremonies which serve to foster Christian devotion.

disorder to this development, but it is certain that those rites did not spoil the harvests.

I know that there are some Tibetan monks who, by sounding a special horn, are able to govern meteorological phenomena. I hope that their directives for conducting religious services have not been so radically changed as to eliminate a tradition of worship and knowledge so useful to mankind.

In the Bible there is also knowledge of numerology. For example, the number 9 appears in many circumstances. The number 9 is dear also to Hindu theology in that it represents the immutability and incorruptibility of the Divine. In fact, the multiples of this number always give 9 when added together. Thus, for example, 27 is still a 9, because 7 + 2 equals 9, 36 (3 + 6 = 9), 7542 still gives 9, etc.... In the Bible, the number 9 has great significance from the 9 tribes of Israel to the hour 9 in the morning when Jesus was crucified; 18 was the number of victims killed by the collapse of the tower of Siloam[9]; God will forbear from destroying Sodom if he can find in it at least 45 just men[10]; 72 is the number of disciples designated by the Lord to preach[11]; 99 is the number of sheep which the Good Shepherd is willing to leave for the lost one[12]; 144,000 is the number of the elect of each tribe[13]; 153 is the number of large fish captured in the miraculous draught of fishes.[14]

It would be very interesting if those who investigate parapsychology were to do an analytic and monographic study on the paranormal and on all the testimony parallel to it in the Bible. I believe that in Western theological learning, there is a serious lacuna in this sense. Parapsychology is certainly an important step towards the discovery of subtler physical levels, which can then lead gradually to the metaphysical.

---

[9]Luke 13.4
[10]Genesis 18.28
[11]Luke 10.1
[12]Matthew 18.12
[13]Apocalypse 7.14; 14.1
[14]John 21.11

One must make sure that one's study in this field is rigorously scientific and serious. Too many people, after having undertaken this inquiry, have allowed themselves to be dragged by the itch of morbid curiosity and have ended up crossing over into a cheap spiritism, if not into black magic. At that point, parapsychology - if you can still call it that - becomes an obstacle to spiritual life. The interest in what is more subtle, which should have led to That which is beyond the most ethereal realm of matter, then drowns ingloriously in an interest in spirits, sprites, devils, possessions, enchantments, cartomancy, fortune-telling, spells, and various forms of witchcraft. In that way, instead of making a qualitative leap and passing from the material to the spiritual, one drowns in a sea of notions and phenomena constructed by one's own mind, trapped by mere speculations which encourage ambition. Instead of surmounting the well-known voracity of the mind, which is already so active on the physical level, one makes the situation worse by providing it with new food to gulp down, a treacherous food, whose effects are not yet fully known. It is like allowing oneself to be tempted by the beauty of a mushroom which has not yet been tested to see if it is poisonous.

Too many people today pronounce theories and edicts on the occult, passing themselves off as experts or as repositories of lofty revelations reserved for a few. These people can play their cards and reshuffle them according to the opportunity of the moment, taking advantage of the incontestability of their subjective "revelations" and of what cannot be proved.

I know various people who, after putting themselves on a path that should have led them to the spiritual, got stranded behind one divining method or another, to the point that they consult their pendulum even to know if they may sneeze. Their talk is crammed with mysterious notions that are a snare for simpletons and the ingenuous. What is worse, they believe they are conversing with the spirits of the dead, from whom they think they are receiving superhuman messages. They forget that among the living there is enough revelation to burst the hearts of six billion human beings!

How clear the warning of Isaiah seems to me now:

And when they say to you: "Interrogate the spirits and mediums who whisper and murmur formulae. Should a people not consult its gods? Consult the dead on behalf of the living?", then cling to revelation, to the testimony. Indeed they will say these things which offer no hope of light.[15]

And again:

It is I who bring to nought the omens of liars, who make fools of diviners; I turn wise men back and make their knowledge foolish.[16]

With these precautions in mind, I found that phenomena like clairvoyance, telepathy, and foreknowledge not only aroused my deepest interest, but also increasingly revealed to me a plane of material existence which I had not thought seriously about before. On the contrary, more than once I had ridiculed, and in public too, the very fact that one could even take into consideration such "irrational" phenomena. I thus declare my guilt in having judged what I did not know, an error which today I am grieved to see in so many people.

As I undertook this study, I entered a world which isolated me ever more from what are commonly considered rational hypotheses, and therefore from all those people whom I associated with and respected insofar as they were rationalists, and who returned that respect for the same reason. Even today it is still hard to give parapsychology the status of a science. The phenomena are so vast that defining which among them are paranormal and which are not is quite problematic. Also, the methods and investigations adopted in the field of official science cannot be used to scientifically prove such phenomena. A future-foretelling dream, no matter how truthful it may be, cannot be "verified," for normally just one person has had the dream. In short, the conclusions paranormal phenomena lead to do not rely on the help of the senses, which are indispensable in scientific experimentation. *Nihil est in intellectu quod prius non fuerit in sensu*, as St. Thomas had already said: There is nothing in the intellect which has not first passed through the senses.

---

[15]Isaiah 8.19-20
[16]Isaiah 44.25

Even today it is still widely debated how to determine which principles are totally reliable in determining if a study is scientific. I will not take this matter further because it does not pertain to this book. I have simply mentioned it because in these first steps of my inquiry, I had to determine if in my investigation I could break through and go beyond the threshold of the sensory without being charged with heterodoxy or madness.

It is certain that the breadth of human knowledge is limited by the very instruments that are used to acquire it. When Galileo had not yet constructed that device, the telescope, which allowed him to observe the phases of the planet Venus and thus to deduce its rotational movement around the sun, the Earth was, in the minds of scholars, a central planet around which the Sun moved. What was scientific in their certainty which in their view was supported even by biblical revelation!?

Everything that is subject to our senses belongs to the past. It is incredible, but true, that in the heavenly vault we observe on a summer night there are many stars which are already extinct, and the perception of them is due to not only the eye but also to the light-years that it takes for those images to reach the eye. And who would ever believe that that plump solar disk which settles on the horizon in the nostalgic sunsets of late summer, almost flattened by the weight of a difficult day, is in reality the phantom of a star which already set eight minutes ago?

If it were possible to have a super-powerful telescope capable of exploring the life which is taking place on a planet more than 2,000 light-years away from us, the use of this telescope would allow the imaginary observer to discover the historic events which happened 2000 years ago on that planet. And so if this observer happened to be 2000 light-years from the Earth, he could see scenes from the history of Jesus or of the ancient Romans. It seems like science-fiction, but if the theory of relativity is true, it is extremely logical! All is Light and without Light the world could not project its illusion.

Where is the truth? Where is the true science, where is its infallibility? How can a scientific axiom be stable when it is grounded on the highly inconstant and unstable line of changing time?

Certainly, when you have the distinct sensation that your son will have a motorcycle accident, but it is only a foreboding and therefore not provable, and others harshly criticize your gloomy pessimism, you come to believe you have no real reason to prevent him from leaving the house. But when the event tragically occurs, you feel like a Cassandra, "never-heeded". For science, the only evidence to consider the warning valid would have been an un-retouched photo of the accident, taken some time before the accident itself.

After having discovered that everything that is scientific is still relative, in that there are instruments of observation which go beyond the five senses, my mind began to believe in the existence of truths hidden to normal sensory perception. I was struck as by lightning by the thought that, beyond the world I saw and felt, there was another one "in existence" of a much thinner physical density and therefore perceptible only by much subtler senses. Of this I was certain, but I could never have taught it in a university.

I asked myself repeatedly how a subjective proof could acquire objective validity. I wondered if in order for a phenomenon to be declared "normal" it is enough to have a majority who uphold it as such. How abnormal is it to mistake red for green? Is it really a defect in the organ of perception, or could it not be rather a decision of expediency accepted by a social community?

The readings I was doing were ever more thrilling. I read something too on hypotheses on the world beyond the grave. E. Bozzano was extremely comforting to me, even though it cannot be said that his works are scientific. What was most important to me wasn't the reassurance that the thought expressed in those writings was shared by the majority of thinkers, but the fact that I felt what I was reading was true.

No matter how many persuasive arguments I might have used with an interlocutor, if he were someone used to "planting his feet on the ground," he would have demolished me. And yet I knew that much of what I was reading, for which I could not have any physical verification, was true; no one in the world could have convinced me of the opposite. The voice which told me "that's exactly how it is" came from inside, from a dimension in which reason is ousted by the infallibility of intuition. This voice, for me, began to be rigorously "scientific."

The discovery of the possible in what I had once believed intellectually inadmissible opened new horizons for me and enabled me to approach the various teachers of truth, who were preparing their appearance in my life.

CHAPTER FOUR

In Search of Saints and Masters

It is not enough if you listen to
the Master's words;
you must put into practice
what He says,
give ear to every word,
carry out each hint.
A hint you have not followed,
a word you have missed
are lost forever,
because He does not speak twice.

Krishnamurti

I had fully exhausted my curiosity about the world of the occult: the questions, like a musical counterpoint, began to burn themselves out one after another in a concert of answers. Now I felt the need to nourish myself with choicer foods. Next to the books on parapsychology, certain volumes were on the waiting list on my desk. I had the *Bhagavad Gita*, Yogananda's *Autobiography of a Yogi*, *Concentration and Meditation* by Swami Shivananda Saraswati, some *Upanishads*, and the *Sutra of Patanjali*.

As a program it was very rich, and I did not know yet how delightful the study of those works would be. I began, if I remember, with the simplest: *Autobiography of a Yogi*. This book already had a certain history in my life, and for me this return to it had a particular significance.

A few months before I had left Rome, a person had lent that book to me. Based on its appearance, it did not inspire much confidence in me. On the cover there was a picture of an Indian with full and flowing hair. My notions of the world of India were terribly compromised by the deep impressions left in me from my years of theological study. In those years theology was taught defensively: one's own religion was held to be indisputably superior, and other religions were undervalued, if not regarded with contempt. India and all its religious apparatus for me smacked of paganism. I had been trained to think that my religion was the only one capable of saving people and that no other theology on earth could surpass that of the Catholics.

The weight of that prejudice was remarkable, but I decided to start reading the autobiography of Yogananda anyway. I must remind the reader that those were the years when I found myself in the dark night of my soul. I kept the book on my bed table, and at night, those interminable nights in which sleep never came to give me peace, I would read some pages in it.

My attitude of diffidence was almost defiance. After reading about fifty pages, I stopped. The book was talking about a saint who gave off perfumes, about another who stuck his arm on again after it had been cut off by two criminals, about tigers that became docile, about vegetarian lionesses that recited the Om. In short, I felt like I had entered into fairyland. My rationalistic mind, combined with a strong dose of ego, rebelled against this information. I closed the book, and giving it back, I said with a rather annoyed air: "This kind of book is not for me!"

Isaiah might say to me: "You have seen many things, but without noticing them; you have opened your ears, but without hearing."[1] In the field of convictions, nothing is more powerful than prejudice. It is like faith; indeed, it is a misplaced faith.

It is only today, at a distance of several years, that I am capable of criticizing myself for that closed attitude; and thanks to that experience I understand how difficult it is for many people to open themselves to something new and disconcerting, or to truths which knock down all the doctrinal scaffolding of a tradition. Fundamentally, prejudice is a bondage which corrodes the very roots of conscience. The conscience of a man full of prejudices is like a bonsai, whose roots are cut off to keep it a dwarf.

Prejudice is a widespread illness. Most people are willing to swear that they wish to take steps to improve themselves, but on the condition that no changes be made in the status quo of their thinking.

---

[1]Isaiah 42.90

In the brains of most people, a sort of program has been installed which can be summed up in the following aphorism: "Transformation is not worth the effort and losses it entails."

Those who are hit hardest by prejudice are naturally those who "have" more, not only in the sense of material possessions, but above all in the sense of cultural patrimony. One who has reached a certain security - whether economic, social, or religious - is content with things as they stand and does not want radical changes. When it comes to spiritual inquiry, the most inflexible people are those who have given their entire brain to a dogmatic faith.

It is in the nature of people to go looking for an authority to give them the security of an apparent order in their lives: this reassures them. Because of this, it is not so astonishing that in two millennia of ecclesiastical history, Christians have not been all that opposed to the idea of delegating to an oligarchy the practices and rites required for them to reach their **own** salvation. Work undertaken on one's own, which is desirable in any investigation of existential and metaphysical realities, has never been encouraged by the precepts and teachings of the men of the church. And yet, in the things of the world, no one would be so ingenuous as to blindly entrust the management of his own financial affairs to an outsider. In this way, a dependent relationship has been created between the faithful and their spiritual directors. Thus authority is born, and with it, its indisputability.

I hope no one who reads my words believes that my relationship with the Catholic Church has developed cracks, or thinks that I am biting the hand that feeds me. I want to clarify now what will become evident in the next pages: I am not fed by that hand. Secondly, I have already said, and I will say it again now, that with this book I intend to reaffirm my love for the Church, whom I consider my mother, even if sometimes a difficult one.

When speaking of the Church in an historical sense, it is good to make a distinction. There is the ecclesiastical organization, a product of the human mind, with all its apparatus, its bureaucracy, its trinkets, its outward appearances, its pomp, but also with its work in fostering human values and discipline: in short, with its merits and faults. There is no reason to bear resentment toward this church: it is nothing but the distillation of all the physical and mental habits of the men who constitute it.

Why get angry at priests or bishops, when it is obvious that they are the product of the environment in which we have all lived and grown for many years? I have met many people who, having been educated in institutions run by monks or nuns, have been left with a profound and searing aversion for anything clerical or ecclesiastical. I don't question that these people have their good reasons for feeling that way, but their rebellion shows how little those people know that nothing in life happens by chance.

Then there is another Church, with a capital C, and it comprises all those people who are thirsty for justice and truth, and who spend the greatest part of their energy finding answers to existential questions, or who dedicate themselves and their time to others with love. Among these are many who never set foot in a church, who do not receive sacraments for the reasons mentioned above, self-styled atheists who do not worship stone idols but serve people with justice and rectitude.

In the ranks of this enormous and invisible community, I have often met people tested by events and free from all hypocrisy. This is the true Church. This is the gathering of all the sheep which are under the guidance of the only Shepherd[2], that Force which pushes people toward goodness and love, that Essence which unifies us all independently of our skin color, our vestments, or our ceremonies. That Shepherd does not need images, though He likes to make use of them in order to make the task easier for humans, who are distracted by many foolish thoughts and superfluous preoccupations. It is a Church which needs neither temples nor institutionalization, but it is powerful and unsinkable because, even if all the institutions of the world were to collapse, there will always be a sea of people who are thirsty for God, and who long for Him with hearts that are sincere and free of preconceptions.

The true duty of the priestly class should be precisely to promote the growth of that Church. The mission of a priest should be to serve as a stimulus to reflection and growth, not by providing packets of

---

[2] John 10.16

pre-packaged answers, but by heightening in each person the latent capacity for investigation and inquiry.

Tradition is useful for everything that is ceremonious, but it becomes an obstacle if it is transplanted into the realm of being. A tradition, with its dogmas, its beliefs, its theories, must necessarily remain static, but an individual's work of transformation cannot depend simply upon a fixed and external set of rules. For example, in a ritual or liturgy, it is necessary to have uniform rules applied in a fixed manner. This assures a steady and correct course for those who want to follow this path. But the fossilization of concepts in the infinite spaces of consciousness would limit that consciousness and block its expansion.

Here we have one of the most obvious differences between Eastern religions and Catholicism. In the East, free inquiry into the Divine is a tradition, while the Vedic ritual is rigorously strict. In the West, it is precisely the opposite: there is rigor on doctrinal questions, which finds its fullest expression in dogma, and extreme flexibility in the rituals, which change with the times and the popes.

The saddest consequence of this is that the ecclesiastical authority has more than once had to resort to repressive methods as the only way to safeguard the integrity of doctrine, while it does nothing about the fanciful initiatives that many pastors have taken in the liturgy. The only purpose of the liturgy is to reveal through symbol and gesture the secret truths concealed in them. But if the symbols keep changing, their implicit meaning is lost. On the other hand, the free inquiry into the Divine, unhampered by constrictions, fears and threats, sharpens the power to intuit the Truth, which cannot be reached by reason alone.

When the function of an authority is reduced to being repressive, it loses its persuasiveness as an educator, and the consequence is the formation of people who are inept and without motivation. If a conscience struggles between what it wants to be and what it really is by its tendencies, inclinations, and promptings, there is no freedom of inquiry, but only conflict: ideology collides with daily existence. This creates further tensions, in addition to those spawned by one's own illusory "ego."

My situation was a paradigm of conflict: a priest who had fallen victim to a number of religious prejudices. This state of affairs is even more unfortunate for priests, because our knowledge of theology, a precious cultural patrimony, often leads us to an unshakable attachment to our own convictions. It should also be said that priests "live from the altar"[3], to use a Pauline expression; that is, in order to live we draw the proceeds from our activity as minister of the rites and preacher. This last reason is surely the most important in solidifying prejudice: you may be able to find a priest who **thinks** differently from the official canons of the Church, but it is very difficult to find one who **expresses** his thought openly without running into great economic or legal difficulties.

These obstacles were taken care of by that loving hand that was guiding me. It was as if His hand was tenderly resting on my head. To support myself I was teaching religion. I worked just a few hours a week -- five -- so as not to injure my health. Along with other income and assistance for which I was never lacking, I had enough for my needs. The classes that I taught in a secondary school in the province of Bergamo showed the effects of my new way of thinking. The children were enthusiastic about all the material I presented to them. I spoke to them about parapsychology as a means of reaching spiritual life, and I made use of very serious and respected texts. I brought them much evidence and a fascinating set of case histories. But at the end of the year, I found myself relieved of my duties as a teacher, without any warning or explanation from anyone.

I understood that I could no longer count on the Curia of Bergamo, which had first proposed my name to the school and now, contravening a precise law, was revoking the appointment. I deemed it necessary to provide for my support in another way, and I looked for other solutions.

The first thing that occurred to me was to enroll in a university, for all the academic titles I had earned from the Lateran University weren't worth a dried fig to the Italian State. But here too the Master

---

[3] This is a reference to I Corinthians 9.13: "The ministers serving in the temple get their food from the temple and those serving at the altar can claim their share from the altar itself."

of Masters, with a very clearly delineated plan, wished me to travel a road I did not yet see. I wanted to enroll in the University of Ca' Foscari in Venice. I thought that my inclination toward Eastern philosophy would have something to chew on in that academy, and I could earn a useful degree allowing me to teach.

The office of the university did not accept the degree that I had earned in Rome as a valid credential for enrollment. Knowing however that for the State an ecclesiastical degree was equivalent to a secondary school certificate, I beseeched the Chancellor to review my position, but I received the same answer. Tenaciously pursuing my intent, I wrote to the Minister of Public Education and went there in person. In the end, I received a reply signed by the minister himself which declared that the university had made a mistake, and enclosed there were the various memos that showed I was right. In the meantime, however, time had passed, and I had sought other solutions. I had applied for a one-year substitute position as an administrative clerk at a school near Bergamo. My name was at a good point on the list, and I was hired.

It was a very hard year, but I discovered that it was exactly what my Master wanted from me: to break down the ego, even in a rather tough way. In a professor's chair, with a degree in Eastern studies, I may have gotten a swollen head, and my fledgling search may have evaporated in a heap of high-sounding notions. Behind a desk covered with rubber stamps and registers, my ego would be scaled down to size.

On the positive side, I was now in an economic position which, at least for a year, would free me from outside interferences. Naturally I surprised many people. I was the only "employed priest" in the province, perhaps in the entire region, if you exclude all the monsignori employed in the offices of the Curia. To those who were so amazed by my position and who asked me why in the world I wasn't teaching religion I would answer: "Why are you amazed that I'm not teaching religion instead of being astonished by the fact that religion is **taught**?"

The Director of my life wanted to bring me gradually to that solitude which would allow Him to reign undisturbed in my heart. Thus He had induced me not to place my hope in institutional supports, in order to give me that security which only He can give. He does not want old clothes worn when He invites people to His Wedding. And by now I was almost entirely undressed, waiting for a new wedding garment.

The freedom of discovery is born when one no longer has any supports. In that freedom a new energy develops which is not rebellion but true innocence.

And so it was that I was now ready to read the autobiography of Yogananda. Prepared by parapsychology, freed from many prejudices, free from the fear of losing a position and even a reputation, that holy book finally flooded into my inner life and revealed to me other mysteries I had not understood before. Now I was no longer scandalized by the perfume-saint, nor did the possibility that there were superhuman beings in the Himalayas disturb me.

From that volume came torrents of beneficial light which showed me with extreme clarity the path to follow. A dream I had had was coming true in which I had seen Yogananda accompanied by some disciples approach me and bless me, while a brilliant ray of light emanated from the center of his forehead and reached mine.

In Yogananda I came upon all those notions which I had studied in parapsychology raised to the level of spiritual truths. Furthermore, I discerned in his writings a noble effort -- I would say a successful one -- to reconcile the religious knowledge of the East with that of Christianity. In the work of this "Supreme Swan" (*Paramahansa*) I glimpsed a thrilling ecumenical mission, to which I wanted to dedicate my energies.

When Catholics talk about ecumenism, they are usually referring to the attempts to foster union among the Christian churches. That Christianity should have divided itself into so many sects and churches is not at all helpful to the goal of diffusing this religion. A spouse who has lived through numerous experiences of separation has good reason to suspect that the responsibility for those divisions lies in himself. If a prospective convert to Christianity were to observe these divisions closely, he might mistrust a religion which has separated itself from many people and has divided itself into many groups: Protestants, Waldensians, Evangelicals, Lutherans, Calvinists, Jehovah's

Witnesses, and so on. It is urgent therefore to find the point common to all these groups.

But I still did not imagine that a union among Christians, already utopian for the Protestants, could be extended to embrace the Churches of the East and religions so apparently distant from our culture. Yogananda had the power to show me instead how close all religions are to each other, and this was the most interesting discovery of my research.

The descriptions in the *Autobiography of a Yogi* were so evocative that after every reading I was left with the desire to go hunting for saints or yogis, if it was true that this planet was still hosting some. On my path I also read of Kriyananda, disciple of Yogananda and author of the book *The Path: Autobiography of a Western Yogi*, another exquisite work which reveals hidden traits of the Master Yogananda. I had the pleasure of meeting Kriyananda and being at his side during several gatherings at a retreat in a community he founded.

In the meantime, another prejudice of mine was falling away, which was the belief that it was only possible to reach sainthood after death. Indeed, death might open the doors to a process of beatification or canonization on the part of an institutional Church, but one can be a saint even in life. Nor can the lack of a declaration of sainthood on the part of the official bodies be taken as a negative judgment. I am profoundly convinced that most of the saints are not yet recognized by the Church. One enters the liturgical calendar for notoriety, for merits acquired through particular feats of charity and abnegation; on God's calendar all those saints are listed who have reached Him through the annihilation of the ego, often in a forgotten and abandoned cave.

I discovered, therefore, that sainthood was the prerogative not only of Christians, but of all those who dedicate their entire energy to the search for God, no matter what creed or race they belong to. I assure you that no matter how obvious or superfluous it may seem to affirm this truth, it is for many priests and Catholics still a solemn heresy. "Only in Christ is there salvation," they would tell you. A sacrosanct truth, but we shall see later what is to be understood by those words, which are used with so much fervor by the champions of Christianity.

It was not long before my yearning for saints was satisfied. While the study of the *Bhagavad Gita* and the *Upanishads* was leading me into authentic paradises, and the brisk demolition of my prejudices about Eastern religions continued, another personage of great stature began to stand out: Jiddu Krishnamurti.

The reading of some of his books stirred me tremendously. His wasn't the sweet and persuasive message of Yogananda, but rather, a continuous call to walk without crutches, with your own legs. In his words I found the highest philosophy. Even though at times his style stunned me like the lash of a whip calling me back to the purest inquiry without supports of any kind, at the end of his discourses I would find that I was different, full of calm, my heart overflowing with gratitude for those words. I felt I could say about him, "Only you have words of eternal life!"[4] Those who do not know Krishnamurti well enough and think he is over-intellectual would be amazed if I told them that his message has the power to make a person dissolve into tears. His arguments do not aim to soften the heart, but basing their leverage on pure reason and a disciplined intellect, they still lead to the same spot, to the seat of all the most noble feelings. His teaching is aimed at leading to the Formless without passing through form and transcending it: not an easy enterprise and suited only to those who no longer have any interest in what is formal, suited to those who understand gold and disdain jewelry.

When I learned that it was even possible to hear his discourses directly, in Saanen, Switzerland, I did not want to miss that precious opportunity.

The trips I was taking to seek out these saints were putting me in contact with other seekers like myself. I discovered, with immense joy, that I was in excellent company. In a world that I was prone to consider as dark and without a future, it heartened me to know that still many people - at least they seemed many, to see them all gathered together - were looking for God and yearned for Him like thirsty deer.

---

[4]John 6.68: "After giving a particularly difficult discourse, Jesus saw that many of His listeners were leaving Him disappointed and he asked the twelve disciples if they wanted to leave Him too. Peter answered, "Lord, to whom shall we go? You have the words of eternal life.'"

After Yogananda and Krishnamurti, it was the turn of a certain Babaji, an experience I cannot pass over in silence.

In the autobiography of Yogananda there is a reference to a divine being who lived on the Himalayas and whose name was Babaji, who was endowed with extraordinary powers and who was capable of staying in a youthful body for millennia. Yogananda relates incredible marvels in connection with this "incomparable Master," those same phenomena that prevent the calloused skeptic from seeing beyond the end of his nose. This Christ-like figure had left his physical body, promising to return later to some cave in the Himalayas.

Well then, during one of the usual gatherings I loved to attend to hear the words of wise men, a young man spoke to me of his encounter with Babaji. "It's not possible," I answered, "Babaji has been absent from the Himalayas since the time of Yogananda." "No," said the young man, "Now he's come back." I thought I was living in a dream world in which everything happens by enchantment. The boy gave me precise indications for reaching that area of the Himalayas. If it were true that Babaji had re-appeared, that unique opportunity was not to be missed.

I bought a book -- the last copy left in the bookstore -- with the title *Babaji, Message from the Himalayas*. It was full of photographs. Some of them, the ones of Babaji during the first years of his present manifestation, corresponded extraordinarily to the description furnished by Yogananda: an extremely beautiful young man, enigmatic, his face similar to that of a Christ, his white garment blowing in the wind, his gaze penetrating. The passage of years had considerably spoiled that enchanting aspect. Now he was obese, his face almost swollen, his hair disordered, his gaze at times frightening, at times gentle. This last image, however, brought to my mind a dream I had had a few nights before, in which a figure which I knew to be Babaji appeared to me, but he did not have the appearance of the Babaji I knew before buying the book. This figure, rather corpulent, dressed in white silk, a few meters away from me, was gesturing to me with his index finger to go to him.

When I saw the picture of him, I recognized the image of the dream, and as I was pointing it out to a person who was involved in a search like mine, she told me that she had had a similar dream the night before: same personage, same identification with the photos in the book.

On my trip to India, in August to September 1982, I threw myself into an enterprise which only a madman could carry out. I organized a trip to the Himalayas, to seek out the immortal Babaji. Even though my physical condition made it clear to me that my kidney disease had by no means receded, my decision was unshakable, and nothing could have stopped me on that path. Nothing, or almost nothing. It was by divine plan that while I was crossing the Himalayan forest, on the slopes of the Kailash Mountains, the residence of Shiva, I was unaware of the terrible animals that inhabited the region: tigers, serpents, and lions. Although I had read it in the *Autobiography*, a veil of oblivion had descended on that information, perhaps to allow me to undertake the enterprise. And so I had the undeserved courage of ingenuousness to cross those blessed, but also wild, areas. Later on, re-reading that passage, and this time without skimming over it, I realized the dangers I had courted. I also understood why, on my trip there, I had seen a Western lady coming down in a sari, escorted by two soldiers with rifles on their shoulders.

The meeting with Babaji lasted only a few days. The immediate presence of that Master did not awaken particular emotions in me, and his attitude was so un-transcendent, so down-to-earth, that it was difficult to discern in it an embodied divinity. Everything was very strange for us new arrivals. A young American whom I met there confided his disillusionment to me on the banks of the Ganges, and I myself did not know how to encourage him, since I found myself in the same position.

Despite the multiple signs and countersigns, even today I am left with a doubt: I am 50 percent inclined to think that this person is of divine origin, and the other 50 percent demolishes that faith completely. I remembered what Yogananda had said about Babaji: "Babaji can be seen or recognized by others only when he wills it."[5]

---

[5]P. Yogananda, *Autobiography of a Yogi*, Los Angeles, Self-Realization Fellowship, 1981.

The hunt for Masters was not yet over. Another experience awaited me which was to have a notable effect on my daily routine and was to bring about a decisive change in my spiritual discipline.

In all my reading there was talk about meditation and yoga techniques to cure the mind's innate tendency to wander. But my understanding wasn't very clear, in part because every book I read proposed different techniques.

Yogananda proposed *Kriya yoga*, but when I asked information about it from the Self-Realization Fellowship in Los Angeles, I was told that as a priest I had to consult my church. I instantly realized how far disciples stray from their Master by entering into labyrinths of organizations and bureaucracies which divide instead of uniting -- the same thing that happened to Christianity and all the other churches of the world.

Krishnamurti had no technique to suggest other than that of disdaining all techniques: observe your thought, he says, for that is meditation.

I was disoriented, but I felt that it was necessary to act on my mind immediately to tame and re-educate it. All the texts of yoga agree that in order to reach *samadhi*, the ecstasy of union with the divine, it is necessary to isolate the mind from all turbulence, and my mind was like an active volcano.

I met a teacher of Transcendental Meditation, who proposed that I take up this technique. It is taught by Maharishi Mahesh Yogi, a Master who is now very old and who has a sizable following, especially in America. As a technique, TM seemed good to me, but I had some reservations about how it was presented.

The technique is taught for a fee, but I was willing to spend the money. I had convinced myself that spiritual realization was well worth even paying for. I did not yet understand that the obstruction to my realization was precisely my eagerness to achieve it, and that money is not the proper currency to gain that type of benefit. After all, I told myself, if to quiet the mind I were to go to a psychoanalyst, I would certainly end up spending more. That's the way I thought at the time. I accepted the "meditation contract." The technique was effective, at least for a certain period. I gained a certain mental calm and a certain stability, but the greatest conquest was that to follow the technique faithfully, I got used to getting up early in the morning, and thus introduced into my life a habit which before had been repugnant to me.

Nonetheless, even today I ask myself how much distance there is between the Indian sage and his organization's marketing. I have too much respect for Eastern sages to believe that they can be reduced to entrusting the power of human salvation to money.

Even though I had some admiration for Maharishi, my feelings for him never reached the attraction that I had for Yogananda or Krishnamurti. It was certainly not by chance that I set out on these paths. The seeker must experiment before finding the royal road. Each experience made its precious contribution in preparing the next step on the path.

Between Yogananda and Krishnamurti, before Babaji and Maharishi, a completely new experience had slipped in, a personage who was to take my entire life, not right away but gradually, with the ability of a god who skillfully lures his own after allowing them to use up all their cartridges. The Master of Masters was waiting for me at the pass, but he was entering my life, not in a dominant way, but gently, so that His power would not frighten me and His heat would not burn me. It was He who had lent an ear to my prayer, my invocation in the confessional of the Jesuit father, and now, after having worked out my rebirth, was presenting Himself with the resolute sweetness of a mother who wants to give back to her son what the son, through distraction, had himself misplaced.

CHAPTER FIVE

The Master of Masters

When your words came,
I devoured them:
your word was my delight
and the joy of my heart.

Jeremiah 15.16

It happened a few months after my return to the area of Bergamo. It was 1980. An acquaintance told me that a great guru by the name of Sai Baba was coming to Italy. With the hunger I had for masters, that seemed like a golden opportunity.

Sai Baba: who was that? The name meant nothing to me, but I managed right away to get my hands on a little book which was supposed to be a brief biography of this personage. It was a book written by an American, a certain Shulman, who was recounting his personal experience of being close to Sai Baba in India. I read it lazily at first, then ever more avidly. The things I was reading were so unheard of that it made me think that perhaps the writer had just dreamed up this wild fantasy just to reawaken an appetite in readers who were tired of being astonished.

Not long after, I discovered that there was another book on the market by another author, Howard Murphet, that dealt with the same subject. It was called *Sai Baba, Man of Miracles*. I bought it and read it with the same voracity as before - except that this time, I could no longer doubt the authenticity of this individual, for it was highly unlikely that two authors, one Australian and the other an American, could be coming up with the same lies or inventions. In addition, all of the phenomena and explanations they discussed were amply supported by the studies I had been pursuing.

The matter was getting ever more serious. This Sai Baba was not really a guru in the common sense of the term, but something far greater, if one was to believe the accounts of what he did. His miracles -I use the past tense because I'm going back to my way of thinking at the time I read the book - were too stupefying. There was something quite theatrical about them: from Those hands would come rings, necklaces, gold statues, even fruits out of season. Why? I asked myself. At least Jesus healed the sick. What's the use of all this show of precious objects, this squandering of ability and powers?

I was too green a reader to understand the profundity of those messages. I still had in me the hurry to know, the impatience to have everything right away and at a discount. I didn't even imagine how far I'd have to travel down the road to understand even one of His smallest gestures, even one of His words. At that time I didn't know that I didn't know, and I thought that knowledge of spiritual and theological matters belonged to me by right of caste. I would look at that frowning face on the cover. Not even his physical aspect appealed to me much, but the expression on his face seemed to say, "You won't escape me either! It's just a matter of days."

By now I had learned not to close books just because of the extravagant things in them. And so in this case it was a matter of resolving one by one all the questions that surfaced in my mind.

First, as far as the "miracles" went, no objection. It might seem rather strange, but I was not particularly astounded by them. If there are people who bend teaspoons or produce ectoplasm from their mouths or light matches by looking at them, why on earth should it stun me or put me off to know that someone exists who can produce from his hand whatever comes into his head? I had understood that it was just a question of levels of matter and of the consciousness of the craftsman.

But, I asked myself, who can that man be who has full mastery over matter, who manipulates it as he wishes, who creates it without tricks? A magician has some purpose such as wealth, success, fame, and he can't make his wonders work all the time; but what about him? What aim did he have in all this? Furthermore, a magician has to produce from a cylinder the doves and rabbits which everyone knows are already hidden somewhere under the table, but Sai Baba had repeatedly demonstrated that most of the objects made by him did not previously exist, but came into existence at that moment: an act of creation, therefore, and an operation that confounds any physicist.

In the case of some miracles, I was struck by the class with which they were accomplished, as for example the necklace of pearls which a wave of the Indian Ocean brought to Sai Baba's feet at the instant he approached the waters: a devout homage of immensity to him who proclaims that he is the Infinite.

To know the repertoire of miracles was not enough. Indeed, Murphet's book is an anthology of miracles, but it gives little space to Sai Baba's thought. At this point, I was about to reach the conclusion that no Catholic would have dared to touch, that Baba, like Christ, is God. It was then that I was attacked by a series of atrocious doubts.

His powers really are stunning, but... what if he were to be a sort of Antichrist? After all, the Scriptures had predicted the coming of that disturbing figure. Now it seemed to me that the devil had put his horns in the whole matter. I'd look at that dark, negroid face, and compare it to the Hollywood versions of the sacred and angelic images of Jesus, the blond, blue-eyed Jesus of traditional iconography, and I'd ask myself: "What if he really is a demon?! I cannot exclude the possibility that he might be, even though for the moment I'm not capable of proving it either." And then, an orange robe. Through all our tradition, what color served to depict the devil and the environment of Hell better than flame-red?

Poor me! I did not realize the absolute irrationality and groundlessness of those thoughts. I didn't see how illogical and infantile the doctor of theology was showing himself to be, who thought he understood an *avatar* simply by looking at a picture of him. And this certified scholar was overlooking the detail that Jesus certainly was not blond with blue eyes, but surely had to be olive-skinned, and that crimson is a color that has the highest dignity in the Catholic Church.

But above all, I didn't understand at that moment how easy it is for the mind to abandon itself to the most infamous stupidities when it gets stuck on an exterior form! Surely, if I had found myself in front of Jesus Christ, I would have objected that He was too short, that His cheekbones protruded, that He had long hair like a hippie, that He looked like a drug addict or a lunatic, that His eyes were too bright - and that therefore He couldn't be the Messiah. Maybe I was one of those who in His time said, "Is it 'in the name of Beelzebub, prince of demons' that He works wonders and miracles?"[1]

Why repeat that mistake?

Many people believe that they have so much faith in Jesus that it is superfluous to look elsewhere. But, apart from the fact that the real test of faith is action rather than beliefs, think how easy it is to believe in a figure that no longer exists physically, and that therefore is also partly glorified by the rhetoric of writers and by His martyrdom. Observe how people like to remember only the happy events in the life of someone who has died, and how they tend to forget all his defects. If this is true for persons who are limited or bad, like a large portion of humanity, the idealization was even greater for Jesus, the "Lamb without blemish."

To avoid misunderstandings, I emphasize that the person of Jesus shines independently of the descriptions provided by history and literature, but I repeat that a glance at a photograph of the Nazarene would certainly have disappointed many people. In fact, many were disappointed even by physical contact with Him. Isn't it curious that so many of the people of His time who did see Him didn't recognize His divinity, while the Christians of this time, who have never seen Him, all do? And after all, why is it that it was not only poor Judas who betrayed Him, but rather all twelve of His closest associates? With the exception of John, who stayed at the foot of the cross, all of them wavered at the crucial moment. Doesn't this general flight lead one to think that the human and historical circumstances of His death momentarily prevented them from seeing the interior Essence of the Christ and His divinity?

My struggle continued. The words of the gospel of Matthew, "False messiahs and false prophets will appear, performing signs and wonders so great as to mislead even the chosen if that were possible,"[2] sounded menacing to me.

And St. Paul too did his part to awaken my suspicions: "It cannot happen until the Great Revolt has taken place and the Rebel, the Lost One, has appeared. This is the Enemy, the one who claims to be so

---

[1]Matthew 12.24.
[2]Matthew 24.24.

much greater than all that men call 'god,' so much greater than anything that is worshiped, that he enthrones himself in God's sanctuary and claims that he is God."[3]

But there's another form of prejudice involved in using Scriptures to condemn things, and that is not to consider the historical setting, the circumstances, and recipients of certain phrases which were said, often in a very severe tone, by Jesus or by his apostles.

It's a standard practice among many Catholics to read the sacred texts haphazardly, and the minute we find a word in them that refers to a particular situation, to think we're making good use of it by citing it against the people it seems to indicate. Actually we are simply trying to hurt them with our accusations. How easy it is to say to a separated couple: "The gospel says, 'Man must not divide what God has united!'" without knowing that couple's sad story, where perhaps the only union between them wasn't even the work of God!

I have noticed many times that the minute I denounce some human weakness in a homily, people whisper in the ear of the person next to them. From the typical and unmistakable expression on their faces, it is obvious that they are saying, "That's meant for X. What he said before fits Y perfectly!"

In some of its severe or threatening passages, the gospel lends itself to being understood as a condemnation, making it easy for the intolerant to fire off judgments with the Bible in hand. This human tendency must have escaped the Holy Spirit that was inspiring the Biblical writer; if he hadn't turned a blind eye to this human frailty, the Bible wouldn't exist.

Moreover, the more the quotations from the Bible are truncated, the more efficacious they can be, and this is an art well-known to those who use them to wound others. The passage from the second letter to the Thessalonians cited above ends with the following sentences:

"Rebellion is at its work already, but in secret, and the one who is holding it back has first to be removed before the Rebel appears openly. The Lord will kill him with the breath of his mouth and will annihilate him with his glorious appearance at his coming. But when the Rebel comes, Satan will set to work:

---

[3] II Thessalonians 2.3-4.

there will be all kinds of miracles and a deceptive show of signs and portents, and everything evil that can deceive those who are bound for destruction because they would not grasp the love of the truth which could have saved them."[4]

The passage is speaking about an Antichrist who is thwarted by the birth of Christ, and about "false miracles" meant to trick those who have not chosen truth. These are expressions that need to be sifted seriously in examining the identity, teaching, and actions of Sai Baba.

In the same vein, in the first letter of John it says: "Children, these are the last days; you were told that an Antichrist must come, and now several antichrists have already appeared; we know from this that these are the last days."[5] It is easy to see that John's declaration refers to a precise and contemporary situation. At the most, one could say that in times similar to those in which Christ came, many rivals come forward, but it can't be concluded that that passage refers specifically to antichrists of two thousand years later. And, even if it were so, given that Scriptures are always also a warning that transcends time, what is the criterion which determines who among all these antichrists of the twentieth century is the authentic diabolical "Rebel" who commands and organizes them all?

It is clear, then, that the real work of the devil is when people prevent someone from pursuing a question and close their minds hysterically against even the possibility of an hypothesis. Right there you can see how such people have not "grasped the love of the truth which could have saved them."

I realized that if I wanted a decisive answer on Sai Baba, the cowardly cautions of those who fear the unknown or who believe they have already absorbed all the truth available to the human mind would be of no help to me. This time, if I wanted an answer, I would have to loosen my moorings, go out into the open water, and dive deep. At the water's edge you never find precious objects, only the refuse of the sea.

---

[4]ibid. 2.7-10.
[5]I John 2.18.

Now my search was beginning to seem like an adventure, and in fact it was the most inspiring adventure of my life. I followed two methods, one destructive, the other constructive. The first consisted in making a clean sweep of certain theological preconceptions, while promising myself to salvage them later if necessary.

I pretended, so to speak, to be a theologian who had forgotten everything he had learned, all his dogmas and beliefs. I became a blank slate, with nothing to defend and nothing to affirm that wasn't the product of the universal patrimony of common sense. Some of my colleagues would have been shocked by my temerity, but today I believe that no theology is superior to the simplest and purest common sense. I began by examining the untouchable idea that mankind was redeemed only by Christ, and by no one else. My concept of Christ was still foggy: I discovered only later that that dogma is profoundly true, but not in the way it is commonly interpreted.

I asked myself, "Can God, to whom every religion attributes all power, wisdom and love, be reduced by mankind to the limits of a single incarnation?" I found myself in a dilemma I could not escape. If I say that God can incarnate more than once, I collide with the Church and its doctrine. If I maintain that God could not have had other incarnations besides Jesus Christ, I rub against the Truth - that is, against God Himself - by implying that God is incapable of doing anything more than what humans can figure out. I do not wish to lack respect for eminent and studious churchmen, nor for a doctrine which has energized many saints. But between the two, allow me to choose not to rub against God-Truth.

Here a very solid prejudice collapsed, one which after many centuries continues to persist in the minds of many good Christians. This was the destructive method. In order to rebuild, you have to tear down the old building.

Then, in order to begin a more detailed examination of Sai Baba's thought, I focused on a precious clarification, also from John:

"The man who denies that Jesus is the Christ -- he is the liar, he is Antichrist; and he is denying the Father as well as the Son, because no one who has the Father can deny the Son, and to

acknowledge the Son is to have the Father as well.[6] And again:

"You can tell the spirits that come from God by this: every spirit which acknowledges that Jesus the Christ has come in the flesh is from God; but any spirit which will not say this of Jesus is not from God, but is the spirit of Antichrist, whose coming you were warned about. Well, now he is here, in the world. Children, you have already overcome these false prophets, because you are from God and you have in you one who is greater than anyone in this world... This is how we can tell the spirit of truth from the spirit of falsehood."[7]

Here began the constructive method. I had to obtain everything possible of Sai Baba's discourses and of his writings, if he had any. Only in this way would I be able to dissolve the serious doubt that this man with the dark skin and hair like a rock singer, dressed in orange, might be the Antichrist. Looking inside him, at his thought, at his habits, studying him in his movements and in his sayings, I would at least know something more about his nature. By interrogating him on who Jesus was for him, that is, by investigating whether he was on Christ's side or one of Christ's antagonists, I would discover who he was.

I was in a state of great mental excitement. My heart told me that I was standing on a diamond mine, and every move I made to scratch the soil filled me with trepidation and emotion. It was as if I were afraid to discover that all that treasure was real and available to me, that it was right there under my feet. I felt like a lottery player who discovers that he has hit the jackpot, and not believing his eyes, goes over the numbers again one at a time, to be sure it is not an illusion. A disappointment of those dimensions could be fatal.

I found the books I was looking for right away. Today, even though ten years have passed, I am still amazed at how fast the angel of the Lord put that holy *dossier* together for me. Even today many people have difficulty in finding the publications of His they're

---

[6]ibid. 2.23.
[7]ibid. 4.24, 6b.

looking for, but I ended up with a lot of them, and right away: a sign that I should no longer delay or loiter in my prior ignorance.

The moment my eyes rested on His words, I felt an instant thrill which transported me mysteriously into a divine atmosphere. I could not tell anymore if the things I was reading were taken from a gospel or if they came from some heavenly book unknown to most people. I was struck by a flash of certainty that what I was reading had to have a divine origin. Above all, I was struck by the authority and magnificence of His declarations.

> *"I am yours, whether you like it or not; you are Mine, even if you hate Me or try to avoid Me.*
> *"I am in you. You are in Me. There is no distance and no distinction. You have come home. This is your house. My house is your heart!"*[8]
> *"Why fear when I am here? Put all your faith in Me. I shall guide and guard you."*[9]

Keeping my place in the book with my finger, I closed it and looked into space, deeply moved: "So you're still here?" I asked with a burst of gratitude toward that benevolent hand that guided my life. "Am I dreaming or am I awake?" There was a photo on the cover of one of the books in which Sai Baba's face now seemed to be smiling at me, and I was even beginning to feel friendly towards that little dark-skinned man.

Forgetting that I was sick, I rushed to a travel agency to book a flight to India. Final destination: Puttaparthi, the place where even now Sai Baba spends most of the year.

If what I had understood was true, I could not afford to reach the end of my life without having seen at least once in the flesh Him who called Himself "the Mother and Father of the whole human race."

The moment of a close encounter was drawing near. I was full of misgivings because I had read that it is not easy to meet Him, and sometimes even to see Him. The books I was reading said that often, when seekers get there, He is someplace else and seems to elude them.

------

[8] N. Kasturi, *Sathyam Sivam Sundaram,* vol.3, p.148.
[9] ibid. vol. 1, p. 99.

No. This could not happen. It was not I who was going to see Him: it was He coming to me to draw me to Himself.

"You did not choose Me. No, I chose you."[10]

---

[10]John 15.16.

CHAPTER SIX

The First Steps Toward the Avatar

I am going to look after my flock myself
and keep all of it in view.
As a shepherd keeps all his flock in view
when he stands up in the middle
of his scattered sheep,
so shall I keep my sheep in view.
I shall rescue them
from wherever they have been scattered
during the mist and darkness.

Ezekiel 34.11-12

The best thing to do, after discovering Sai Baba, is to study Him. Nothing in my life has given me as much joy and filled me with so much bliss as studying this person. This in itself is extraordinary. When in school I was forced to study such personages as Napoleon, Cavour, Mazzini, the emperors of ancient Rome, or the popes throughout history. All I got out of it was an overwhelming boredom and a fervent desire for the end of class. But when I devote myself to the study of Sai Baba, His work, and His teaching, I never get tired of it, even when studying things that I already know (or think I know). In fact I always benefit from it: it is always uplifting and refreshing.

I have noticed ever since I first found out about Baba that people never tire when they talk about Him. You can go on for hours describing His divine games and miracles, His encounters with His devotees, His ways of drawing them to Him, and you forget even to eat.

Another thing I have observed ever since I have been involved with Sai Baba is that talking about Him warms you and recharges you with new energy. At times, remembering a story about Him or recalling one of His characteristic gestures moves the heart so deeply that unless you are talking to someone who does not know Baba, you are liable to dissolve into tears of joy. Often, when I speak of Him, I have seen tears in the eyes of people whom I was meeting for the first time, people who until that moment had always felt distant from faith and religion.

To **study** Sai Baba! Especially to those who know Him, this idea will seem presumptuous. Someone who proposes to study Sai Baba might remind them of a frog who is fed up with his own confining little bog where he knows every nook, so he decides to go to the ocean in order to understand its secrets.

Although Sai Baba complies with even a skeptical scientific curiosity, my "study" was not really a challenge to His greatness, but rather an investigation to learn more about Him. When you come across someone with whom you feel an affinity, it's only natural to want to enter into that person's life. And then if the encounter goes well, you want more than simple acquaintance; you desire a close friendship, intimacy...

For me, then, to study Sai Baba meant first of all to see Him, then to investigate His activity, and third to understand His thought, His message. Although I expected to take these steps one at a time, I soon discovered that they are not separable. Sai Baba began to be a message from the moment I first saw Him. Because of this, someone who sees Him has already received an enormous gift. I don't say this rhetorically, because the things you understand upon meeting Him may be enough to revolutionize your life, but they still are only an infinitesimal part of what you did not understand at the time and will gradually discover in the course of subsequent events.

If I wanted to make such an unfamiliar journey, I had to get some information from someone. The books I had gave an address in Turin where a Sai Baba center had been set up, the first one in Italy, I think. I decided to turn to them to get detailed information for the trip to Puttaparthi.

I entered into a comfortable garret, after they made me take off my shoes. There was a lot of light. Prominently placed in the middle of the central wall was a big photo of Sai Baba. Beneath it was a picture of His feet, immersed among bouquets of flowers. A number of incense sticks diffused a typically Eastern perfume. I was very surprised by all this, and as a first impression, it wasn't very reassuring. When I saw that the men and women were sitting separately, facing images and singing in an incomprehensible language while swaying to the accompaniment of drums, cymbals and harmonium, I understood clearly that those forms of worship did not attract me at all. For a priest who performs rites and ceremonies every day, seeing other cults can't trigger much interest. I felt that I had ended up smack in the middle of some idolatrous and pagan sect. But I didn't swerve from my resolve; I didn't want to give up just because of exterior forms. I asked what I wanted to know, that is, what I needed to bring to Puttaparthi, if there were any accommodations, what the meal arrangements were - in short, everything one needs to know to go to a place that is unfamiliar and full of logistical difficulties. The advice I was given was very sketchy: I was told to bring at most a bedsheet. But the most important thing that I was told, and it remained impressed upon my memory, was this phrase, "Swami severely tests the people who go to Him."

Swami is a Sanskrit word that means "master" or "teacher," and Baba's devotees often use it when they talk about Him.

A gentleman with a marked southern accent asked me if I had some *vibhuti*, the sacred ash materialized by Sai Baba that I had often read about. I had never expected that I could have a pinch of that miraculous ash even before reaching Puttaparthi, and so when he handed me a packet of it, I felt so fortunate that I was overcome by deep emotion.

I knew that in Sai Baba's ashram, that is, in the sort of monastery or sanctuary where Sai Baba lives, one is not allowed to eat meat or fish or eggs. For fear that I wouldn't be able to be faithful to so many Lenten Fridays in a row, I tested myself before going and decided in one moment to stop eating meat.

To most people this might seem a trivial decision, but for me it was not, for two reasons. The first was because of health. The acute illness I was suffering from had crippled my kidneys: the inflammation typical of this disease affects the exchange of glomerules at the capillary level, creating a disorder in the retention of nutrients and the expulsion of wastes. In short, my body was losing many precious nutrients, particularly proteins, and was retaining residues that it should have excreted. My surgeon friend who had placed me in his ward begged me to offset that loss with a diet rich in protein (at least 120 grams a day!) and low in sodium. Meat and fish seemed perfect for my situation. Such a radical change in my diet would perhaps further compromise my health.

But I stopped eating meat anyway, and I replaced it with milk-based products. I hadn't known it would be so easy to quit, but above all I couldn't believe my eyes when a few months later I discovered that my condition had improved decisively, even with the reduced protein that I was now getting only from milk products, and modest amounts of them at that.

The second reason I decided to opt for vegetarianism was in order to discipline my mind. I had read a great deal on the subject, and I was by now convinced that just as the saying "a sound mind in a sound body" is true, so is its opposite, "a sound body in a sound mind."

My studies had persuaded me that the mind depends on the chemical and subtle products of the food we eat. I would later find extended and detailed explanations of this fact in the teachings of Sai Baba. I knew from my studies in parapsychology that the violence and the death-stress connected with the slaughter of animals are not mere hypotheses, but verifiable facts that have a precise influence on the life of anyone implicated in them. In sum, by eating the animal, one assimilates its history: its fears, its stresses, its rebellion against death, its desires and passions. We know that in a single cell there is the entire program which will define the future of the creature, with colors, forms, and appearance all clearly delineated. So why not think that in that cell there is also its future mind, the *antahkarana*, that is, the "interior instrument" of Sankhya philosophy - obviously in potential form, as in a seed, but full of energy like a seed?

I know these arguments are difficult to document, yet one knows them intuitively. Much has been written and much is still being written in defense of vegetarianism. Today even official medicine better appreciates this type of diet, recognizing its great advantages in many types of therapy.

Yet the body cannot heal simply with a change of diet. It is not merely a marvelous chemical machine that reflects chemical products and reactions. In the body there is much more: it hosts the Lawgiver, and when the mind becomes sensitive enough to detect His presence, the laws can also follow a different course. This is what would happen for me, and for many others, in the years to come, thanks to my meeting the "object" of my studies.

I was able to personally experience the influence of meat on the psyche. Here, to the delight of those who like to balance accounts, I must confess a weakness that nonetheless turned out to be a *felix culpa*, a happy fault. I would be a hypocrite if I led the reader to believe that I was strong enough to be perfectly faithful to my Lenten resolution. There was one moment in particular when I gave in. It was at the time when I started to meditate with the Transcendental Meditation technique. The TM instructors assured me that being vegetarian was a stress I still needed to overcome, and that's why the problem of eating meat kept surfacing in my mind. I hadn't yet completely resolved my desire for meat - they told me - and so the repressed desire was floating to the surface. It is a fact that the minute I would sit down to meditate, the most succulent meals would pass in front of my mind, full of fragrant roasted chickens and various sausages.

What to do? If I was going to ruin all my meditations for a roast chicken, it would be better to eliminate the problem by facing it head on. And so, after about three years of strict vegetarianism, I decided to get rid of the desire once and for all by satiating myself with a meat dinner. After all, I told myself to quiet my sense of guilt, "It isn't a crime to eat meat, and I can't say that because I'm vegetarian I'm better than many people who are carnivorous."

It was almost a traumatic experience. I remembered an analogous experience of Gandhi's that he recounted in his autobiography. Convinced by a friend that India could be liberated only by the grit of someone who ate meat, he hid himself on a river bank to consume some barbecued baby goat meat, and the next night he could feel bleating in his chest. Needless to say, I am not a *mahatma*, merely a little aspirant who strayed on the shoulder of his spiritual path because of dietary desires, and not for a noble motivation like Gandhi's, and yet I can assure you that instead of enjoying the coveted snack in peace, the minute this little faith-breaker set his teeth into the cruel repast,[1] he was himself bitten by remorse and anxiety. I kept seeing the animal alive in front of me, and this inhibited the desire that was so enticing when it was simply mental.

I immediately noticed some other effects, physical as well as psychic. My intestines held that food much longer than they kept vegetables, and my sense of smell, made sensitive by several years of vegetarianism, was able to detect the odor of the cooked animal on my skin. It was a disagreeable sensation. As for my psyche, I noticed that my mind, which during my three-year "Lent" was no longer seriously agitated by unwanted thoughts, suffered a set-back from that "carne-vale" (meat-festival): polluting thoughts started to enter again in triumph.

It was a lesson. As always, it is experience, more than words, that has the greater power of persuasion.

The decision to adopt a vegetarian diet was motivated also by a religious factor. I knew that I was going to a sacred place where the Avatar was living in person. It seemed right to prepare the body for such an important moment.

In the second half of August of 1981, I reached Puttaparthi, after a long plane trip and exhausting waits in airports. From Bangalore it was still about 150 kilometers by taxi to reach Sai Baba's ashram. It took four hours to cover that distance. The road was narrow, and it crossed an inhospitable savannah dotted with little rocky mountains that looked like meteorites fallen from the sky and smoothed for millennia. The car, an old Fiat 1100, promised neither comfort nor safety. My kidneys hurt like they were in pieces.

The driver stopped to get gas and drink a coffee. The heat was suffocating, and the minute the car stopped, a beggar came up asking for alms. The moment I gave him some, a flock of other beggars, some of them lepers, clustered around stretching out their hands or arm stumps. It seemed like an hallucination. I had been travelling two days. The night before, a taxi driver had taken money from me that was supposed to have been provided by the travel

---

[1]A reference to the famous story of Ugolino and his sons in the *Divine Comedy*: *La bocca sollevò dal fiero pasto / quel peccator...* (And that sinner raised his mouth from the cruel repast...) (*Inferno* XXXIII.1). [Translator's note].

agency. I knew very little English, and no Indian-English. I could not take it any more. I closed the window, and on the verge of desperation, I asked myself, "What on earth made me come here into this hell? What an idiotic idea to have had!"

It was the moment of the test. The time had come to determine how much I was willing to suffer to have the greatest thing possible. Even mythological tales often relate that the great treasures hidden in the crypts of mysterious ruins are usually protected by fierce animals and poisonous snakes. Only the daring adventurer gains access to those riches, after having overcome all the obstacles.

In those circumstances, though, I was not inclined to philosophize, and I would have considered it a real miracle if a helicopter were to arrive and kidnap me and bring me home. Actually, a real miracle was taking place, given that in a sense I was already kidnapped, and I had no possibility of undoing my decision. The road was the one that was to bring me with no possibility of delay into an Abode of Highest Peace. It was no longer my responsibility to do anything to bring myself back to the true Home.

There was someone who was watching over me and was planning my return. No matter how much I struggled to escape that grip, it would have been fatal to me to loosen it, and He to whom I had entrusted my salvation could no longer allow it. The love of a mother is great, even when she chases her child because he refuses to take his medicine and she grips him firmly in her arm to make him take it!

Finally, Prashanti Nilayam: Sai Baba's house, and indeed, as the name says, the Abode of Highest Peace. The things I had read had convinced me of the extreme difficulty of meeting the Divine Master, but when one tempts fortune, one always hopes for the best. And so it happened, because I barely had time to leave my suitcase in the Accommodations Office when I was informed that there was about to be a *darshan*.

Darshan means "a sight of," and it is a word commonly used in India to indicate the moment in which a religious personage shows himself to his devotees. Some time ago, I read in the Vatican newspaper an article about some Southern Indian bishops who had had a meeting with the Pope. One of them, when addressing the customary greeting to the Holy Father, began his speech by referring to the last darshan that had been recently granted by the Pope.

Even if it is true, as older people used to say, that the spiritual power of a blessing can go through seven walls (actually it can go through any number of them), still any good Catholic would rather receive the Sunday-noon papal blessing directly in St. Peter's Square rather than on television. In the same way, Indians too commonly believe that the physical presence of a saint is much more effective than a simple spiritual communion.

Until man is able to transcend every form in order to unite spiritually with the Formless, everything in the external world that reminds him of the Divine is useful, and must be observed very carefully in that light. Someone who is beyond all form can do without vehicles and spiritual practices to reach the Divine, but only when he is no longer at all affected by the senses. Here no one can cheat: no one can claim to have overcome all external forms if he still has so much love for a good dinner, for the comfort of a luxurious villa, for a car with all the options, for companions who give him a fleeting ecstasy. The man who has lost all interest in the objects of the senses is ready to fuse with the Formless, but as long as he still has the slightest dependence on the sensory world, he needs a form even when he is in search of God.

Ten years ago at Prashanti Nilayam, there wasn't the huge crowd there is now. I did not know back then how lucky I was to have all that space and all those opportunities to see Sai Baba from up close. In the sacred area in front of the temple, there were no more than three straight rows of people seated on the ground, of fine red sand. Now there are many rows and the entire area is filled with people.

I hastened to enter this area, which was surrounded by an ornamental wall. In front, there was the temple. A figure in orange was coming out with a calm and solemn step, like that of a great priest. His thick curly hair, which made a large crown around his head like a regal diadem, was blown by a soft breeze that tempered the humid heat of the last days of monsoon season and revealed his timeless face to those present.

The group of men was a lake of white, that of the women a rainbow of colors. The temple was pink and blue, the trees an intense green. In that festival of colors, which seemed an enchanted garden full of lilies and meadow flowers, His robe stood out vividly. It was bright orange and fell straight, totally covering His feet, so that He seemed an eternal tree solidly planted in the ground. And the wind, to make Him even more fascinating, caressed His tunic, making it cling to a body that was both slender and powerful.

There was an ineffable silence in that atmosphere. Yes, there were a lot of crows that were croaking and songbirds and parrots wheeling here and there, etched against a deep blue sky with swift passing clouds - and yet the overall impression made by the scene was that of a great silence. All those birds and clouds seemed nothing but the image of our thoughts that come and go in an incessant whirlwind with a tireless pace. The silence was like pure consciousness, which watches thoughts pass without being affected by them.

Everything happened without conflict. It seemed as if time had ceased to exist. No thoughts of family, problems, weariness, or physical ills crossed my mind.

I was mesmerized by that Presence. Now He was approaching the spot where I was sitting. Now and then He would accept letters, or He would make a gesture with His hand, as if to say "Wait. Tomorrow. Patience! Stay seated." He would stop, bend down over someone who was making a request, and with a sweet and innocent voice, ask "Eh?" like someone who hasn't understood, or who was pretending not to understand and wants to have the question repeated. Occasionally He would stop, move off a little bit and make circles with His hand, and a white powder, vibhuti, would flow from it. It all seemed normal to me; everything corresponded to the accounts I had read in the books.

While I was watching Him materialize the sacred ash, I noticed that I considered that action ordinary, and I was astonished by the fact that I wasn't astonished. "How's this?" I said to myself. "You're seeing something extraordinary and you're not even surprised?" I was scandalized by my own indifference.

He passed in front of me and gave me a wide smile, like the one a public figure might give to a friend whom he's known forever when he makes him out in the crowd, as if to say, "Oh, you're here too? Hi there!" I looked behind me because I was afraid that I had presumed to deserve an attention that maybe was not for me, given that I had just arrived, but there was no one there.

After He passed by, I had a shiver of indescribable joy that I could calm only by shedding a flood of tears. Yes - because our little bodies cannot tolerate joy either when it is excessive, and if we do not want to explode, it has to find an escape valve. Next to me there was a Japanese, or maybe a Thai, gentleman, who with unperturbable dignity slipped a tissue from his jacket pocket and kindly offered it to me.

Everyone who goes to Prashanti Nilayam nurtures the keen hope that one day or another he will be personally received by Sai Baba. I was no exception, but given the idea I had formed of this man who scrutinizes the minds and hearts of people, I did not dare to imagine that that good fortune could happen to me, too. Sai Baba usually receives people in groups, where there is always someone who dares to ask for an interview, as these private meetings are called. To ask for an interview for a group seems fair and legitimate, but that a single person should push for being personally received to me seems not only unseemly but presumptuous.

One day, a gentleman next to me, named Francesco, found out that I was Italian, and he told me that if the Italian group was called, I should follow its members. Our talk was like a pre-rehearsed scene. He certainly couldn't have known that a little later Sai Baba would call the Italian group.

When that small and powerful Being in orange appeared in the doorway of the temple that day, I watched all his movements. He passed the women first, then the men. One of them stood up to whisper something to Him in a pleading tone. Sai Baba asked something, and then, after pausing a moment with His gaze fixed in space, He made a commanding gesture with His finger, from which it was very clear that the monosyllable that He uttered in English had to be "Go!" In fact, I saw a small group of people get up promptly and head in an orderly way toward the rooms of the temple. Francesco took my arm and said, "Come on, let's go!"

I was not sure about what I was doing, and I was afraid that when I went in, Sai Baba would say to me, "Who called you?", thus relegating me to the fate of the wedding-guest in the famous parable of Jesus, who was ejected by the master because he was not wearing the proper wedding garment. I was like a little, trembling, lost puppy in the hope that no one would get the idea to send me back. Baba returned, and with a sure step entered the interview room, followed by all of us. I gave a sigh of relief.

Now we were there, men on one side and women on the other, waiting to see the Man of Miracles face to face. With a very natural air, Sai Baba turned on the fan, and then went to sit down on a chair in the corner of the room. He was very small, and there He no longer had that imposing appearance that He takes on at darshan. Let's say He was very "human," and my brain was already beginning to devise theories.

"So this person here is supposed really to be God in flesh and blood? He doesn't look like a god, he looks more like a cunning little wizard." Evidently, my mind, which was busy searching for plausible explanations, presumed already to know what God looked like! Otherwise it would not have mistaken Him for a common magician. The smile of the friend who had taken me in so amiably now seemed a suspicious ruse. I really do not know what was coming over me.

The skin of His face was extraordinarily luminous, and only later thinking about it, I realized that I didn't see it olive-toned as it usually is, but bluish, like the clouds of a mid-summer thunderstorm. The luminosity of His face gave the impression that under the translucent skin there was a light that was shining through. It certainly was not the face of a 56-year-old man, but rather of a pure and angelic adolescent.

The minute He was seated on the chair, His eyes fixed mine and He asked me, "How are you?" My English was halting, but I had encountered that phrase in all my English courses, and I knew how to answer it: "Fine, thank you!"

It was like a farce in which one of the actors, I, in this case, had gotten stuck on the only line he knew. Sai Baba, who had leaned forward a little to ask me that question, drew back a bit with an expression that meant, "Are you sure?" while I was biting my tongue for having answered in such a foolish way.

Then Sai Baba made a circle with His right hand, and from it came some vibhuti, which He gave to a young man seated on His right. He made another circle and produced a little medallion, which he bestowed on a child who was seriously ill. The third materialization was a ring, which He put on the finger of that child's father. All in the space of a few seconds, and at such a short distance that I could distinguish the objects as they came out shining brilliantly, fresh from the mint of His hand. There was a wave of emotion among those present.

After this, He turned His attention to me again to ask me a second time, "How are you?" I was deeply grateful to Him for having giving me that second chance so I could correct my previous answer.

I had no intention of asking Him for a physical cure. I had left Italy with a very clear purpose. I knew that He had not only the power to manipulate matter and to heal, but also the power to touch the hearts of men to show them the main road that leads to the final destination. But to speak to Him in front of everyone about my moral state and my desire to receive directions so that I could get on that road seemed immodest to me. So, having no alternative, I answered Him by saying that I had problems with my kidneys.

"Yes," He said, "I know." And He began a detailed description of the disease. Francesco translated. The gist of His whole discourse was that I should not worry about the illness, that He would take care of me, and that the origin of all ills is in the mind. "Dispel depressions," He said to me, "and don't think about the future." These two admonitions made a deep impression on me because they were a perfectly accurate description of my mental state at the time: emotional highs and lows and deep torment about the future.

I asked myself why on earth He had devoted so much of His precious time to give attention to a problem that for me was not important. Perhaps precisely because it should have been. When you meet Sai Baba, everything happens as if in an extrasensory dimension; you are stunned and you no longer understand anything of what is happening around you. You understand the message He leaves you with only later, often much later.

Thus, while at the time I didn't understand why He was emphasizing my illness when what I wanted to ask Him was of a spiritual nature, later I understood that you can only attain spiritual discipline and final realization when you have refined and cared for the basic instrument, which is the body. And I had to care for my body - it seems like a contradiction - by "neglecting" it, that is, by not concerning myself with it more than necessary.

Physical illness is a consequence of moral illness, and it arises due to a misplaced confidence in the body, as if it were something to be exploited for one's whims instead of being an instrument for spiritual realization. The more you devote yourself to activities that do not lead beyond the physical realm, the more you necessarily dread the loss of the vehicle that lets you perform those activities, the more you depend on it. Fear is born, and with it, sickness.

Having finished His lesson on my ills, Baba turned to other people. To one lady He said: "At darshan, you kept asking yourself, 'Why doesn't He look at me? Why does He turn His gaze elsewhere?'" And the lady, acknowledging that she had thought that, dissolved in tears. There were a few more humorous remarks interspersed among very simple and practical teachings, all in an atmosphere of the sweetest familiarity, and then He got up.

Sitting with my head down, lost in thoughts I do not remember, I had not noticed that Baba was passing near me in going out and that He had stopped in front of me. I saw this orange robe in front of me, and then I felt the softest hand pass under my chin and raise it, as one does with sulking children, in order to look into my eyes, and when our eyes met, He gave me a gentle slap on my left cheek and continued towards the door.

We all got up. There was a bit of a crush around Him. Now that I was standing and I saw Him pass under my nose, I realized how small in stature He was. His thick hair reached literally to my nose. We were very close, His body brushed against mine, and I had a great desire to embrace Him. I was extremely happy without knowing why, and with the familiarity that one has with people towards whom one feels a natural sympathy and a boundless love, I felt like saying to Him: "You're so adorable, it makes one want to eat You up!"

We were invited to sit down in a small adjacent room. From there Sai Baba called a few people one at a time. Between the two rooms there was nothing but a little curtain, and yet you couldn't hear a murmur, not a word, not a breath. It was as if that fragile separation had become an armored door. When the people came back, they were each full of emotion and their faces were transfigured.

Afterwards Baba took a basket like the ones village women use for shopping, and drew from it handfuls of packets of vibhuti, which He distributed to all of us.

We all went out with our hearts full of silence. We were like people who had been invited to a banquet and who were going out satiated, intoxicated with the nectar of an infinite love that we had never experienced before that moment. The other devotees would stop us, as students do to their classmates after an oral exam, and ask us such questions as, "How did it go? What did He say to you? What did He ask you? How lucky you are!"

During my stay in the ashram, I was able to observe that His presence leaves a mark on nature, too. One evening -- it was already dark and the moon was covered with clouds -- a few moments before entering my room to go to bed, I saw a large rainbow vividly etched against the sky. I had never seen a rainbow at night before. I thought perhaps it was not an unusual event in the tropics, but an Indian who was nearby, joining his hands with the grace characteristic of that nation, hastened to tell me, "It's one of Baba's miracles!" The next day everyone was talking about the nocturnal rainbow.

One day at darshan, a little before Baba came out from His rooms, a monkey entered the precinct of the mandir. Monkeys are clownish animals who seem made especially to distract people, because there is nothing they know how to imitate as well as man, by caricaturing him. So whenever a monkey walks in front of you, it's always a funny and entertaining spectacle. At the moment that Baba came out to go towards His devotees, two crows descended in a synchronized dive. They looked like two F-16's from an aerobatic team. They dove headlong onto the back of the monkey, scaring it and evicting it, so that it ran away.

The climate was still that of monsoon season. Even though the weather was about to improve, there were still many days when the sky was overcast and there would be sudden downpours without warning. I noticed that on many rainy days, even when it looked like there was no hope that there could be darshan, at the last moment the weather would suddenly turn, it would stop raining, and a blue patch would appear in the sky over the temple. All around, it would be gloomy, black, and rainy, but the devotees could go in and enjoy their encounter with the Divine Master in peace.

On another occasion, at the same moment that Baba came out from the temple, an intense fragrance of jasmine spread through the air. And don't think you can dismiss the coincidence by attributing it to jasmine bushes in the ashram, because many people noticed that the wind was blowing in only one direction, and the fragrance was detected in every corner of the mandir.

These might seem like chance events of little significance, but try adding up a good number of these small anecdotes, and you'll see that you have a picture of a reality that is not ordinary. I do not think that in our daily life it happens that we always have good weather when we have to go out for the weekend, or that remote-control birds chase away the dog that is howling and disturbing our lesson. We would want miracles to be ever more prodigious. After having seen the saint of Assisi speak with birds and tame a wild wolf, we would want to see him fly over the rooftops in order to believe in the miracle that already surrounds us - the miracle that we are. If we were to see him fly over the rooftops, there would always be someone who would ask why the house did not fly with him, too.

The miracle is precisely this order of nature, which man can fit into and be part of, when he wills it. The miracle is the flower that spreads its perfume in a hidden corner of the forest, the miracle is the spring that never tires of producing fresh water, the miracle is the sun that never tires of warming us. When humans mess things up so that we lose these benefits, the springs begin to lose their purity, the sun ceases to shine and the flowers wither even before blooming, then we discover that everything we had was a miracle. The continuing miracle is that nature possesses an enormous power of self-protection, an incredible will to live, and an amazing energy to reconstruct everything that humans destroy. We must not bring nature to the point of depletion.

Man could subjugate all of creation at his feet, but he does not do it because he does not believe in the power he is. Man substitutes the ego, a second-hand power, which only has limited energy. If he learned to live in harmony with the world, to desire the great goals of the cosmos, the cosmos itself would bow before man and serve him as a god.

I was very happy to have been able to see Sai Baba right away. I had not hoped for so much. I felt welcomed and felt that it boded well for the future. Indeed, there are no ill omens under that sky, and everything that happens is only for the good of those who take refuge under it.

Everything becomes desirable when we are near a man who is free from all desire.

CHAPTER SEVEN

Another Religion
Or a Single Faith?

Ut unum sint
Let them be one!

Jesus

After my return to Italy, I had to face a series of difficulties. As I said, my appointment as a teacher of religion was revoked in one of the two schools where I taught. But I was so happy that I would have borne anything in order to shout my discovery to the world. The fleeting events of life no longer concerned me at all. My only satisfaction would have been to spread the news of what I had discovered. But I found out that the world around me was cold and indifferent to my announcement.

A few days after I got back from India, I telephoned my sister, a catechism instructor and faithful parishioner, who I knew was more-than-usually receptive in religious matters. She knew about my trip to Puttaparthi, and although she respected my opinions, in the bottom of her heart she did not approve of it. "You know," I told her, "He really has returned. I assure you, He's still here!" But on the other end of the line, the answer was an embarrassing silence that was meant to dampen my enthusiasm.

When I would go to celebrate Mass, people would ask me about my trip, and I could not refrain from talking about the sensational things I had seen. But, to no avail! In response to my comments, they would look at me as if they were examining my face to determine if I was mentally sound or insane, and it would all stop there. Some people felt sorry for me, marveling at what my sickness had done to me.

I remember that during one Sunday homily - it was the Feast of the Epiphany and the church was full of people - while I was explaining that God's creative power had not limited or depleted itself with the birth of Jesus, I could not keep myself from saying some sentence like: "You do not know what surprises God has reserved for this era, and these eyes of mine have seen unmistakable signs of His living presence in the world." What I was saying came from the fullness of my heart, and frankly, I thought an assertion like that might produce some reaction or at least a little curiosity. But not a single soul took me aside after Mass to ask me: "What were you talking about? Can you explain? What did your eyes see?"

Evidently, the time was not yet ripe. It is also true that when a truth is so momentous as to overturn all the positions of one's creed, rather than face the shock, people do not want to make the effort to understand. Laziness, that good ally of fear, takes over, and people conclude, "It might be, but I don't believe it."

Today I understand the value of the lesson I received not too long ago from a nun who was very faithful to her vow of obedience. One day, noting how disappointed I was about certain seditious articles that condemned anything that came from the East as being sectarian (it was the time of the famous letter of Cardinal Ratzinger), this sister said to me placidly: "Don Mario, don't worry about these obstacles. The truth is like light: When it wants to make headway, it doesn't need other lights, it sets out alone!"

I realized that the phenomenon that is Sai Baba transcended not only science with all its laws, but also theology, insofar as it too is a science subject to the power of reason and therefore as limited as human reason itself. I understood that if medicine or physics had to upset all their conclusions and surrender before the "phenomenon" that is Sai Baba, theology could not escape having to do the same in front of the "revelation" that is Sai Baba. In short, either revolution or surrender.

I would say to myself, "What does it matter if the world does not want to recognize Him? This too is part of His plans. Why should I worry about a task that is fully His responsibility? It would be sad if I let myself be blinded by fear. It would be sad if I succumbed to the instinct to protect my respectability, and re-entered the circle of skeptics simply in order not to upset theories that have become sacred and inviolable. If I did that, what use would I be? It would serve no purpose to complain about the indifference of others if I allowed myself to be swayed by the same laws of apathy."

Immersed in these thoughts, I decided that Sai Baba's teachings should be actively pursued. Now that I have seen and met Him in person, I hope I am no longer afraid of misunderstandings and retaliations by the authorities. At least for now, I must move forward courageously.

I still had a lot of things to understand, and that is what I'll try to explain to the patient reader in these next pages. I will not draw any conclusions, but rather offer points of reflection that I hope will be useful to new seekers. The only conclusions that I shall not try to disclaim are the ones that come naturally through my presentation. I apologize to those who might be upset or disturbed by them. In my defense, I can say that I would have to be like a pearl-diver who tries to describe only the habitat, color, and shape of pearls and the water conditions that make it possible to retrieve them, without ever mentioning the exalted experience of being in the under water world. In the same way it would be a terrible repression for me to limit myself to describing the "Sai Baba phenomenon" with just the eyes of an experimental scientist. Allow me an occasional moment of rapture!

From the outset I have to state an important premise. Everything I am about to say is the fruit of my own personal inquiry. The reader should not be misled by the idea that just because the person writing is a priest, what he is expounding is the official opinion of the Church. This is a mistake into which many Catholics fall, and non-Catholics, too. Many people are of the opinion that an ecclesiastic is like an official in the army, that he should no longer have a mind with which to think, and that everything he says should be rigorously sifted by an authoritarian censor. This is certainly valid for the fundamental truths that cannot change according to the nation and the times. The eternal truths in fact are the only ones on which we should all feel unity and brotherhood, and their survival does not depend on being defended from pulpits because they are the common patrimony of all people.

Thus, in pointing out that I conducted my inquiry as a free thinker, I invite readers to use their discrimination and critical sense, so as not to accept everything passively as being from the voice of authority.

One should not be afraid of inquiring into things that can change; there are many things that can change in the world. If even Russia has freely adopted a policy of political openness, why should we of the church, who should be relied on to set a crystal clear example, be afraid to be transparent in front of mankind? How many times have we had to change our minds about some conditional truth? The fear of changing is a fear of evolving. In the world of thought, everything is in flux, and it is right that we should seek to climb ever higher, transcending thought itself.

I realize that what I will say might be called into question, especially by the solemn doctors of official theology. I am not afraid of a discussion as long as my interlocutor shows the willingness to have a friendly conversation, without the air of an inquisitor who is ready to condemn because he thinks he has already understood everything. I will say what I think about Sai Baba, in the same way as many priests have given their opinions about the sightings at Medjugorje. Some people have already taken the liberty to say everything they thought about Sai Baba, condemning Him *a priori* or with very dubious arguments. If we tolerate those who condemn others, then I invoke the same tolerance for those who refuse to repudiate a personage as enigmatic and unfathomable as Sai Baba.

After having been concerned all these years with a figure as controversial as the "barefoot saint" of Puttaparthi, I have concluded that it is not legitimate to take into consideration the opinions of anyone who has not seen Him, who has not heard Him, who has not read His discourses, who is unfamiliar with the environment in which He was born, the religious and social context in which He lives, or who has no elementary notions of science and theology. To understand a fraction of Sai Baba's reality, it is not enough to have just one of all the qualities listed above, you must have them all, at least to some degree. And yet there are already groups, often among Catholics, who pronounce judgment, who have already declared that Sai Baba must be a demon or a powerfully mystifying magician. But if you inquire further, you will find that they have only seen a photograph of Sai Baba and heard something about Him. They are people who are afraid of competition or of the intervention of a God who might come and overthrow their kingdom or overturn their money-changing tables.

There are at least three factors which trigger a sometimes-passionate theological reaction. Chief among them is the fear that the phenomenon called Sai Baba, which is drawing the attention of millions of human beings, could threaten the stability of established religion and encourage sheep to stray from their fold. This worry is rather noble when it derives from a sincere impulse to defend or spread faith. It is sometimes necessary to be willing to vigorously defend one's faith, but when that impulse deteriorates into a polemical aggressiveness, you begin to suspect that it springs from an intense fear, that is, from the person's deep-seated insecurity that what he believes in is not sufficiently believable in itself!

Connected with this motivation, there is a second factor, parallel to the first, and that is that the great power of attraction exercised by Sai Baba might prevent so-called "pagans" from reaching the "truth," the truth that every religion believes it has found. There is also the fear that those who have distanced themselves from religious practice for various reasons (not always justified), might be distracted by the East, thus annulling the effort to bring them back to their own religion.

I shall respond to this objection immediately. I have seen thousands of Sai Baba devotees, and I have observed that most have a great desire to return to their original church with renewed fervor. Moreover, this return is often prevented by pastors who have in effect excommunicated the devotees, by singling them out in their sermons as traitors to their faith. Nonetheless, there are some parish priests with open minds who have realized that an authentic spiritual conversion has taken place in these people baptized in the "Light of the East," and that it is a conversion worthy of complete respect.

The third factor responsible for self-justifying reactions is the conviction, by now rooted in many Christians, that their own religion is the only one born from a first-hand Revelation, while all the others might indeed be valid, but none can compare to Christianity.

In the "Declaration on the Relations of the Catholic Church with Non-Christian Religions," a very short document which is better known in ecclesiastical circles by the title *Nostra Aetate*, the Second Vatican Council "admonishes Christians...if possible, as far as is within their power" to remain "at peace with all men" of every creed and race, and about the various non-Christian religions it says the following:

> *"The Catholic Church does not reject anything that is valid and holy in these religions. She regards with sincere respect those ways of acting and living, those precepts and those doctrines which, while they differ on many points from what she herself believes and teaches, nonetheless not infrequently reflect a ray of that truth which illuminates all men.*
> *"Therefore She announces, and She is obliged to announce, the Christ who is "the way, the truth, and the life" (John 14.6), in whom men must find the fullness of religious life and in whom God has reconciled all things to Himself."*[1]

These are no longer the anathemas of the Council of Trent, where every proposition began with a menacing "if someone should say that" and ended with the condemnation "he shall be cursed."

The Second Vatican Council brought the Church to a level of tolerance that is much more... tolerable. Nevertheless, deep down the conviction remains that anyone who is not in the Catholic Church still lacks a large share of the benefits that only the Christ has granted to His sheep. That is why the document quoted above affirms in no uncertain terms that people **must** find the **fullness** of religious life in Christ. Even though the expressions **fullness** and **must** seem to be quite peremptory and to exclude any alternatives, rather than being disputable, they are profoundly true.[2]

---

[1] Nostra Aetate, § 2.

[2] In the *Declaration on Religious Freedom* (known as the *Dignitatis humanae*), the Second Vatican Council re-asserted the presumed supremacy of the Catholic Church in these words: "The Sacred Council professes that the same God has made manifest to humankind the path through which men, by serving Him, may find salvation in Christ and become blessed. We believe that this single and true religion exists in the apostolic and catholic Church, to whom the Lord Jesus has entrusted the mission of communicating it to all men." (§ 1)

Nevertheless, in the *Lumen gentium*, the *Dogmatic Constitution on the Church*, the Council admits that "the plan of salvation embraces also those who recognize

The error of church officials lies in their need to have absolute control and a monopoly on the christic truth. The christic truth really belongs to the entire human race, and it does not necessarily have to meet the expectations or the models of Western culture. The Christ who is "alive yesterday, today, and always," who is "Beginning and End" of all things, who is "the Alpha and the Omega," transcends the world of rites and doctrines and reaches every heart, crossing continents and oceans by Himself, and making use of every form that seems appropriate to Him.

Given that the Christ is not an entity wandering in space, but is rather the Truth innate in every heart, It belongs not only to Catholics, but to the entire human race. It is superfluous, not to mention counterproductive, to impose doctrines on others. If the Christ-Truth is already in the heart of each human being, it can be revealed only by right and just conduct: when a person has learned the art of loving his neighbor, he becomes a missionary of that love and that truth. "By this love you have for one another, everyone will know that you are my disciples."[3]

Thus everything rests on determining what the concept of Christ encompasses, what is the true flock, in what forms the Shepherd manifests Himself, and who are His sheep.

There is an amusing and dramatic story that illustrates the kind of spirit that still today exists among men of the cloth - and not just Catholic ones.

In Belfast, Ireland, a Catholic priest, a Protestant minister, and a Jewish rabbi were engaged in a heated theological discussion. Each one of them was giving a different interpretation of the same Biblical passage. Even though the conversation had started on sacred topics, their inner fervor was degenerating into open polemics, and resentment was growing among them. None of them was able to convince the others. When talking about God, they accused each other of heresy, apostasy, and religious betrayal; and

---

the Creator" and that "God is not even far from those others who search for the unknown God in phantasms and in idols, because He gives life to all and breath to all things, and as Saviour wills that all men be saved." (§ 16)

[3]John 13.35.

so they began to hate each other.

Suddenly an angel appeared among them and said: "God sends you His blessing. Express a wish that will foster peace and the Almighty will grant it."

The Protestant minister said:"Make all the Catholics disappear from our beautiful island, and then peace will reign undisturbed."

The Catholic priest said: "Let there no longer be a single Protestant on the sacred soil of Ireland and this island will have peace."

"And you, rabbi?," asked the angel. "Don't you have a desire to express?"

"No," answered the rabbi. "As long as the wishes of these two gentlemen are fulfilled, I'll be happy."[4]

The various religious communities that have ended up institutionalizing themselves as churches -- a phenomenon that affects virtually all religions -- give great emphasis to ideology, theological subtleties, the polemical reading of sacred texts and their factious interpretation.

A person who feels protected by a church, who defines himself as religious or devoted, who adheres totally to that institution while following his own personal interpretations of the Scriptures, ends up refusing to believe that God is still capable of manifesting Himself as **He** wills. Such a *homo ecclesiasticus*, or man of the church, is not very *sapiens*, or wise: he wants God to obey his interpretations, but God is absolute and unconditional freedom.

In the course of the history of the various churches, the fundamental purpose of holy Scriptures, of the preaching of prophets and sages, of the presence of avatars, has gradually been lost. The goal of all these divine interventions has always been to change how people live in practice by leading them to knowledge of, and identification with, the Divine.

Theologies and ideological movements exalt the human intellect. They feed on intellectual games and lose sight of the most concrete goal: to live out in practice the message left by Great Men.

---

[4]The story is freely drawn from *La preghiera della rana [The Frog's Prayer]* by A. De Mello (ed. Paoline).

Instead of clarifying that message, theological debates obscure it with the turmoil they provoke and the disharmony that they almost always leave behind them.

Man has enough clear-sightedness to perceive the need to use his strength and energy towards discovering his own identity. Why does he end up so ingloriously in quarrels and divisions?

His inquiry is fine at the beginning, but then as it progresses, his mind is swayed by its attachment to its own intellectual discoveries, and by the desire to protect the nest of security and certainty that it has constructed for itself. The desire for security stems from the ego. Initially individual, it becomes collective, and what was once a psychological defense mechanism now becomes an organizational mechanism of power.

In order to protect this artificial security, man reaches the point of acting dishonorably toward his fellow men, because it is precisely in their freedom of thought that he sees the greatest threat to that security. And so instead of seeking truth, the long-time seeker seeks and defends himself, his own ideology, his own interpretation.

The same obstinacy that serves to divide two theories can be used to unite them. I became aware of this possibility in my recent studies, when I discovered that what divides theologians in their assertions is only an attitude that ranges from laziness to close-mindedness. If that is all, don't you think that the effort of the discussion should be to promote union?

What we need today is people and theologians who seek this unity with a sincere heart - practicing it in daily life - and who in their studies disregard the points of disagreement that kill, embracing instead all that unites!

This is what the poet Kabir says:

What use is it if the scholar ponders words and concepts,
If his heart does not overflow with love?
What use is it if the ascetic dons saffron-colored robes,
If inside himself he is pale?
What use is it if you display morality
To make it shine in front of men,
If there is no music inside it?

The truths which unite are discovered through humility and purity of heart. Everything which divides stems from pride and ill-will.

Sometimes what makes it difficult to come to agreement is obstinacy and wilfulness. In that case, the only solution seems to be the art of maintaining silence. If the truth lights its own way, it is wise to avoid instigating conflicts in cases where we know they will only end up killing the peace.

The essential thing is to realize that in conducting their searches, all religions have always aimed at the same goal. They use the most diverse methods - one travels by boat, one on a raft, one in a ship - but they are all in the same water.

One of the most serious faults that prevents people from seeking union is presumption. There are people who are convinced that they are doing the will of God even when they persecute, kill, and torture others. It is worth observing how easily the new religious movements that have sprung up almost everywhere give in to the temptation of thinking they have certainties to impose on others, and those who denounce the slaughter of the Inquisition become in their turn Inquisitors. Perhaps the reader too has already encountered born-again Christians, Jehovah's Witnesses, fundamentalist Christian groups, who are ready to swear that they have already received the revelation that Sai Baba is Satan incarnate. Even the Hare Krishna movement, who could easily find out for themselves how many qualities their beloved Krishna has in common with Sai Baba, turn up their noses when they enter a house where they see a picture of Sai on the wall.

There is nothing to be done. Maybe another five thousand years will have to pass before another movement arises -- the Hare Sai, whose members will go door to door to spread the stories about Baba's games and about how He was loved by His *gopis*[5], shepherdesses devoted not to cows, but to computers. And these "Hare Sai" will know that the Divine is still there at their side to sing in every tune: "Love one another, as I love you. I will always

---

[5]The shepherdesses among whom Krishna spent His youth. In their total surrender to the Divine Incarnation of that age, they symbolize true devotion to the Lord, grounded on the total renunciation of all attachment.

descend to earth to teach you this."

Spiritual people stay clear of all fanaticism. They do not care whether people sing one way or another, whether they wear a *japamala* around their necks or a cross on a chain; rather, they desperately seek every point of union with others, all the while taking care not to agitate others' hearts.

Sai Baba does not compete against religions. That is His greatness. He is a person on His own who transcends religion itself, and He is not interested in having initiates or followers. He does not add or remove a single iota from scriptures, but rather explains them, showing how they have been distorted or forgotten.

Those who see in Sai Baba a man who is organizing villages and colleges for the love of power and money forget that He who has at His disposal all the gold in the world, He who knows how to draw pearls and diamonds from the ocean with a simple movement of thought, has no need to beg for alms. They fail to realize that with their foul and miserable yardstick they are judging an extraordinary Being, someone with immeasurable powers, someone who can draw from the inexhaustible reservoir which sustains them too, even though they are ignorant of this and ungrateful. They do not realize that what they see in Him is a reflection of *their own tendencies.*

Sai Baba's unlimited love flows with compassion toward our religions, which are foundering in a state of corruption and decadence. To approach Sai Baba, the essential prerequisite is a heart open to truth and closed to prejudice. Then, and only then, does Sai Baba reveal Himself.

Part II: The Teachings of Sai Baba

CHAPTER EIGHT

The Message of Miracles

In the heavens, on the earth,
in the ocean, in the depths,
Yahweh's will is sovereign.

Psalm 135

What generally makes the greatest impression on people when they first come into Sai Baba's physical presence, is the ease with which He performs miracles. One could say of Him what John affirms about Jesus at the end of his gospel: "There were many other things that Jesus did; if all were written down, the world itself, I suppose, would not hold all the books that would have to be written."

Sai Baba's *leelas* (a sanskrit word meaning "divine play", or "small miracles") include many kinds of phenomena. They may be grouped under the following headings:

1) **Materializations.** From the time of His birth, these are His most frequent miracles. A simple motion of His hand, with the palm facing down as if to churn the air, and the most diverse objects emerge from the void: statues of various dimensions, rings, necklaces of various metals and designs, rosaries, medallions, fruits out of season, food in enormous quantities, *lingams*,[1] sacred images, crucifixes, and

---

[1]"The Lingam has the form of a mathematically perfect figure, the ellipsoid. It has neither a front nor back, and is without an end or a beginning. It has no protuberances or irregularities jutting out from its smooth surface, which might give it some character. It's form is based purely on a geometrical figure, the ellipsoid, and hence it cannot be identified with any other known physical form in the universe except another mathematically perfect ellipsoid, which is another Lingam. It is so

miraculous unguents. Sometimes He will blow gently on an object and it will change from one substance to another or instantaneously change shape. At other times, if one is in a good position to observe closely, one can even see how in the space of a few seconds a small, shining lump forms in Sai Baba's palm and rapidly takes the desired form. It is like a *poof*! in the comics, a little cloud of luminescent energy that in a short time forges a jewel, which remains hanging in the air for a few instants, oblivious to the law of gravity. When it is presented to the recipient, it is very bright, shiny and warm.

With the exception of a few cases that could be counted as examples of translocation, a phenomenon well-known to those who study parapsychology, His materializations are for the most part authentic manifestations of matter created at the moment. It is as if His hand is able to collect atoms and molecules of various chemical and organic compounds from some dimension beyond space, and recombine them all according to some new plan of His, completely independent of the physical laws known to us. Or rather, it is as if He commands the atoms of the air under His hand to come together in a precise way.

I hope the expression does not seem exaggerated, but "acts of creation" would be the most accurate description of these leelas. Artists are said to "create" works of art, but in fact all they do is reuse pre-existing elements and recombine them in a new way. The artist's "creation" takes place in his imagination, which is capable, with the help of his hands, of shaping already existing matter into completely original forms. At other times, he will take a familiar object and vary it slightly with a touch of his personal interpretation. In Sai Baba's case, He supplies the material that He then uses to create whatever He wills or desires, and He does not need any models.

Christian doctrine has always maintained that creation is "to draw things out of the void." Even though the word "void" seems inadequate and ingenuous in respect to modern scientific knowledge, classical theology could not use a better term to describe the birth of

---

much devoid of character, that the author is almost tempted to call it a formless form. Therefore, Baba has said that it is *the fittest symbol for representing the formless Divine Essence, that is God.* Thus, when the Lingam emanates from Baba's mouth it is symbolic of the birth in time and space of THAT which is formless and eternal, within a simple geometrically perfect entity, the Lingam." (E.B. Fanibunda, *Vision of the Divine*, p.51).

an object from an invisible dimension, and it uses this word to try to explain the birth of the Universe.

When I first started studying Sai Baba, that continuous production of shiny jewels annoyed me more than a little. At that time, I was not aware of the numerous and profound messages contained in those manifestations. The fact that most of the jewels were made of precious metals excluded the possibility that they were simple magic. A magician could not long sustain such a Pharaonic expense. Often the jewels are rings and necklaces in solid gold, platinum, with precious stones like surprisingly large diamonds, pearls, topazes, and emeralds. Sometimes the objects are of very modest materials, but of very high spiritual value, like rosaries (called *japamala*) of simple crystal, or the vibuthi itself, the sacred ash.

Certainly, the doubt can always arise that a small object like a ring or medallion could easily be concealed in the sleeves or at the wrists of a magician. However, it remains difficult to explain how you could hide objects as big as solid gold statues, sometimes more than a foot high, like the ones Sai Baba often materialized in earlier days on the shores of the Chitravati river.

While from the material point of view vibuthi is the most modest gift that Sai Baba constantly gives to devotees, it is really the one richest in powers and meanings. I can no longer count the number of seriously ill people whom I have seen healed by vibuthi, and I shall refrain from citing as examples all my own sicknesses, like fevers and various pains, which allowed me to experience first-hand how the symptoms subsided completely with the use of vibuthi. Besides its powerful healing properties, this holy ash embodies a particular spiritual meaning.

Chemically, ash represents the final stage of matter: a state that is incorruptible, stable, aseptic, pure, and purifying. In fact, ash is free from bacteria, and it can be placed without worry on a cut as a styptic that promotes healing. For farmers in past times, it was often the first and only first aid in cases of amputations or accidental cuts while working, and housewives would even use it in the wash as bleach. Older rural women could still tell you the procedure that produced the fragrant white bedsheets of past times.

Symbolically, ash represents a redeeming death, or rather a state of death that is a prelude to life. In Sai Baba's discourses, the concept often recurs that from the death of the ego, from its being reduced to ashes, man rises to the state of imperishable divinity. By "ego" is meant the complex of passions such as anger, envy, jealousy, lust, and ambitions that constitute it, which are the real death of the inner life of man.

This mystical symbolism of vibuthi calls to mind the Christian liturgy of Ash Wednesday, when the priest places holy ash on the foreheads of the faithful and says these words: "Remember, man, that you are dust and unto dust you shall return." It seems to me that this formula encourages the idea that we are the body and that our existence ends with it. On this occasion, I take the liberty of amending the text to say: "Remember, man, that your **body** is dust and unto dust it will return." The body dies, but we do not. *Vita mutatur non tollitur*: "Life only changes, it is not eliminated."

The meaning suggested by Sai Baba is applicable to that liturgy and gives it even deeper significance: reduce your "I," the cause of all ills, to ashes, and you will rise again to divine life as perfect and incorruptible as the ash itself.

If all the objects created by that extraordinary hand were to be gathered together, your house would not be large enough to contain them all. This assertion may seem like hyperbole, but instead I think it is an understatement, if you consider the testimony of N. Kasturi, Sai Baba's principal biographer, who lived at His side for years until his death. This venerable writer affirmed in 1961 that Sai Baba materializes about a pound of vibuthi a day, and that already at that time, if all the ash He had created were gathered together, it would make a mound weighing 5 tons! Just think that twice each day Sai Baba usually gives interviews to one or more groups at the end of darshan, and in each interview He presents several objects which He materializes on the spot.

But what is the purpose of all these creations? The motives for which Sai Baba creates these objects are infinite, and they are often as inscrutable as His Will. Nonetheless, it is possible to understand a few of their meanings, both from what He has said about them and from listening directly to the beneficiaries of these extraordinary gifts.

Sai Baba has provided an explanation: "Do not pay too much importance to miracles. They are just my leelas, divine play. I first give people what they want, so that later on, they may want what I have come to give."[2]

This explanation is valid for all of Sai Baba's miracles, but it is especially applicable to the various objects that He bestows on devotees. To give someone a necklace or something of value is a gesture of great love, something usually only done for a beloved. These gifts do not come from jewelry stores, but from a world unknown even to the world's most expert physicist. Their creation thus represents a complete mastery over matter, and shows an intimate knowledge of it.

Another meaning of the creation of talismans is that they protect the devotees who wear them. This was explained by Sai Baba himself, who said that in a moment of danger, the object worn by the devotee acts as a kind of radio transmitter: it connects with Him who created it so that He can send energy to overcome the moment of difficulty.

One day Sai Baba put a ring with a diamond of at least 15 carats on the finger of a dear friend of mine. Since he was an expert engineer, this person knew his gems, and when the shock of that miracle passed, he estimated that the stone was worth about half a million dollars. Sometimes Sai Baba comments ironically on the monetary value of the gems that He produces, and by making them appear so rapidly and effortlessly, He wants to show how illusory matter is and how important it is to pursue higher and more lasting goals. On August 5, 1988, in the course of a talk to a large international group, He said:

It is hard for you to understand Sai. Sai talks like an ordinary person and He moves freely among you. But you would be deceiving yourselves if you thought that Sai is like any other human being. It is not so. Sai can transform the entire world in an instant. Gold, diamonds, everything is in Sai's hands. See for yourselves: with a movement of His hand a large diamond will suddenly appear (as He said this, He waved His hand and a gigantic diamond appeared) *and, as you see, with a breath from Swami it will disappear.* (He blew on the stone and it disappeared). *Everything that Swami wills must happen. The true nature of Divinity cannot be understood by everyone. For this faith is necessary.*

---

[2]N. Kasturi, *Sathyam Sivam Sundaram*, Part II. p. 12.

2) **Cures of physical illnesses.** I specify "physical illnesses" because the miracles that Sai Baba performs on the souls of people -- miracles that are harder to verify by objective analysis -- are far more numerous than the bodily healings.

I myself have seen with my own eyes cures of cancerous tumors in their most advanced stages. The patients, realizing that their days were numbered, would find out about this last hope: holy ash, or water that had been sanctified by a lingam, created for the purpose by Sai Baba himself. Perhaps prompted by the extreme circumstances of being seriously sick, they would have great confidence in the remedy and would be healed. But even without having to resort to serious cases, which certainly are more sensational, I have observed that in almost all the cases in which I gave vibuthi or lingam water to people who asked me for them, they recovered.

It must be understood that often the problem was not solved in exactly the way the person had hoped. But by invoking Sai Baba's grace for a healing, even if the person is not physically cured, he will certainly obtain a greater mental acceptance of the illness. I have seen many people hope for a cure and not receive it, but gain instead from their appeal great strength to overcome more difficult obstacles, including death itself.

One of my sisters developed a breast tumor. By the time the tumor was discovered, the operation to remove the mass of the tumor itself was no more than a temporary remedy, because the cancer was already in advanced metastasis. The doctors said that it was too late. I put vibuthi on her forehead before and after the operation, and I suggested that she spread some on the incision, too. She told me later that she overcame all her anxiety about the operation in an instant, and that even the doctors were astonished by how fast the incision healed and she regained her strength. She lived another two and a half years after that operation, when the prognosis was no more than a year, but the most amazing thing was that she reached the end of her days without any of the physical pain that usually accompanies the late stages of cancer.

People have such a will to live that they would want miracles to confer immortality on the body, but the purpose of a miracle is not to make a mass of decomposable organic elements eternal. It is rather to delay the call to the other world so that the extra days granted may be utilized for better and further progress than what was expected. Even Lazarus, restored to life by Jesus, in the end had to give up that miraculously healed body a second time, but this in no way diminishes the importance of his resurrection.

3) **Dominion over the forces of nature.** I have already mentioned how rain clouds would miraculously disperse at darshan during my first trip to Prasanthi Nilayam, but this does not seem like a very great miracle when you think that once Sai Baba made the waters of the Chitravati River retreat, when it had flooded and was about to wash away the village of Puttaparthi. Howard Murphet's book talks about a perpendicular rainbow. N. Kasturi's biography gives a delightful account of miracles of this kind, too.

On November 24, 1990, in the middle of the dry season, Baba said the following to a crowd of hundreds of thousands gathered in the great stadium of Prasanthi Nilayam, who were all surprised by the unusual weather of those days:

You were all witnesses to what happened yesterday. The whole sky was filled with dark rain clouds. At 7:30 in the morning, all the clouds had gotten thicker, and looked threatening: a violent rainstorm seemed to be approaching. But instead the clouds served as air conditioners and offered shelter from the burning sun, and then dispersed.

4) **Resurrections.** Here many people are ready to raise the barrier of suspicion and skepticism. They can accept that He heals people or creates objects from nothing; but that he raises people from the dead, no, that cannot be - that's impossible!

When you analyze it closely, this mental block in Christians derives from the opinion that only Christ was capable of a miracle so great as raising people from the dead. Many Catholics should be surprised at their own ignorance, having forgotten that the Acts of the Apostles recount how Peter raised up Tabitha at Jaffa[3] and how Paul resuscitated a boy who fell asleep during his talk and fell from a

---

[3]Acts of the Apostles, 9.36-41.

window.[4]

Granted, one doesn't hear about resurrections on the evening news, but to deny that they could happen is excessive. On the contrary, if we question these, what's to stop us from questioning those recorded in Holy Scriptures?

In Chapter 13 of his book, Murphet[5] describes the resurrection of a certain Radhakrishna, with details that very much recall the episode of Lazarus in the Gospel. Sai Baba has performed others as well, observed by numerous eye-witnesses. I myself know of a lady who had just expired in one of the sheds of Prasanthi Nilayam, and who regained her life and strength when Sai Baba passed by. Several years ago, I was told about a student in one of his colleges who was brought back to life. I wonder how many of these miracles are not known to the public, and how many marvels occur in the world without anyone knowing about them!

This is not the most appropriate place to examine all the other cases of "re-animation of the corpse," as they are termed by Dr. Rosati, with the typical terminology of doctors. (For love of science, doctors stay clear of any possible contamination of reason by faith.) Here it is enough to observe that Sai Baba's power encompasses even this possibility. Anyone who wants to know more about it will have to study all the case histories, and not just at a desk!

Sai Baba affirms: "Let me tell you this: mine is no mesmerism, miracle, or magic. Mine is genuine Divine Power. I am *Sarvadaivattwaswarupam*. I am the Indweller of every heart."[6]

Now, without sliding into a boring theological treatise, I would like to address the question of "miracles" from a Christian perspective to determine whether Sai Baba's power to work miracles can be considered to be of divine origin. My inquiry required that I carry out such a study, because I had resolved to put Sai Baba through an "exam." The exam consisted of sifting through the case histories of His miracles using the conditions established by theological schools, especially those schools bent on defending the Catholic faith. It is

---

[4]ibid. 20.7-12.

[5]H. Murphet, *Sai Baba Man of Miracles*, York Beach, Maine: Samuel Weiser, 1973.

[6]*Sathya Sai Speaks*, Vol. VII, p.369

precisely these schools that have put out theses intended to defend religion from possible attacks and counterfeits. Even biblical theology offers numerous starting points for a strict analysis of Sai Baba's miracles. By comparing Him with these studies, I would be more certain how to regard Sai Baba's human form.

The notion of "miracle" is quite ambiguous, because while some people go off seeking prodigious events, really all of creation in its immense and perfect order should be considered miraculous. All of creation seems the object of loving care that defies the randomness that many people still want to believe controls the eons and infinite spaces of the universe. The rationalistic school of criticism at the beginning of the century, represented by A. Harnack, contested the truth of miracles, seeing them as a "violation of the laws of nature."[7]

But no matter how many rational explanations are advanced to explain extraordinary events, the true exceptions to the normal laws of nature, the fact is that these marvels are merely unusual events that still obviously depend on the natural order of things. That is, Nature cannot go against herself and against her own laws. If the famous aphorism of Leibniz about evolution, "Nature does not skip steps", is true, it is also true for phenomena that cannot be explained by the common understanding acquired by humanity up to our time. In other words, if something happens in nature that seems to disrupt the theories we have devised, the apparent contradiction derives from our ignorance of deeper laws that embrace that exception.

Really, from this point of view, there are no miracles. That is, there is nothing in the world that man cannot understand, at least potentially, and what should really amaze us is not the miracle, but the fact that we cannot understand it. At the time it was invented, the locomotive was considered a diabolical instrument. Computers, with the innumerable possibilities of development they offer and the speed with which they are transforming the exchange of information, could be considered a miracle in relation to what was known about electronics just a few years ago. And the best is yet to come!

People are paying more and more attention to the power of the mind and to cures achieved by spiritual healers or by the power of

---

[7]A. Harnack, *Das Wesen des Christentums*, Leipzig 1908, p. 17; Italian ed., p. 26.

concentration. There are even sacred liturgies which when performed, sometimes result in instant healings. As long as they are not the result of hysteria, these phenomena deserve attention. They show that God is not an external power that intervenes arbitrarily to help man, but rather that He is a power within man.

It is not geniuses who are extraordinary or "out of the norm"; rather, everyone who isn't a genius, that is, most of humanity, is abnormal. The condition of genius should be the normal state of humanity. If a person has not reached the level of consciousness that enables him to live in perfect harmony with the laws of nature, it is not because it has been decreed that the lowest level is the norm, but it is because of his or her own ineptitude. The causes of this ineptitude must be thoroughly investigated to find the appropriate remedies for it.

In the Old and the New Testaments of the Bible, setting aside the distinction between what is "providential" and what is "rationally justifiable," great importance is given to the religious significance of miracles, both those that constitute the enchanting order of nature and those that constitute the "exceptions" to the ordinary course of events. Indeed, miracles constitute an essential part of the Gospels: it is not possible to reject miracles without rejecting all the rest of the gospel.

Jesus performed miracles in order to prove the truth of His assertions. It is too hasty to conclude *a priori* that Sai Baba's miracles derive from a "love of the marvelous," while those of Jesus originated from "the love for those who suffer," and to "establish the Reign of God," as was asserted in an article in the Italian magazine *Famiglia Cristiana (The Christian Family)*.[8]

Judgments about miracles run the risk of not being very reliable when the people making the judgments don't know much about the mission of the person performing the miracles. Nor should it be forgotten that the Master of Galilee let slip some pretty sensational miracles, too. If the water in the jars at the wedding of Cana had not been changed into wine, and good wine at that, no tragedy would have occurred; in fact, the less-temperate guests might have remained more lucid. The miracle of the coin that materialized in the mouth of the fish to pay the tax could have been substituted by taking up a collection. Was not the transfiguration of the Lord on Mount Tabor

---

[8]*Famiglia Cristiana* No. 5 / 1990.

spectacular? What about the fig tree shrivelled in an instant because it failed to bear fruit? Who knows all the criticism Sai Baba would get in the *Times* and the *News* if he made a herd of two thousand pigs fling themselves headlong into the Chitravati river! Who can scrutinize a divine mind and judge whether it would be more or less appropriate for it to act in one way rather than another? What human mind, unaccustomed to divine matters, can determine whether a miracle was performed for the love of the spectacular instead of for the Reign of God?

In his treatise *Catholic Dogma*, M. Schmauss, a noted professor at Monaco, asserts that Christ worked miracles "not for a pure and simple sense of compassion towards those who suffer, nor to arouse wonder or to satisfy human curiosity. That He did not perform them just for compassion is clear from the fact that the number of those He healed was small in relation to the huge number of sick people. On the other hand, He did not perform them just for display or for self-glorification (and in this He distinguishes himself in a fundamental way from miracle-workers and Hellenistic magicians). This is revealed by the fact that He would not perform any miracles where faith was lacking (Mc. 6.5). The miracles were intended to develop faith in Him and in His mission. Therefore, when He encounters a hardened heart and a blinded spirit, He does not act, not because He lacks the power but because the sense of His miracles would be misunderstood."[9]

Why not admit, at least as a hypothesis, that the same thing is happening with Sai Baba? Sai Baba does not heal everyone indiscriminately, but He bestows a loving attention on everyone who approaches Him. This can lead to the healing of the body or of the mind. He cannot act against the will of others, because He who has defined Himself as *Narayana* - the Faithful One in the heart of each person - would abhor any violence to Himself: He is the conscience in every human being.

The reasons for having recourse to miracles are well laid out by John the Evangelist, who clearly shows that the purpose of Jesus' signs was to develop faith. *Semaia* (signs) is in fact the word John uses to indicate Jesus' miracles, and it is surely the most appropriate term if you keep in mind the preceding reflections.

---

[9]M. Schmauss, *Dogmatica Cattolica*, vol. II, Marietti. pp. 163-164.

"Many believed in His name when they saw the signs that He gave."[10]

Nicodemus, an important man among the Pharisees who would go to Jesus secretly so as not to be criticized by the sect he headed, turned to Jesus with these words: "Rabbi, we know that you are a teacher who comes from God, for no one could perform the signs that you do unless God were with him."[11]

Saint Thomas Aquinas underlines the divine origin of miracles: "Only God can perform miracles."[12]

And Jesus, disheartened by the incredulity and the hard-heartedness of His people, exclaimed one day when He was summoned to heal the son of a court official: "So you will not believe unless you see signs and portents!"[13]

Like Sai Baba, Jesus did not attribute much importance to His "signs." In fact, the Nazarene would prohibit the people He healed from spreading the news of the miracles. He would do His best to get away from the enthusiasm of the crowd, and would refuse to perform miracles on request. He would reprimand those who were gluttons for the extraordinary: "It is an evil and unfaithful generation that asks for a sign!"[14]

Do not give importance to miracles. Do not exaggerate their significance. The greatness of My power does not reside in these miracles, it consists only in My Love. It is true, I can change heaven into earth and earth into heaven. But Divine Power does not fritter itself thus to reveal itself. It is only for the sake of love that Divinity descends as an Avatar. All the ostensible miracles are only droplets of that Ocean of Love. Do not be dazzled by the droplets. Recognize the ocean and come to dip yourselves therein.[15]

It is foolish for people to think that I am just a man of miracles

---

[10] John 2.23.
[11] id., 3.2.
[12] *Summa Theologica.* P. I, Q. 110, art. 4.
[13] John 4.48.
[14] Matthew 16.4.
[15] R. Ganapati, *Baba: Sathya Sai*, Part II, p. 108.

and no more. The kind of feeling which an elephant gets when a mosquito lands on its body is exactly like what miracles are for me. These miracles have an insignificant place in my totality. Sometimes I feel like laughing at the ignorance of people when they attach importance to my miracles. People talk of only such small things and forget the much bigger aspect in me. [16]

The signs of Jesus, and His actions and His life, prove His divinity and His role as the Messiah. In short, Jesus did not stop just at asserting His own divinity, but confirmed it with the miracles that surrounded Him as well as with the teaching that always accompanied the signs. We must consider these characteristics in order to distinguish a true sign from a false one. As Pascal said, "Miracles identify the teachings, and the teaching identifies miracles."

The question today is whether the author of miracles is God or the devil. Many people reject Sai Baba for their own idiosyncratic passions. They accuse Him of performing miracles through demoniacal, rather than divine powers. They blindly repeat what was already described in the gospel, namely when Jesus was accused of expelling demons "in the name of Beelzebub, prince of devils."

Jesus' answer could only confirm His supreme wisdom:

"Every kingdom divided against itself is heading for ruin, and no town, no household divided against itself can stand. Now if Satan casts out Satan, he is divided against himself, so how can his kingdom stand? And if it is through Beelzebub that I cast out devils, through whom do your own experts cast them out?" [17]

To ask whether it is God or the devil who works miracles shows how deeply men are trapped in the snare of dualism. In fact, there is only one Divine Energy, there is only one Inventor of all things, only one Law that governs all. Obviously He is not the direct author of evil, but He is its Witness. In this dualistic play put on by an inscrutable Will, good and evil are two categories that have a precise purpose: to reveal the Principle that gave rise to the whole play, and

---

[16]*Summer Showers in Brindavan* 1974, p. 282.
[17]Matthew 12.22-27.

to lead all things back to the Totality.

In this game, which the capricious human mind rejects as incomprehensible and absurd, the Supreme Principle, the Without-a-Cause, does not enter into the competition. He does not participate in it by rooting for the good, nor does He manipulate events so that the good people are on the winning team. The "I am" of the Bible is the Pure and Simple Witness, the Absolute Observer of all happenings, recognized by Him as being perfectly in harmony with His Law. Everything derives from Him. How could He take sides? The distinction between good and evil, ethics, moral codes, all originate from man and vary according to the times, the place, the era, and the nation.

The only immutable code is that which Eastern philosophy defines as the Eternal Law, *Dharma*. "Wisdom is the Law that stands forever," it says in the book of the prophet Baruch.[18] And Luke the Evangelist says: "It is easier for heaven and earth to disappear than for one little stroke to drop out of the Law."[19]

To entertain doubts about who engenders miracles, and to maintain that the energy that produces them could be evil, would be like asking whether all the suffering seen in a war movie is actually made by a Hollywood film director. It makes more sense to ask what the purpose and message of a miracle is. When the intent is clear, even though the contrasting forces of good and evil will still be part of the picture, it will be clear that the overall purpose is to lead beyond the dualistic categories of good and bad.

That is how Saint Thomas rephrases the question, to then answer it with the crystal clearness that characterizes his deductions. The Angelic Doctor dedicates a special section to the problem: "Whether demons can lead men astray with certain miracles."[20] He answers: "If one understands the term miracle in its proper sense, devils cannot perform miracles, nor can any other creature, but only God." Nonetheless, citing Saint Augustine, Saint Aquinas observes that God permits Satan to perform miracles as signs of falsehood, insofar as "the signs of the Antichrist serve the purpose of leading man into

---

[18]Baruch 4.1.
[19]Luke 16.17.
[20]op.cit. P. I, Q. 114, art. 4.

falsehood."

I will study the question of whether Sathya Sai Baba wants to lead men into falsehood in the section dedicated to His message, which is based essentially on five values: Truth, Righteousness, Peace, Love, and Non-Violence.

There are Christian-inspired groups or sects who have not made any serious inquiries into who Sai Baba is, and have not read a single word of His discourses, who declare peremptorily with a no-appeals-allowed kind of air that Sai Baba is the devil himself. When I hear this, I feel like repeating the bitter complaint that Jesus directed toward His contemporaries:

"What description can I find for this generation? It is like children shouting to each other as they sit in the marketplace: 'We played the pipes for you, and you wouldn't dance; we sang dirges, and you wouldn't be mourners.' For John came, neither eating nor drinking, and they said, 'He is possessed.' The Son of Man came, eating and drinking, and they said, 'Look, a glutton and a drunkard, a friend of tax collectors and sinners.'"[21]

And these people, in whose name do they cast out their demons?

Another doubt that can arise about Sai Baba's miracles is whether they are done through magic. Saint Augustine makes a sharp distinction between the miracles of magicians and those of saints:

"If magicians do things similar to those done by saints, it is for an ulterior motive and for a very different reason. They do it looking toward their own fame, while saints do it for the glory of God. They do it for some private business, while saints do it for the universal economy and by command of God, to whom all created things are subject."[22]

This point too will be clearer when we discuss the work and actions of Sai Baba.

---

[21]Matthew 11. 16-19.
[22]Quoted by Saint Thomas, in the op. cit. above.

But are Sai Baba's miracles real? In short, are they an effect of illusion or can one believe in them as true and authentic?

Renan declared in his controversial *Life of Jesus* that rather than assert the impossibility of miracles, what he could affirm was that no miracle had ever been verified;[23] but Sai Baba makes it possible for all to observe and verify the incontrovertible proof of His miracles. There have even been scientists anchored in a stubborn skepticism who have gone to observe Sai Baba's miracles with the precise intent of exposing Him, but despite their challenge, all they could do was verify objectively that the phenomena that they observed with their own eyes were real.

In classical theology, there are four indispensable requirements that determine whether miracles are authentic. They are principles officially adopted by the Church both for examining all the case histories connected with the healings at Lourdes, Fatima, and other recognized sanctuaries, and also for the process of beatification or canonization, which elevates people who died with a reputation for saintliness into objects of worship.[24]

---

[23]E. Renan, *Vie de Jésus*, Paris, 1891, p. 20.

[24]I have consulted a specialist in the field, a monsignor Delegate appointed for procedures of beatification and canonization in the Diocese of Bergamo. From the interview he graciously granted me, the following principles emerged, which show that the process for making people of outstanding virtues into objects of worship is very strict. This reveals the extreme prudence used by the official agencies of the church in judging appearances of the Madonna, for example, or any other case which seems to reveal the intervention of the Divine in the human.

Here are the requirements for making a servant of God an object of veneration, either as "Beatified" or as "Saint":

1) The foundation of any process of beatification or canonization is heroic virtues. This heroism is confirmed through investigations by the Ecclesiastical Tribunal, and validated by the Sacred Congregation in two bodies: the Theological Commission and the Cardinal's Commission.

2) The Church requires a miracle both for beatification and for canonization.

3) The healing must be obtained through the intercession of the person proposed for beatification or canonization, and it must be of a physical disease (all mental and psychic illnesses are excluded) that is incurable by any means known to medicine or surgery.

4) The healing must be instantaneous and immediate, and the illness from which the person is healed must not recur within the span of 10-15 years (sic!).

5) The healing must be verified and unanimously certified by a team of

1) To be real, a miracle must be a historical event, verifiable with certainty. Miracles are unusual events that depart from normal known laws, and precisely because they are unusual, one must be sure that one has not fallen victim to a hallucination. For example, to get well in itself is not an unusual event, but to be healed from a cancer in its final stages of metastasis is. When the miracle occurs infrequently, obviously the suspicion that it is not real is greater than when it is re-occurs regularly. If we only know of an event through the reports of other people, then it is much easier to contest its authenticity.

W. Bousset maintains that "miracles that have not been personally verified are not real miracles. Because then it is not the miracles which support faith, but faith which has to support the miracles."[25] Although this hypothesis is very strict, it is understandable when you keep in mind how easily "men deceive themselves or lie," as David Hume said. [26]

2) For an event to be considered miraculous, its supernatural character must be established with certainty. This is not an easy project, but in some situations it is indeed possible. It is very difficult to establish the boundary line between the "natural" and the "preternatural." The most common objection hinges on the power of suggestion or the placebo effect. We don't know exactly to what degree auto-suggestion can enter directly into the facts of life and manipulate them, but we certainly are capable of establishing what it cannot do. If the power of suggestion were unequivocally confirmed as a cause of healings, there would no longer be rooms for radiation therapy in the hospitals, no dialysis wards, and many operations could

---

specialized doctors, drawn from the Medical Council of the Congregation for Canonization of Saints in Rome.

6) Having been declared unexplainable by official science, the miracle must be recognized by the Church (the Theological and Cardinals' Commissions) as deriving from a supernatural intervention.

7) When on the other hand an incurable or almost-incurable disease is healed by medical efforts, even if those treatments very rarely work for that disease, it cannot be termed a miracle, but an extraordinary occurrence. In fact the Catholic Church draws a sharp distinction between miracles in the strict sense, that is super-natural interventions, and prodigies, that is extraordinary events which do not necessarily imply a special divine intervention.

[25]W. Bousset, *Das Wesen der Religion*, Halle 1920, p. 209.

[26]D. Hume, *An Enquiry Concerning Human Understanding*, section 10.

be avoided.

Saint Augustine says: "We know that a bean will not sprout from a kernel of grain, nor a kernel of grain from a bean."[27] It is not necessary to know all the natural causes of an event in order to recognize it as miraculous. The fact that people must cite unknown forces as the hidden causes of the event only confirms its extraordinary character. The proof of a miracle is often precisely the inflexibility with which skeptics deny its historical truth.

3) Another requirement for calling an extraordinary, Divinity-revealing event a miracle is first to rule out whether there were any diabolical influences. For example, A. Lang (from whom I draw many of these reflections) asserts that "New creations and destructions, both real or the equivalent, can only be the work of the omnipotence of the Creator Himself...A miracle worked by God will only serve His purposes; while spirits contrary to God will always betray themselves by their intentions, which are hostile to God. You will be able to tell them by their fruits (Mt 7.16)."[28]

4) Miracles are intimately connected with truth: they are either a declaration of Divinity, or a message revealing truth. In this connection, A. Lang says: "We do not need to decide the question whether all miracles serve to propagate faith, but one cannot deny *a priori* the possibility that God, even outside Christianity, might, through miraculous means, come to the aid of a man who fights for religion or morality. Nevertheless it is certain that God will never validate error in itself through miraculous signs. If God is called as a witness, He cannot serve as witness except for the truth."[29]

As far as miracles are concerned, Sai Baba completes and passes my "examination" with a perfect score. In fact:

1) Sai Baba has allowed thousands of people to observe His miracles with an unprecedented frequency, and still today anyone can go and verify them with the proof of direct observation.

2) One cannot even suggest that there might be mesmerism or even a collective hypnotism, because the objects He creates remain as

---

[27]*De Genesi*, 1.9, c. 17, n.32; PL 34.406.
[28]A. Lang, *Compendio di Apologetica*, Marietti, p. 116.
[29]Id. p. 117.

testimony to the miracle, and it is impossible to attribute a placebo effect to the vibuthi; for example, even animals have been healed by vibhuti. Even if one were to prove that animals are susceptible to the placebo effect, it would still not apply in cases when the vibhuti was administered without the patient knowing about it. Besides -- miracle of miracles -- the sacred ash has worked even on inert matter, for example, to reactivate or fix cars!

We know from Saint Augustine that a kernel of grain cannot be born from a bean. There is a tamarind tree on a hill in Puttaparthi that overlooks the village. On many occasions, at Sai Baba's command, the tree produced five different fruits in the same instant.

3) If what Lang asserts is true, that creation and destruction can be the work only of God, the continuous materializations and de-materializations worked by Sai Baba demonstrate the origin of His power.

4) The purpose of Sai Baba's miracles is always strictly for human salvation. Besides its immediate healing effect, each miracle exercises a moral effect on the beneficiary. When Sai Baba heals someone, He always underlines the fact that human ills all derive from the disorder of the mind, and He exhorts the person to abandon himself to the Divine will, because it is precisely this surrender that triggers the miracle.

When He bestows a gem on someone, He always explains its meaning, if it is not obvious from the image it bears. For example, diamonds for Him are a symbol of mental peace, and therefore of the death of the ego-plagued mind. Sometimes He plays on the resemblance in sound between *diamond* and *die-mind*. Some gemstones symbolize emotional life, the desires and attachments from which a person must free himself; a ring may be a token of God's response to the faith of the devotee, or a symbol of the sacred wedding between God and the devotee, or between two persons.

People who have been witnesses or recipients of one of Sai Baba's miracles are always transformed and shaken by the experience; and often they rise from a life that is meaningless or full of mistakes to a tranquil and happy existence, in harmony with others, with the world, and with themselves.

Really, this is His greatest miracle.

One must not forget that God's capacities were not exhausted by, and did not stop with, the creation of the universe. The cosmos is a continuous miracle that is only a small testimony to the magnificence of God. The events man calls miracles are really exceptional signs which seem to be beyond the order of nature. They have a precise purpose: to reveal to man the Essence from which he and everything around him was born.

CHAPTER NINE

Sai Baba and Jesus
Two Redeemers, A Single Redemption

Do not seek to know Me
with your physical eyes.
When you go to church
and pray in front of the image of God,
you close your eyes, no? Why?
Because you feel that only the Inner Eye
of wisdom
will reveal Him to you.

Sai Baba

The effort to study Sai Baba has two opposing aspects, one which helps it and one which hinders it.

In the effort to study the figure of Jesus Christ it is a disadvantage that what we have available to us as sources of information are gospels written after the time of His historical existence. There is very little testimony about the *ipsissima verba Christi*, the exact words of Jesus. On the other hand, in the case of Sai Baba a vast repertoire of first hand writings and experiences are available, including some experiences that are even more reliable because they are one's own.

The early history of Christianity gives abundant testimony that the Tree of Christ bore good fruit, while in our age, contemporary to Sai Baba, the fruits are still germinating. Thus those who do not dare to judge events except by observing them through the filter of the past might deem it premature and imprudent to pronounce a favorable judgement on Puttaparthi's Saint in orange.

Nevertheless, the most stimulating question that arises, whether in regard to Jesus or to Baba, is: Who are You? Who do You say You are? How do You define Yourself?

Such questions are natural. None of us likes to deal with people who do not introduce themselves. We want people to identify themselves when we talk to them on the telephone, and when meeting people, we give considerable importance to how they present themselves, how they speak. Even though the opinion people have of themselves does not always correspond to the truth, nevertheless the assertions and behavior which accompany that opinion are the basis of one's final judgement about other people. Even in court, when a defendant is allowed to speak, his declaration of innocence is important even if grave charges have been levelled against him. Whether he is actually innocent is then determined by the facts.

The mission of Jesus was marked by a clear consciousness of having been "sent," "charged", "anointed". If the word "Messiah", which has been used to describe Jesus, is traced to the Hebrew *Masci'ah*, it means "anointed", like the word "Christ."

Of the four Evangelists, John is the one who very clearly sets forth this distinctive trait of Christ's coming.

"I have come here from God - Jesus says about Himself -; not that I came because I chose, no, I was sent, and by him."[1]

"I have come from heaven, not to do my own will, but to do the will of the one who sent me."[2]

"My teaching is not from myself: it comes from the one who sent me."[3]

Jesus was fully aware that He was the Messiah, and He asserted it openly, to the point that most of the disputes with the Pharisees stemmed from this claim. Even the evil spirits proclaimed Him "the Saint of God." The whole public life of Jesus centered on His mission as having been sent by God, and it culminated in a trial in which this declaration became the principal charge against Him.

Now, two thousand years later, when it is no longer possible to physically crucify Jesus a second time, not only is no one surprised anymore that He should have been sent by God in flesh and blood,

---

[1] John 8.42.
[2] *ibid.* 6.38.
[3] *ibid.* 7.16.

but it is considered scandalous to assert the contrary. Was it perhaps the disappearance of Christ from earth which made His divinity more apparent, and allowed the fledgling churches to formulate theories freely, without the benefit of direct proof, and with no debate?

While He was alive, Jesus was openly attacked for His claim that He was the Messiah. Once He disappeared, people cried out what a scandal it was to have killed the Son of God. Feeling the earth tremble, the centurion at the foot of the cross exclaimed, "So He really was the Son of God." If the earth had trembled when He was alive, would they perhaps have said that it was the devil that made it tremble?

Sai Baba presents Himself with the same clarity, but with a different connotation. The first scandal Sai Baba provokes is by affirming His identity. He does this with very strong expressions, which only a being of pure divine consciousness or a madman could use:

My Reality is unreachable. Unreachable it will be, not only today, but even for a thousand years; though the thousand years are spent in ardent inquiry by all the people of the world, acting in unison. But the bliss emanating from that Reality is within the reach of all the nations of the earth, and you can partake of it.

My Shakti, My Power, My Mystery can never be understood, whoever may try for however long a period, by whatever means.[4]

Sai Baba does not present Himself as having a precise mandate to fulfill. It would not be correct to say about Him that He is a Messiah, but we do not have a term in the West that corresponds to "Pûrnâvatâr," "Full Avatar." In speaking about Himself Sai Baba makes no reference to any authority higher than Himself. His Word

---

[4]Arjan D. Bharwani, *The Spring of Divine Sakthis*, p. 2.

is peremptory and full of force, like that of Him who possesses All in His own hands.

Some people wonder why this announcement isn't made solemnly, in a way that would reach the most people possible in the shortest possible time. When the high priest asked Jesus the crucial question, in the name of the living God, "Are you the Christ, the Son of the Blessed One?", and the Messiah answered, in front of the competent authorities, "I am!"[5], the reaction was that the interrogator ripped his clothes and cursed the "blasphemy" he had heard. So what was achieved by this holy declaration?

Today, in an age when Alì Agcha, the assassin who tried to kill the current Pope, declares that he is the reincarnation of Christ, what use would it be for someone else to use similar expressions to identify himself? Every once in a while you read in the paper about someone who claims he is the Messiah. In neuro-psychiatric hospitals it is not uncommon to meet people who believe they are Napoleon, Julius Caesar, or the Messiah himself. However the test which reveals who a person really is consists not in words, but in deeds.

Just as in the case of Jesus, His identification as the Messiah did not come simply from His declarations, but mostly from His work of salvation. In the same way Sai Baba does not worry about making everybody know who He is right away, but He works in the hearts of men, redeeming them.

The world does not change because of someone's declaration that he is the Messiah. The world will change when man discovers that he is himself divine.

Jesus did not correct those who declared that He was the "Son of God" or "Christ" or the "Messiah." Even during his triumphal entry into Jerusalem he condemned the Pharisees' effort to suppress the crowd's homage of the "Hosannah." He always displayed an extreme reserve in regard to the titles people attributed to Him. This was not due to false humility; it was because of the false concept of Messiah that His contemporaries had developed in their minds. They were hoping for a political and nationalistic messiah, one who would solve all their little social and economic problems.

---

[5]Mark 14.61-62.

In the same way even today there are many people who charge Sai Baba with indifference to the sorrow that weighs on the world, and they ask themselves, "If He is so powerful, why doesn't He eliminate all the suffering there is in the world?" These people would like to change the mission of the Divine Incarnation. Jesus Christ did not change the sorrowful state of the world either, neither in His own time, nor afterwards. Everything that had to happen - bloody revolutions, wars, destruction, persecutions, poverty, epidemics, etc... - it all happened on schedule.

Even at His birth all the children under two years of age were slaughtered, by the insane command of a criminal king who was afraid he would lose his kingdom. The same kind of thing had already happened at the time of Krishna: Kamsa had all his sister's children killed, because she had been told that her eighth son would suppress his wicked uncle.

It is never the task of a Redeemer to resolve human errors with a magic wand. Doing so would ensure that the errors would continue to be committed. It is not the mission of an elementary school teacher or of a parent to do the students' homework. If that were to happen laziness would triumph, diplomas would be given unjustly, and degrees would soon prove deleterious to the whole society. No one among us would willingly go to a doctor who had received his certification by buying all his degrees! The project to perfect society is based on understanding one's own errors and on the effort we make to avoid them.

Some people who have seen Sai Baba pass in front of so many sick people, often without even looking at them, think they detect a mark of cruel insensitivity in this behavior. The truth is that His apparent indifference to illness, which is nothing but a tiny episode among so many existences, contains a deep message: it is not your bodies which move Me to pity, - the great Master would tell us - but only your mental state. Heal your minds and then your bodies too will no longer undergo suffering. First remove all the causes which have brought on the pain, and you will have perfect health.

I shall not get involved in recounting the birth and life of Sai
Baba, because several thick books would be required for that.[6]
However I'd like to stress one extraordinary detail of His
conception, given in the first pages of the volume *Words of Jesus
and Sathya Sai Baba*:[7]

"One day, while Baba was sitting surrounded by His devotees,
there was an unexpected interruption. A *pundit*, Mr. Rama Sarma,
well-versed in the holy Puranas, suddenly had the impulse to ask a
question: 'Swami! Did you incarnate by entering the world directly
(*Pravesa*), or through human conception (*Prasava*)?' Baba turned
to His Mother, so that she could answer the question herself. And
His Mother said: 'I had had a dream in which an angel of God
(*Satyanarayana Deva*) told me not to be afraid if something should
happen to me which depended on the Will of God. That morning,
while I was at the well to draw water, a great sphere of blue light
came rolling toward me. I lost consciousness and fell to the
ground, and I felt it slip inside me.'

Baba turned to Rama Sarma smiling: 'There's your answer! I
was not born through conception. It was *Pravesa*, not *Prasava*. I
was born through a descent, not from human contact.'"

It was foretold that Sai Baba would come as *Avatar*, and that is
what a great number of people consider Him to be.[8] "Avatar" is a
Sanskrit word which means "Descent of God in a physical form."
In the Hindu theological and religious tradition, the concept of a
divine incarnation that manifests itself in human form, as a
recurring phenomenon in human history, does not cause any
astonishment. In our Western and Christian culture, however, the
Avatar in an absolute and unrepeatable sense is Jesus, the Christ.

---

[6]See N. Kasturi, *Sathyam Sivam Sundaram* (Sathya Sai Books & Publications
Trust, Prashanti Nilayam, 4 vols.), and the bibliography at the end of this book.

[7]The volume was edited by Dr. H. K. Takyi and Kishin J. Khubchandani
(Prashanti Printers, Bombay, 1986).

[8]Another subject that would deserve attention and study are the prophecies
about Sai Baba. It is not easy to interpret prophecies, because more often than
not they can only be understood when they have come to pass. Prophetic
language is hermetic, esoteric: it is such that those who think they understand are
confused, and those who are confused understand.

In the *Bhagavad Gita*, Lord Krishna reveals His identity and divine mission to Arjuna: "O descendant of Bharata, each time that in some place in the universe religion declines and irreligion advances, I come in person. I incarnate from age to age in order to rescue the pious, to destroy unbelievers, and to re-establish the principles of religion."[9]

Jesus said, "I, the light, have come into the world, so that whoever believes in me need not stay in the dark any more."[10] "I was born for this, I came into the world for this: to bear witness to the truth,"[11] was Jesus's answer to Pilate, when he asked if Jesus was a king. In a letter, the author of this same gospel affirmed that Jesus had "appeared in order to abolish sin" and "to undo all that the devil has done," words that strongly call to mind the passage quoted from the Bhagavad Gita.[12]

But while a Hindu has no difficulty believing in the divinity of Jesus Christ, and worshiping His form along with those of Krishna or Rama or the other avatars of Vishnu, for a Westerner this would be apostasy.

The concept of *avatar* deserves close study on the part of Christian scholars. It may be that the whole problem, which makes us think that we are in some antithesis with the East, stems from a faulty interpretation of dogmas, or in an irrational and self-serving respect for opinions that have been catalogued as unquestionable and presented as immutable for all time. In fact people change, and with them their collective and individual level of consciousness also changes. If man changes, his thought will change too.

The position taken by the Christian Church (and not just by Catholics, in other words) on the figure of Christ does not see any other possibility of redemption in the course of human history than that linked with the name of Christ. The affirmation in the Acts of the Apostles (4.12) would not seem to leave any room for discussion: "For of all the names in the world given to men, this is the only one by which we can be saved." The name "Jesus" in fact

---

[9]*Bhagavad Gita*, IV, 7-8.
[10]John 12.46.
[11]*ibid.*, 18.37.
[12]I John 3. 5, 8.

means "God saves", and this sentence, drawn from Peter's speech before the elders, scribes and high priests of Jerusalem, underlines the saving power of that name and of the work of Jesus. Not many years had passed since His crucifixion. At that particular moment the apostles were not investigating what names and forms God takes in order to save humanity; their concern was to spread the news that a great act of redemption had occurred.

No human being has the authority to declare that God can only incarnate a certain way, or that He cannot choose to spread His message as He wills, not only through prophets, but also by incarnating as the Christ, that is, as avatars. It would be an unforgivable theological and philosophical absurdity to deny the Divine Power the right of taking human form in other epochs, among other nations, and in other physical forms. On this point there can be no contrary dogma, because this truth is self-evident, and even a child can understand it: God cannot be limited by anything; much less by a human mind. If we want to have some mental concept of God, the first attribute we must give Him is all possible freedom.

Lang writes: "God created the world with free will; after the creation of the world He can also, by free choice, enter into personal relationships with rational creatures and graciously reveal Himself to them. The world is not a pastime, nor a need, of God; it is a free manifestation of His power and of His love which He bestows. It would present a poor concept of God to be willing to admit that His possibilities were exhausted with the creation of this world, or that His love was fully used up by it. It is not within the province of man to impose limits on God or to raise doubts in His regard. We do not know how great His power is, and what love He is capable of. Man must have the courage and the humility to allow himself to be vanquished by God, and to consent to His unpredictability."[13]

To compare two figures like that of Jesus and that of Sai Baba is difficult not only for those who see them as similar because their mission is the same, but also for those who are unable to reconcile them. In fact, because those who see them as similar do not see any

---

[13]A. Lang, *Compendio di Apologetica*, Marietti 1960.

contradiction between them, they risk being tempted to define the position each occupies in the Divine Plan of Salvation. People who see no way to reconcile the two figures, perhaps because they have been conditioned by a certain interpretation of passages like the one from the Acts of the Apostles quoted above, are not aware that they have fallen into a giant trap: For them it is impossible to reconcile the two incarnations, that is, two physical forms. The forms, however, are simply bodies, and like all bodies, they are subject to change and annihilation.

There is no need to reconcile two different bodies. Why insist that two twins are identical, when you know that in fact they can't be, but only seem to be? Certainly, people who make everything depend on the form would have a lot fewer difficulties if Baba were physically Jesus's look-alike! Jesus's body is no longer among us, at least in the form of a living being, but the Christ continues to live among us: that is, Jesus's teaching and the Grace of the Christ, a Mystical Energy that is omnipresent and immortal, incorruptible and non-decaying.

The same thing will happen with Sai Baba's body, which He has foretold He will abandon at the venerable age of 96. But though He may abandon His body, the Being Sai Baba represents will never abandon His devotees, whom He has promised to look after for ever.

I am not Sathya Sai Baba. That is only a name by which you designate Me now. All names are Mine. I am the One God who answers the prayers that rise in human hearts, in all languages, from all lands, addressed to all forms of the Deity.[14]

Every attempt to enclose beings as exalted as Jesus the Christ in definitions, ends up shipwrecked in doctrinal conflicts and controversy, which in fact fill the history of all the Churches. Councils and counter-councils, Eastern Churches and Western Churches, Protestants and Catholics, have fought endless battles which have not contributed to peace. Instead of affirming together the truths which can be easily deduced, they have divided

---

[14]Ganapathi, *Baba - Sathya Sai* Part I, p. 91.

themselves by making precise distinctions, with tiresome fastidiousness, in questions which are marginal to the problems which interest religious people.

The great religious wars were undertaken for motives connected with situations, persons and formulations of belief that belonged to a particular historic setting. They were as fleeting as clouds and after a century or two, obsolete.

The Christ-Baba dualism is therefore only morphological and physical, not ontological. The differences between the two depend simply on the type of incarnation which the Single Reality has taken on. Historically they are two bodily sheaths, two temples of the Supreme Spirit: that of Jesus, which hosted the Christ, and that of Sai Baba, another cathedral of God, in a different manifestation.

It is obvious that not a stone of either temple can remain permanently in place. However, if they willed it, the Divine Guests could rebuild the temples in three days or less: Their bodies are a direct manifestation of their divine will, and obey their will entirely. The important truth is the living Divinity in them never dies. The Sai Baba we see with our physical eyes is nothing but an exterior casing, corruptible and subject to death, which with the powers it mediates has the purpose of representing a dimension that is infinite, spiritual, metaphysical, eternal, and - why not? - Christic. The body which has received the responsibility of giving form to that One Truth must die, because it was born: everything that is born, develops and grows, also dies. It is an Eternal physical Law, it is the Divine Law, it is the *Dharma* of the entire Universe and of all it contains. Moreover, the death of that sacred body imparts a teaching that can be summed up as the supremacy of the Spirit which, while it redeems Matter, at the same time transcends it.

How can one recognize Christ as an incarnation of God, based only on His form? And how could one believe that Sai Baba is really an avatar by simply looking at what appears on the surface?

Jesus of Nazareth claimed a divine authority, which did not derive solely from His mission, but was implicit in His very person: He put Himself above Jonah, above Solomon, the temple, the Sabbath.[15]   And yet he often referred to the authority of the

---

[15]See Matthew 12.6; 8.41.

Father, with whom He had a direct relation, and whom He often addressed with the expression "My Father."

Sai Baba has no relationship of dependence upon a divine Authority or Paternity, but presents Himself as the Father and Creator of all:

See in Me yourself, for I see Myself in you all. You are My life, My breath, My soul. You are My Forms all, when I love you, I love Myself; when you love yourselves, you love Me! I have separated Myself from Myself so that I may love Myself. My beloved ones, You are My own Self.[16]

He presents Himself as a Being which cannot be touched by suffering, even though He takes upon Himself the suffering of many:

To take upon Myself the sufferings of those who have surrendered to Me is My duty. I have no suffering and you have no reason to suffer too when I do this duty of Mine. The entire give-and-take is the play of Love. It is taken over by me in Love, so how can I suffer? Christ sacrificed His life for the sake of those who put their faith in Him. He propagated the truth that sacrifice is God.[17]

In August of 1988, Sai Baba had an "accident." I happened to be at Prashanti Nilayam at the time. The Avatar slipped on a little piece of soap in the bathroom and fell, breaking His thigh bone. For several days He did not come out, and He was not giving darshan. But one day, August 26, he came to the Purnachandra, the huge hall of Prashanti, and gave a discourse for the Holy Day of Onam.

The faith of many people was shaken by this "accident" of Swami's. They did not understand that that was a test and also a lesson through which Baba demonstrated how we should behave when we are in pain. Here is an excerpt from that discourse, which

---

[16]N. Kasturi, *Loving God* (from back cover).
[17]Ganapathi, *Baba - Sathya Sai,* Part II, p. 171.

He gave standing, for an hour and a quarter, with no signs of being tired, without a single grimace of pain:

Swami's capacity of control and endurance cannot easily be understood... Only doctors and those who have suffered a similar fracture know something of it. I was directed to rest for four weeks. But I do not know what rest is, I do not feel the need for it. I have My duty to fulfill... Many people have written to Me to say that I should heal Myself immediately of this tiresome fracture. But no, there is no need. They are little things which can happen occasionally. I am not sick... It is almost impossible for Me to stand, the pain is so unbearable... but I smile about it, and this is a sign of My Divinity. Some devotees pray and think that Swami could heal Himself in a moment. Even though this is possible, Swami is not a person affected by egoism. When someone is wounded or sick, I do not heal him immediately. Everything has its time... it is necessary to suffer, until the proper moment arrives. Nonetheless it is possible to develop the power to divert the mind in order to control the pain and not to allow oneself to be overcome by problems and difficulties... Why should I worry about this body? This body is not Mine, it belongs to you and I don't want to interfere. Your bodies, on the other hand, are Mine, and if they cause you troubles, I take care of it... Nothing can make Me suffer. Nothing can harm Me.[18]

Sai's word rings like that of the Creator in person. We would have a thousand reasons to doubt Him, when He asserts things that can only be attributed to God the Father, if He did not demonstrate with His actions that He possesses absolute powers of creation and destruction:

There was no one to know who am I till I created the world, at My pleasure, with one word. Immediately mountains rose up, rivers started flowing, earth and sky were formed, oceans, seas, lands, and water-sheds, sun, moon, and desert sands sprang out

---

[18]*Discorsi* 1988/89, vol. I, II (20.24.81).

of nowhere to prove My existence. There came all forms of beings, men, beasts, and birds, flying, speaking, hearing. All powers were bestowed upon them under My orders. The first place was granted to mankind, and My knowledge was placed in man's mind.[19]

Just as all the criteria and solid principles of science waver in front of Sai Baba, so also theology, insofar as it is a science, lacks the wherewithal to explain and justify a presence as extraordinary as that of the Avatar of this age. The most serious obstacle, which to our theology will seem insurmountable, derives from attributing the title Only-Begotten exclusively to the avatar Jesus, known as the Christ.

Only when we look from a narrow perspective does the problem seem impossible to resolve. In my opinion, where some Catholic theology has erred is in fusing and confusing together the two realities of Jesus and of the Christ. Traditional theology says that Jesus was true man and true God. Naturally! But the notion "Only-Begotten" principally regards His Divine Essence. In fact that is the sense it is given by all the classical teachings, and by Thomistic doctrine in particular.

It is overly-reductive and simplistic to attribute the uniqueness of the "Only-Begotten Son of God" simply to the fact of a single incarnation in one maternal womb. This is so even if we accept that "the brothers of Jesus" mentioned in the gospels can be validly interpreted as "cousins", as traditionally done, and we admit that Jesus was Mary's only child. I think it is legitimate to ask how having blood siblings could possibly detract anything from the greatness of Jesus and His messianic role. But tradition has always venerated the Mother of the Savior in Her spiritual and also physical Virginity "before, during, and after the Birth." Frankly I don't think it's worth raising questions about a problem which, in the Economy of Salvation, is surely of secondary importance.

That in ancient times the word "Only-Begotten" was not used to refer to the physical person of the Messiah, but rather to His metaphysical dimension - that is to the Christ and not to Jesus of

---

[19]N. Kasturi, *Sathyam Sivam Sundaram* Part IV, p. 105.

Nazareth - is clear from the Discourse against the Pagans of Saint Anastasius:

"I think about the living and acting God, about the Word of the good God, of the God of the Universe, about the God who is distinct and different from all created things and all creation. It is He who is the only and proper Word of the Father, He who gave order to the Universe. He is the One, the Only-Begotten, the good God, who proceeds from the Father as from a fountain of goodness, and who orders and contains the Universe."[20]

Saint Thomas drives home with even greater clarity the hypostatic process whereby Divinity, that is the Christ, was hosted in the Divine Incarnation of Jesus: "So that we could share in His Divinity, the Only-Begotten Son of God assumed our human nature, in order that, after having made Himself man, men might become gods."[21]

And here is St. Augustine: "That only Son, born from the substance of the Father, was the Word identical with the Father in divine nature, Him for whom all things were made."[22]

Every Sunday Christian believers, by reciting the Creed, profess their faith in the Only-Begotten Son, precisely understood as the emanation of God from all eternity: "I believe in Jesus Christ, Only-Begotten Son of God, *born of the Father before all ages.*" The notion of "birth" is hard to reconcile with that of "eternity, before all ages," but once again the intuitions of the spirit are imprisoned in narrow constraints by our language.

Therefore in order to dissolve the common objection advanced by Christians who are unable to believe that God could incarnate again, because for them there was only one incarnation of God and that was Christ, it is necessary to emphasize the eternal and unrepeatable dimension of the Only-Begotten. We need to distinguish this eternal and unrepeatable dimension clearly from the physical-historical

---

[20]See *Patrologica Greca* vol. XXV, 79-83.
[21]*Opusc. 57*, "On the Feast of Corpus Christi", 1-4.
[22]From the *Discourse on the Shepherds*, Disc. 46.11.

dimension, which can repeat itself through the centuries under various forms, according to the will of God.

At this point one final question arises, after which there is no choice but to surrender: who can assure us that Sai Baba is what He himself says He is? Could this mysterious being in the flame-red tunic be deceiving himself? Maybe he wants to deceive us all!

In asking the same questions about Jesus, Lang says that this would be "in strident contrast with the intellectual and moral greatness of His personality as evidenced in the Gospels" and that "His personality is therefore the guarantee of the truth of what He affirmed about Himself."[23] "If Jesus of Nazareth is not the Messiah, ... either He has to be pitied as a morbid psychopath, or else He has to be branded as the coarsest liar in history. There is no possibility of escape from this inexorable dilemma, as the liberal Jesus-movements tried to do: *si non est Deus, non est bonus*, if He is not God, He is not good.[24]

The same reasoning applies to Sai Baba, and the question which remains open is: could he be an ecstatic, a psychopath, or a deranged person? This question is groundless, because anyone who has seen or met Sai Baba or heard Him speak, has come away with an experience of love, security, truthfulness, and fullness. Everyone who has made contact with Sai Baba, after an initial shock which overcomes anyone not accustomed to an Omnipotent Energy, feels he has contacted a higher Reality, full of peace, of mercy, of sweetness and forbearance. It is ultimately the direct experience of Sai's physical presence which proves its reliability and truthfulness against all censure. That is why anyone who has had no experience of it cannot pronounce any judgement.

As long as the sweetness or sourness of a fruit is merely described, one can doubt the descriptions, though perhaps a little less when they come from a great number of sources. But no criticism or judgement can condition the experience of actually tasting the fruit. Only an illness can render the palate incapable of tasting, or cause nausea when you eat a delicacy. In the same way, no one can condition the experience of the bliss and love which

[23] A. Lang, *op. cit.* p. 199.
[24] *ibid.*

radiate from the person of Sai Baba. No one whose heart produces sound feelings can resist being fascinated by Him. Not even those who are hostile to Him can hold out very long against His power of attraction.

After reading these lines, a few people will probably think that the person who wrote them is a zealot. To categorize ourselves as bigots or liberals does not help us to understand an event. In any case, every one in the world is a partisan for something. What people dismiss with scorn as fanaticism is nothing but the desire for happiness, the motivating energy which gives life. You might be a fanatic for a woman, for a soccer team, for your favorite album, for your furniture, or for your high-powered car.

Fanaticism implies intolerance towards those who think differently from you, and it generates violence. Christianity too, along with other intolerant religions, has been deeply stained by bigotry. Therefore those who write about "sects", listing them in order to condemn them, should not forget that early Christianity was condemned as a sect, and accused of secretly propagating unmentionable crimes, such as infanticide, sacred prostitution, etc... If you are inclined to assault someone who touches your idol, then you are a zealot.

As for me, I try never to grow angry with those who do not see, because the blindness of a friend does not justify one's own ire. Nor do I desperately seek to proselytize. What for? I know instead that even the resistance to Truth is the divine play of Truth itself. Therefore I limit myself to saying: if your palate is developed, taste in order to believe! Only the tasting will lend credibility to your judgement.

The Pharisees complained that the world had run after Jesus.[25] The same enthusiasm is drawing the world towards Sai Baba, while some people, without having tasted this Divine Fruit, consider it poisonous and work "against" the Truth.

But this is normal; in God's fields there is room not only for the good grain, but also for crabgrass! Every plant, good or bad, has its own particular nature, which in the end reveals the Divine to us. Therefore the crabgrass too deserves all our respect and love.

---

[25]See John 12.19.

CHAPTER TEN

The Work of Sai Baba

*The Lord
will never abandon
His Children.*

Sai Baba

Whenever we hear someone being praised, we cannot wait to see that person in action. Ultimately it is concrete action which causes the downfall of the imposter and exalts the man of truth. Words are not enough; indeed, it is very easy to talk.

The preaching of Jesus Christ culminated on the cross, where He fulfilled His own example by sacrificing His body, so that the world might be redeemed, and might learn from this sacred symbol to sacrifice the ego, the cause of all evil.

In the same way, Sai Baba's declarations culminate in His activity, which can be divided into three principal areas: education, spiritual direction, and the example He Himself sets.

Education

The first time I went into "Sri Sathya Sai Baba's Kingdom," I was thunderstruck to see all the constructions that began sprouting up from that arid and barren land as I approached the village. These are His colleges, institutes and boarding-schools, which house students who have been selected one by one by Sai Baba Himself. Those gigantic constructions (which in 1981 were only a small part of what has been built in the last decade), host boys and girls from all over the world, but especially from India, all of whom can study free from elementary school through college.

But Sai institutes have not been established only at Puttaparthi. There are some at Whitefield (20 kilometers from Bangalore), and others scattered throughout India. The importance Sai Baba gives to the field of school-instruction and education merits all our attention. Our schools would have a lot to learn from the method used in the Sai institutes.

Anyone who has the good fortune to go to Prasanthi Nilayam can see from a first glance what effects Sai education has had. The boys gather silently in the *mandir* to wait for the Master. They often have books or notebooks full of mantras, and sitting cross-legged for hours, they study, they review, they write notes, or they pray. You do not see a single grimace of impatience or intolerance, you do not see a single boy, even among the youngest, move restlessly or look around distracted. It is an astonishing rank of angels "in white garments," which calls to mind John's prophetic vision.

The method of instruction offered by Sai Baba is guaranteed to improve humanity and to lead it to the highest level of consciousness. It is based on five values, which Baba Himself calls Human Values: Truth, Right Action, Peace, Love, and Non-violence. It constitutes a complete method, like our Montessori or Pestalozzi methods.

The great merit of the Sathya Sai system is that it works. Wherever it has been tried, it has had excellent results. The improvement in behavior surpassed all expectations. The students who follow the method gain a psychic equilibrium and an intellectual level which no other system is capable of providing.

The educational system based on Human Values begins from the premise that in a splintered society which lacks moral values, it is not enough to teach a few notions in school. The fruits of study must be applied in daily life, and dividing barriers must not be constructed among the various scientific disciplines, given that they are all based on one universal principle.

The main goal of the Sathya Sai method is to foster a healthy and well-balanced development of all the aspects of the human personality: physical, intellectual, emotional, psychic, and spiritual. The target group are children from 6 to 15 years old, the age in which thought processes form and behavioral patterns develop.

It is worth noting that this method does not interfere with ordinary scholastic programs, nor does it suggest modifying them.

It is therefore a method which can be applied in any school in the world.[1]

Sai Baba shows a special concern for the students of His colleges. He really oversees each one individually; He admonishes them, He scolds them with both severity and love, He encourages them and caresses them, often bestowing on them not only His much sought-after Presence, but little gifts or sweets which He creates with His hand on the spur of the moment. You will often see Him lingering under the veranda of the temple, with His hands behind His back, interrogating some student on some subject, or asking someone a question which always has a precise message, often known only to the person asked!

Because Sai Baba has no difficulty reading anyone's mind, often when He passes through this throng of white angels, He will tell someone to discipline his mind, order his thoughts, and focus them on God, all simply by touching His head with His index finger.

All of Creation is a University - says Sai Baba. - In this University of the Universe, Nature is the first Teacher. When he is born man is like an animal, and the effort of the parents is to provide him with an education so that he can transcend that condition. Parents, therefore, are the second teacher.

Having understood that it is not enough to develop some human qualities in the child, the ancient Sages perfected an educational system consisting in rites leading to initiation, for his growth and spiritual transformation. ...

It is in the way a human being thinks, his habits and actions, that his humanness is manifest. Therefore every type of study that is undertaken must serve the body, the mind, and the spirit. Instead modern education stops at the physical aspects and does not go beyond the intellect to reach the heart. People speak of Education in Human Values, abbreviating it EHV, but in my opinion, one should develop the 3HV, rather

---

[1] In Italy a team has formed, headed by Dr. Francesco Polenghi, to provide various didactic materials for the study of the Sathya Sai system. It is organizing training centers for any teachers who wish to adopt the system.

*than the EHV. In fact, what is needed are the three "H"
values, which are Head, Heart, and Hands.*[2]

In all His discourses Sai Baba constantly re-iterates the virtues
essential for creating a radical change in the current systems of
education: the coherence among thought, word and deed, right
action, keeping one's word, discipline, self-confidence, the good
example of the teacher, the love of silence, the condemnation of
wastefulness, common sense, sweetness in speech, punctuality,
discrimination, and wisdom.

At times, His tone becomes firm and severe:

*I have decided that from this year an iron discipline must
reign in our institutes, without giving in to sentiments of pity.
The instruction we give is free. To receive money would force
us to compromise, while it is the students who must adapt to
our discipline. Know that this discipline and these decisions
have only one objective, your good.*[3]

Spiritual direction

When Sai Baba receives devotees individually, it is to give them
advice, warnings, recommendations. Once, to a devotee who was
asking Him for some rules of behavior, Sai Baba listed some
maxims of conduct, prefacing them by saying that they were "some
selected jewels." People are astonished and attracted by His
continuous creations, but His most precious jewels are the teachings
He bestows so freely. Here is the garland of 46 pearls which He
created for that devotee:

1. Prema, Love, should be considered as the very breath of Life.
2. The Love that is manifest in all things equally, believe that the
   same Prema is Paramathma [the Supreme Soul or divine
   Emanation].

---

[2]*Discorsi 88/89*, XX, 1-3.11.
[3]*ibid.* 27.

3. The one divine Emanation [Paramathma] is in every one, in the form of Love [Prema].

4. More than all other forms of Prema, man's first effort should be to fix his Love on the Lord.

5. Such Love directed towards God is Bhakthi [Devotion]; that is the fundamental test, the acquisition of Bhakthi.

6. Those who seek the Bliss of the Atma [Spirit] should not run after the joys of sense objects.

7. Sathya, Truth, must be treated as life-giving as breathing itself.

8. Just as a body that has no breath is useless and begins to rot and stink within a few minutes, similarly, life without Truth is useless and becomes the stinking abode of strife and grief.

9. Believe that there is nothing greater than Truth, nothing more precious, nothing sweeter and nothing more lasting.

10. Truth is the all-protecting God. There is no mightier Guardian than Truth.

11. The Lord who is Sathyaswarupa [the Embodiment of Truth] grants His *Darshan* to those of truthful speech and loving heart.

12. Have undiminished kindness towards all beings and also the spirit of self-sacrifice.

13. You must also possess control of the senses, an unruffled character and non-attachment.

14. Be always on the alert against the four sins which the tongue is prone to commit: 1) Speaking falsehood; 2) Speaking ill of others; 3) Back-biting; 4) Talking too much. It is best to attempt to control these tendencies.

15. Try to prevent the five sins that the body commits: Killing, Adultery, Theft, Drinking intoxicants and the Eating of flesh. It is a great help for the highest life if these also are kept as far away as possible.

16. One must be always vigilant, without a moment's carelessness, against the eight sins that the mind perpetrates: Kamam or craving; Krodham or anger; Lobham or greed; Moham or attachment; Impatience; Hatred, Egoism, Pride. Man's primary duty is to keep all these things at a safe distance from himself.

17. Man's mind speeds fast, pursuing wrong actions. Without letting it hurry like that remember the name of the Lord at that

time or attempt to do some good deed or other. Those who do thus will certainly become fit for the Lord's Grace.

18. First give up the evil tendency to feel envious at the prosperity of others and the desire to harm them. Be happy that others are happy. Sympathize with those who are in adversity and wish for their prosperity. That is the means of cultivating love for God.

19. Patience is all the strength that man needs.

20. Those anxious to live in joy must always be doing good.

21. It is easy to conquer anger through love, attachment through reasoning, falsehood through truth, bad through good and greed through charity.

22. No reply should be given to the words of the wicked. Be at a great distance from them; that is for your good. Break off all relations with such people.

23. Seek the company of good men, even at the sacrifice of your honor and life. But be praying to God to bless you with the discrimination needed to distinguish between the good men and the bad. You must also endeavor, with the intellect given to you.

24. Those who conquer states and earn fame in the world are hailed as heroes, no doubt; but those who have conquered the senses are heroes who must be acclaimed as the conquerors of the *atma*.

25. Whatever acts a good or bad man may do, the fruits thereof follow him and will never stop pursuing him.

26. Greed yields only sorrow; contentment is best. There is no happiness greater than contentment.

27. The mischief-mongering tendency should be plucked out by the roots and thrown off. If allowed to exist, it will undermine life itself.

28. Bear with fortitude both loss and grief; try and search for plans to achieve joy and gain.

29. When you are invaded by anger, practice silence or remember the name of the Lord. Do not remind yourself of things which will inflame the anger more. That will do incalculable harm.

30. From this moment, avoid all bad habits. Do not delay or postpone. They do not contribute the slightest joy.

31. Try as far as possible within your means to satisfy the needs of the poor, who are really Daridranarayana [the Creator Himself, come to reside in them]. Share with them whatever food you have and make them happy at least that moment.

32. Whatever you feel should not be done to you by others, avoid doing such things to others.

33. For faults and sins committed in ignorance, repent sincerely; try not to repeat the faults and sins again; pray to God to bless you with the strength and the courage needed to stick to the right path.

34. Do not allow anything to come near you, which will destroy your eagerness and enthusiasm for God. Lack of zeal will cause the decay of the strength of man.

35. Yield not to cowardice; do not give up Ananda [Bliss].

36. Do not get swelled up when people praise you; do not feel dejected when people blame you.

37. If among your friends any one hates another and starts a quarrel, do not attempt to inflame them more and make them hate each other more; try, on the other hand, with love and sympathy to restore their former friendship.

38. Instead of searching for others' faults, search for your own faults yourself; uproot them, throw them off. It is enough if you search and discover one fault of yours; that is better than discovering tens of hundreds of faults in others.

39. Even if you cannot or will not do any Punya or good deed, do not conceive or carry out any Papa, or bad deed.

40. Whatever people may say about the faults that you know are not in you, do not be concerned; as for the faults that are in you, try to correct them yourself, even before others point them out to you. Do not harbor anger or bitterness against persons who point out your faults; do not retort, pointing out the faults of those persons themselves, but show your gratitude to them. Trying to discover their faults is a greater mistake on your part. It is good for you to know your faults; it is no good your knowing others' faults.

41. Whenever you get a little leisure, do not spend it in talking about all and sundry, but utilize it in meditating on God or in doing service to others.

42. The Lord is understood only by the Bhaktha [devotee]; the Bhaktha is understood only by the Lord. Others cannot understand them. So, do not discuss matters relating to the Lord with those who have no Bhakthi [devotion]. On account of such discussion, your devotion will diminish.

43. If anyone speaks to you on any subject, having understood it wrongly, do not think of other wrong notions which will support that stand but grasp only the good and the sweet, in what he says. True meaning is to be appreciated as desirable, not wrong meaning or many meanings, which give no meaning at all and cause only the hampering of Ananda [Bliss].

44. If you desire to cultivate one-pointedness, do not, when in a crowd or bazaar, scatter your vision to the four corners and on everything, but see only the road in front of you, just enough to avoid accidents to yourself. One-pointedness will become firmer if one moves about without taking one's attention off the road, avoiding dangers, and not casting eyes on others' forms.

45. Give up all doubts regarding the Guru and God. If your worldly desires do not get fulfilled, do not blame it on your devotion; there is no relationship between such desires and devotion to God. These worldly desires have to be given up some day or other; feelings of devotion [Bhakthi] have to be acquired some day or other. Be firmly convinced of this.

46. If your Dhyanam [meditation] or Japam [prayer, repetition of the name of God] does not progress properly or if the desires you have entertained do not come to fruition, do not get dispirited with God. It will dispirit you even more and you will lose the peace, however small or big, that you might have earned. During Dhyanam and Japam you should not be dispirited, desperate or discouraged. When such feelings come, take it that it is the fault of your Sadhana [spiritual practices] and endeavor to do them correctly.

It is only when in your daily conduct and in all actions you automatically behave and act in this manner and along these lines that you can attain the Divine principle, very easily.[4]

It is not difficult to see in all these principles an expansion and completion of the advice of the Gospel, especially as it is found in the Sermon on the Mount.[5] I hope that anyone who still lives in the doubt that Sai Baba might be the Antichrist will come upon these strictly evangelical counsels of His with a pure heart, and will have the humility to change his mind.

Another characteristic of Sai Baba, which makes you reflect deeply, is that He knows all the Sacred Scriptures, both those of the Eastern tradition and those of the Western tradition, and He knows all the scientific principles and laws of Nature. He can move from an extremely simple discourse, which even a child could understand, into a treatise of physics or philosophy, providing exhaustive answers to eminent scientists or theologians or pundits. And He possesses all this knowledge without ever having studied it! With His divine Wisdom He can give answers to the deepest unresolved questions that trouble many hearts, about God, about man, about present and future life, about the body, about the soul, about society and the individual.

Like His Person, His teachings too know no national limits, no restrictions dependent on time or geographical conditions. His love flows to all without distinction, whether Indians or Westerners, good or evil, intelligent or ignorant.

He does not call upon His powers to overcome the normal barriers created by man: the language He speaks is Telugu, the language of His earthly origins, the environment is that of Puttaparthi, the food He eats is that prepared by Indian cooking; but all this is nothing but an exterior aspect. The content of His message transcends nationality, it is extratemporal, universal. His words sound familiar to anyone, they know no obstacles of age, profession, social class, ethnic origins or culture. Whoever reads

---

[4]*Sandeha Nivarini - Dialogues Dissolving Doubts*, 1979, pp. 41-48.
[5]See Matthew 5-7 and parallel passages.

His discourses, whether he be Mexican or Japanese, finds there the Truth he has always sought, which he has always longed for.

One could say that the source-spring of Sai's teaching are the eternal Truths contained in all Scriptures, especially in the Vedas, the holy writings which gave birth to all other inspired books. But when you hear His voice live, you are moved to exclaim, like the Jews astonished at Jesus: "How did he learn to read? He has not been taught."[6] "Where did the man get all this? What is this wisdom that has been granted him, and these miracles that are worked through him?"[7]

There is no evolution or development in His teaching: it remains always identical to itself. If at times it seems that there are contradictions between what He said some time ago and what He says now, it is simply due to the fact that He adapts His teaching to the individual, the time, the culture.

His respect for the original culture of each person is almost unbelievable. To a group of Catholics He can narrate the story of Jesus in terms which correspond exactly to the Christian tradition; He never upsets the sensibility or beliefs of a people, even when the truths they profess could be formulated with greater clarity. To Indians He will speak openly of reincarnation or *karma*; to Westerners He will allude to it with veiled words, or He will not raise the issue at all. He knows and teaches that one must say the truths which unite, not those which divide. This does not prevent Him from sometimes breaking traditional schemes, and thus challenging overly-humanized conceptions of divine mysteries. Obviously discourses addressed to Indians can be read by Westerners, and this is where often men massacre His message, because they do not consider the time, the place, who is being addressed, or the circumstances in which a discourse was given.

Sai Baba often propounds the Truth through the clarity of parables. Jesus too liked to speak through images. "By their nature parables are part of the art of teaching. Parables are based on

---

[6]John 7.15.
[7]Mark 6.2b.

clarity, on the appeal to living, concrete, irrefutable examples, in order to force the mind to assent."[8]

The example set by Sai.

The third aspect of Sai Baba's activity is the concrete example He Himself sets. His life is free from sin. The purity of His discourses permeates also His life and His character. The fact that some people murmur and slander Him is not a proof of His guilt.

What is He accused of? Of favoring rich people, of accepting money from them. But as far as I can tell, He also receives and counsels the poor, and He accepts their offerings too. You only need to attend a *darshan* to see who the majority of people are whom He allows to enter the interview room: there is no distinction of caste, religion, or race.

He never receives women alone. This is a norm that used to be enforced also for us priests, and which we should still observe in order to avoid trouble. Sai Baba does it to set a good example. But this, along with the gestures of fatherly sympathy and maternal concern that He occasionally bestows on young men, has prompted a few malicious people to accuse Him of homosexuality. "The thief thinks everyone is like himself," says an old and wise Tuscan proverb!

Wasn't Jesus accused of loving sinners and prostitutes? In fact He Himself would forgive sins, provoking the astonishment of those present, as when He healed the paralytic, or the adulteress.

There have even been people who have insinuated that all of Sai Baba's activity is nothing but a business to attract people from all over the world and thus to improve the miserable condition of India. Granted that a just re-distribution of the world's wealth would not be so immoral, I would ask these persons if they know some way that people can avoid transferring money from one country to another when they travel, or if they know some technique that would allow people to live near any of the sanctuaries of the world without eating and without lodging... In addition to giving lodging almost free, Sai Baba never advises any

---

[8]L. Algisi, *Gesù e le sue parabole*, Marietti 1964, p. 78.

one of his "guests" to waste his money in useless acquisitions. In fact He insists on not wasting money, food, or energy.

Sai Baba sums up in Himself all the virtues man would like to possess. His equilibrium is exceptional: He never allows Himself to be dominated by passion, or to be possessed by anger. When He wishes to show a severe side of His complex reality, He does it only on the surface, without being affected by it. He is full of goodness and sweetness, but without being effeminate or weak. His gaze is full of love, without being sentimental. Sometimes He assumes a humble attitude, but He preserves His full regality: it is the humility of a mother who teaches her stubborn child, it is the simplicity and modesty of a friend who wants to win back his unyielding companion. He is understanding and lenient, but He becomes severe with anyone who takes advantage of it.

His life is free of struggle or of interior or exterior conflicts. His step is sure both in walking on the paths at darshan, and in enacting His history. He remains unmoved in front of virtues and licentiousness, but everything He does aims to remove injustice from the hearts of men and thus from the world. There is always a divine atmosphere around Him, and everything occurs with a divine precision, even incidents which to human eyes seem like tragedies. A holy light radiates from His face. His words are full of truth and peace. Anyone who listens to them takes away with him a patrimony that he did not know he possessed.

Jesus Christ already distinguished the Good Shepherd from the mercenary in the discourse recorded in the Gospel of St. John, "The good shepherd is one who lays down his life for his sheep. The hired man, since he is not the shepherd and the sheep do not belong to him, abandons the sheep and runs away as soon as he sees a wolf coming, and then the wolf attacks and scatters the sheep; this is because he is only a hired man and has no concern for the sheep."[9]

For years, Sai Baba has done nothing each day except come out among the waiting crowds, bless, give advice, accept petitions, letters, prayers, and requests. Every day He distributes vibuthi to heal, comfort, and indicate the royal road of becoming nothing in the presence of God. He gives rules of conduct to the poorest man,

---

[9]John 10.11-13.

He listens to the richest and most powerful man in town. He distributes food to poor children, clothes and blankets to the needy.

I have often put myself in the mentality of someone seeing Him for the first time, and asked myself: why does someone who has such powers do such boring things every day? What patience and forbearance! What politician or religious leader would do the same? In the meantime Sathya Sai keeps buildings sprouting with fantastic rapidity in the various locations He has chosen, and He pursues the educational program they house.

Sai Baba is like a prisoner of mankind. He is there, like a father of so many prodigal children, waiting for anyone who will return to Him. When a dissolute son returns, He does not let him recite a self-accusation like a sinner. He prepares a great banquet, He places a precious ring on his finger, He gives orders that the returned son be treated with full honor, and He reminds him that he was always His son, even when he was far from home...

The qualities that anyone can see in Sai Baba's personality demonstrate His holiness and His Divine Essence with absolute clarity. Above all He pays no attention to money, and even though He gives it a divine value insofar as it is a means to provide charitable care and assistance, He does not depend on it. Rich philanthropists have offered Him colossal donations, only to have Him refuse the offers; He accepts money only from those He chooses, in order to maintain the building program and operating costs of Prasanthi Nilayam. I was personally present when the Governor of the Andhra Pradesh region, who had gone to have an interview in August, 1990, had to solemnly wait to be received. Every corner of the ashram was patrolled by Indian soldiers, and invaded by government vehicles, but the Governor had to wait his turn, because Sai Baba does not need powerful people: it is they who need Him, and the first condition for meeting Him is to be humble and patient.

Anyone who has been to Prasanthi Nilayam knows very well that he can be assigned to a shed, with lavatory facilities, at no cost. Otherwise he can be lodged in a simple room or mini-apartment that is more Westernized, at the modest expense of 5-10 rupees a day (about 25-50 cents). All the guests can eat in a canteen or cafeteria, where there are dishes for both Indian and European palates, and where a complete meal costs the token sum of 6 rupees. Someone staying at Prasanthi Nilayam might spend a total of 50 cents to a dollar a day: an expense which is modest even by Indian standards. No one can possibly insinuate that Sai Baba makes any money from pilgrims, at that rate. On special occasions, like His birthday celebrations, He has even fed hundreds of thousands of people from all over the world free food, in such abundance as to astonish the cooks, who knew how little food was in the warehouses.

Theologians or churchmen who always demand unending proofs in order to certify a miracle, just to make sure they will not be laughed at, would never be satisfied with the testimony of a simple cook, not to mention the testimony of the people who were fed. But the Divine Power is still more awesome when it mocks human calculations and overcomes them, throwing the skeptic's endless questioning into confusion.

The work through which Sai Baba incessantly manifests His sanctity and His grace is His most amazing miracle. "Come" - He says - "and take by the handful."

Anyone who has been to Him would want to have hands as big as the world in order to hold even a little of what He gives!

CHAPTER ELEVEN

Man is God

*God makes Himself man
so that man may be God.*

Saint Thomas Aquinas

According to Sai Baba, man's position in creation is even higher than certain Biblical passages suggest. While Psalm 8 says that man was created "little less than a god," in Sai's discourses man has the status of a god, a Divinity that through an error of ignorance lives unaware of its own dignity and wealth. So man is like a wretched and hopeless beggar sleeping on a safe full of diamonds. All he has to do is wake up in order to rediscover those riches and make full use of them.

Man is divine; he has the Lord dwelling in his heart, yet he is bound, miserable, limited, weak, agitated. Why? He is ignorant of his reality. He imagines himself weak, limited, bound, and he is so shaped by the mind, which is the source of that imagination.[1]

Man is unaware of his glory. He is the Divine poured into a human mold, just as everything else alive or inert is, but it is the privilege of man alone to be able to become aware of this precious truth![2]

Baba takes the Biblical phrase which says that man is an image and likeness of God and expresses it with greater force. There is not a discourse of Baba's which does not begin with the expressions

---

[1]*Sathya Sai Speaks,* vol. V, p. 203.
[2]*id.,* vol. VIII, p. 111.

"Incarnations of the Divine Essence," "Incarnations of Divine Love," "Incarnations of the Holy Spirit."

That man is divine is surely one of the most difficult teachings for a Christian to accept. Nevertheless, two thousand years ago Jesus taught the same truth. Through the centuries, that truth has been supplanted by a sense of guilt, feelings of unworthiness and of self-contempt, and the expectation of a redemption from outside man, solely by the grace of God. It is certainly true that only the grace of God, that is, His Love, can save man, but this Love should not be evicted from its natural residence: the heart of man.

John the Evangelist recounts that one winter day during the Feast of the Dedication, when Jesus was walking in the temple of Jerusalem, He was surrounded by several Jews who asked Him to declare His identity. Jesus declared for the umpteenth time that He was in union with the Father, but the questioners picked up stones -- it was not the first time that they did this -- to stone Him.

> *"I have done many good works for you to see, works from my Father; for which of these are you stoning me?" (asked the Master). The Jews answered Him, "We are not stoning you for doing a good work but for blasphemy: you are only a man and you claim to be God."*

> Jesus answered: *"Is it not written in your Law: 'I said, you are gods?' So the Law uses the word **gods** of those to whom the word of God was addressed, and scripture cannot be rejected. Yet you say to someone whom the Father has consecrated and sent into the world, 'You are blaspheming' because he says, 'I am the Son of God.'"*[3]

It is a passage which needs no comment. Although many passages are read and explained in the churches, many Christians would not even know that this one comes from a canonical gospel. Instead, sermons repeatedly emphasize the idea that we are sinners and good-for-nothings. This is the power of conditioning, which spreads a veil over everything that can awaken one's divine nature!

---

[3] *John 10.32-36.*

In case anyone thinks that I have interpreted this passage in a way that is too flattering to man, I'll cite another one, also from John, which will dissolve that doubt:

I tell you most solemnly, whoever believes in me will perform the same works as I do myself, he will perform even greater works, because I am going to the Father.[4]

The reader is sure to meet people who are scandalized and angry when confronted with the truth often repeated by Sai Baba: "You are God!" These people deduce that anyone making such an assertion must be sent by the devil, and they bring up the point that the serpent in the Garden of Eden said the same thing to Adam and Eve. People who think this way sometimes even have a certain background in theology, but their faith does not dare to step beyond the limits of some theologian's or preacher's personal interpretation of the Bible. Because they are followers of some "specialist," they end up seeing only a part of what Scripture teaches, and they see even that only from a certain angle. Falling into the pattern of the Pharisees, they think, "If there is anyone who dares to declare the divinity of man, he is ranting, he is a blasphemer, and what he says must be condemned as contrary to Christ's mission. May he be cursed!"

But if we have the patience to work side by side in our inquiry like old friends and if we give up the desire to attack each other, we will discover that our stumbling block is a set of truths that have been catalogued as if they were a dead language. To exhume that language is to bring back all the life that was buried with it: it is to dig up hidden and immortal meanings, which were lost in the labyrinth of disputations and theorems and suffocated by material concerns.

In this age of ignorance, in which truth is presented as falsehood and only error makes the news, Someone has taken it upon Himself to remind humans, in their state of total amnesia, who they are, what their hidden reality is. This person is the *avatar* Sai Baba, that is, Being itself. He has come down in human form, drawn by the longing of saints of all times and religions, to pick up the thread of the story

---

[4]*id.,* 14.12.

where it was interrupted and to repeat: You are God! You are My offspring, you are the child of God. Therefore, if you are My child, you are also My heir!

Some people continue to believe that this inheritance can be acquired only through the sacrament of baptism, because according to them it is the only way to enter into the kingdom of God. Nevertheless, Saint Paul declared:

> *"Everyone moved by the Spirit is a son of God. The spirit you received is not the spirit of slaves bringing fear into your lives again; it is the spirit of sons, and it makes us cry out, 'Abba, Father!' The Spirit himself and our spirit bear united witness that we are children of God. And if we are children, we are heirs as well: heirs of God and co-heirs with Christ, sharing his sufferings so as to share his glory."*[5]

We become children of God even before we are baptized by the rite of any particular religion. Baptism is really a solemn promise to live like children of God, and it guarantees the grace and assistance of the Spirit to all who do. Someone who lives far from God (I do not mean far from the rites of a religion) annuls that grace, even if he is baptized. Merely baptizing people is not enough in itself to make them give up their evil conduct. Their baptism begins to take effect when they themselves take a step toward the Divine.

The real source of original sin is to think, as people did in the centuries after Christ, that man's declaration of his divinity caused his fall. Original sin does not derive from a boastful claim to be God, or from wanting to be God. If anything, it springs from asserting the opposite, that is, that one is diabolical. This "offends" Him who made us, just as any parents would be offended if their child blamed them for his having been born with bad qualities. The Being who has the nature of both Mother and Father would say to us: "You cause your Father great displeasure when you insist on saying that you are disabled, an idiot, a sinner. Have you forgotten how I welcomed the prodigal son? The fact that you have mistaken yourself for a sinner is

---

[5]*Romans 8.14-17.*

the error which has caused you to forget your divine origin and has kept you in a state of suffering. Therefore know yourself! Know who you really are, and be happy!"

In the course of the many centuries of the Christian tradition, humans have spread a cloak over the intelligence of their fellow human beings, for concealed personal motives. Only humans could make such a mistake. It almost seems as if someone got pleasure out of inverting all the road signs, turning them upside down and brutally rewriting their directions. Among the early Christians the awareness of being a divine emanation - and therefore the awareness, to put it simply, of being God - was not uncommon, but the mists of time have led the pilgrims off course. We priests are expected to read the Breviary, and I assure you that this obligation is especially comforting when you come across a passage in it like the following:

I command you: awaken, you who are asleep! Indeed I did not create you in order that you should remain a prisoner in Hell. Rise from the dead. I am the life of the dead. Rise, work of My hands! Rise, My likeness, made in My image! Rise up, let us leave this place! You in Me and I in you; we are, in fact, one indivisible nature.

The enemy made you leave the land of paradise. I however will not put you back in that garden, but I shall place you on the throne of heaven.

Now I shall have the Cherubim adore you, as is fitting for God.[6]

------

[6]The passage is from an ancient *Homily for Holy Saturday*. See the *Liturgy of Hours*, vol. II, p. 446 (in Latin, *Liturgia horarum*, vol. II. p. 405). The fear that the Latin text contained an "exaggerated" assertion led the person who translated it into Italian not only to soften it, depriving it of all the force it had in the original, but even arbitrarily to add an expression - "even though you are not God" - which absolutely does not exist in the Latin. So in the Italian version of the Breviary, the sentence runs: "Now I shall have the Cherubim adore you almost like God, even though you are not God." The Latin simply says: *Facio ut cherubim, pro eo ac Deum decet, adorent te*, "I shall have the Cherubim adore you, as is fitting for God."

The unknown but ancient author of another text in the Breviary says:

According to the Apostle himself (Paul), Christ comes first, because He is the author of his resurrection and of life. Then come these "Christs," that is, those who live according to the example of His holiness.[7]

A passage drawn from the Jerusalem *Catechism*, and recommended to priests for their spiritual reading, confirms the expressions quoted above. It reads:

Having become participants in Christ, you are not improperly called "christs." Therefore God has said of you: "Do not touch my christs" (Psalm 104.15). You became "christs," in fact, when you received the archetype of the Holy Spirit.[8]

---

[7]From the *Easter Homily* of an ancient author, in the *Liturgy of Hours*, vol. II, p. 522. The Latin appears in *Patrologia Latina* XVII, 696-697. Here too one should check against the original Latin version (*Liturgia horarum*, vol. II, p. 480): *Initium, Christus, id est, auctor resurrectionis et vitae; deinde hi Christi, id est, qui in forma puritatis eius viventes, de spe resurrectionis eius securi erunt...* In the Italian version, *hi Christi*, literally "these Christs", was translated as "those who belong to Christ." What motivated the translator to change it?

[8]From the Jerusalem *Catechism*, in the *Liturgy of Hours*, vol. II. p. 547. (Source: *Catech. 21, Mistagogica* 3.1-3; *Patrologia graeca*, XXXIII, 1087-1091.) It is painful to have to say it, but even here the translator has made additions which obscure the original meaning. Here is the Latin text (and consider that this is already a translation from the Greek): *Participes igitur effecti Christi, christi non immerito appellamini; deque vobis dixit Deus: Nolite tangere christos meos. Christi autem facti estis, dum Spiritus Sancti antitypum accepistis.* In the Italian *Liturgia delle ore*, this is translated as follows: "Having become participants in Christ, you are not improperly called *christi*, that is people who have been consecrated. Therefore God has said of you: Do not touch my consecrated ones (Psalm 104.15). You were consecrated when you received the sign of the Holy Spirit." The translator's zeal pushed him beyond the bounds of careful reading, and here too he added an explanation - "that is people who have been consecrated" - not called for in the original.

I would like to end this series of citations from Christian sources with a very explicit passage from Saint John of the Cross. It should dissipate any doubts about our nature, if any still remain:

> *The soul united and transformed in God lives in God and for God, and reflects to Him the same vital impulse that He transmits to it... It must not be considered impossible for such a sublime thing to happen in the soul. In fact, if God grants the soul the grace to be formed like God and united with the Holy Trinity, it becomes God by participation. Then another life of intellect, perception, and love becomes possible in the soul. This life is realized in the Trinity, in union with the Trinity, and is similar to that of the Trinity itself.*
>
> *Therefore souls possess by participation the same goods that God possesses by nature. Because of this, **they are truly God by participation, identical to Him, and they are His companions**.*
>
> *O souls created for and called to such heights, what are you doing? What are you lingering over? Do you wish to be blind to so much light, and deaf to calls of such authority?*[9]

Sai Baba does not miss any opportunity to remind us how sacred a human birth is. There are many discourses in which He calls being born in human form a rare good fortune:

> *To be born as a man is a very sacred thing. That is, among all the animals that are born, to be born as a man is something very difficult and very sacred. Even devas (angels, gods) at one time want to have a human birth. One must make the determination to use all the organs in the body for sacred purposes.*[10]
>
> *Man is essentially divine.*[11]

---

[9]From the *Spiritual Canticle of St. John of the Cross*, strophe 38.
[10]*Sathya Sai Speaks*, 1978, pp. 228-229.
[11]*Upanishad Vahini*, 3rd ed., 1975, p. 1.

Someone might object: if that's how things are, then why is there so much suffering in the world? If man is God, then why has the world fallen so low? Why does it continue to moan in pain, loneliness, poverty, disease and death? Man's sin is precisely that he has forgotten his true origin. The cause of all his problems is his ignorance: because he is unaware that he is God, he continues to act, more often than not, like an animal. He pursues money, worldly pleasures, success, possessions and sensual loves. It is not wrong to aspire to happiness: this need is in our veins from the moment we are born. Where humans go wrong is in the type of objectives they pursue to gain happiness. What is temporary cannot give the Eternal; what is born from the ephemeral cannot produce What never fails.

> *Man is Atmasvarûpa, an embodiment of Spirit, of the nature of Atma, which is Truth, Beauty, Goodness, Peace and Love. But he craves against his nature for the false, fleeting, the crude, the inert and the chaotic. This is demeaning and disgraceful. Man must turn his face away from these and seek in himself the source of strength and joy. He must always have God, of whom he is a an expression, in view when he does any act.*[12]

The source of all man's ills, the foundation of his ignorance, is his conviction that he is his body. He thinks that everything that he sees happening to his body is happening to himself. If the body suffers, he thinks he is suffering; if his emotions are depressed, he thinks he himself is depressed; if he injures a limb and bleeds, he is instantly worried. When he thinks about death, he says, "When I die, bury me there," while in fact only his physical body dies. It would be more correct to say, "When my body dies, bury it there." When we know that our body has some ailment, even if we don't feel pain, we say, "I'm sick," as if our entire being were ill.

The perception that we are our bodies stems from nature itself, which plays a game of illusion. Everything that manifests itself to us as nature is only an appearance. Even though it seems real, it is only a dream. Illusion accompanies our life inseparably, just as our shadows follow the shape of our bodies.

---

[12]*Sathya Sai Speaks,* vol. VI, p. 36.

It is natural for every human being to aspire to joy and pleasurable things while avoiding pain and sorrow. Man has always made a ceaseless effort, night and day, to experience this joy without any interruption, but he has not succeeded in obtaining it. Why? The reason for this is that he deludes himself by thinking that he is his body and his sensory organs. With the aim of satisfying them, he is willing to make any effort to provide them with something that will satiate them. But the joy man seeks and longs for does not belong to the external world, it is not found in the senses, nor in material objects. You do not find it even in the persons that surround you.... The joy you incessantly seek to obtain is yourself, yes, yourself![13]*

Our physical bodies are the temple of God. When do they become this? Only when they are filled with thoughts of God... Sanctify your body, consider it as sacred as a temple. What care or respect wouldn't you show for a place where you know God resides?[14]

If it is true that man is divine, how could he have been misled by the perverse idea that he is simply a physical and mental body? This question was already answered by the inspired author of Genesis, the first book of the Bible.

That book tells us that the Garden of Eden was rich in plant life and full of fruit trees. But it was forbidden to eat the fruit of one of the trees, the Tree of Knowledge. In fact, God had set this condition: "You can eat the fruit of any tree in the garden, but not of the tree which infuses the knowledge of all things. If you eat that, you will be destined to die!" This was not so much an obligation as a loving warning: the death that would follow this indiscretion would simply

---

[13]*Discorsi 88/89*, XXXIV, 1-2.

[14]*id.*, XXX, 25. The passage is a clear echo of I Corinthians 3.16-17: "Are you not aware that you are the temple of God, and that the Spirit of God dwells in you? If anyone destroys God's temple, God will destroy him. For the temple of God is holy; and you are that temple." Cf. also II Corinthians 6.16; Ephesians 2.21-22; Hebrews 3.6.

be an automatic result, such as the result of deliberately putting your hand in a nest of poisonous snakes.

A tree's fruit is like something that is earned through effort, after a long wait. A fruit tree will not bear fruit unless it is first planted and then properly tended. No one in the world would carefully cultivate a tree and then let its fruit fall to the ground and rot. The fruit of the tree can be seen as the complex of desires which ripen every season in the human mind. Here you can see a second sign of the Creator's Love: He does not categorically forbid eating any fruit at all. He does not cut off the appetite or aspirations of His children, but rather offers them all the fruits with divine abundance, except one.

Why this exception? Is it a trap? It is true that human nature is such that if someone warns us not to touch something, it triggers an uncontrollable impulse of curiosity in us, so that we are really heroic if we resist it. The treacherous serpent which arrives to craftily exploit this natural impulse is nothing but the power of illusion, called *maya* in Eastern philosophy. Like a magician who creates and dissolves the illusions he stages, maya, the great Illusionist, makes what is false seem real, and what is real seem false. Maya is like God's shadow: it accompanies Him everywhere.

> *Someone who cloaks himself in ignorance cannot gain the vision of the Divine. There is a little story which explains this.*
>
> *One day the Lord called Maya, Illusion, and said: "Look, because of My many manifestations, everyone describes Me as being veiled by Maya, and this has given Me a bad name. I have gained a bad reputation, because you are constantly with Me. From this moment on, leave Me alone, stay away from Me and go where you please."*
>
> *Maya answered: "My Master, I am ready to obey Your orders, but first You must show me a place where You are not, so I can go there."*
>
> *God smiled and said: "Indeed, there is no place where I am not. We are like twin birds. I put this question to you, to see how you would answer."*[15]

---

[15] *Discorsi 88/89*, XXII, 9.

In the Biblical story, the serpent plays the part of maya to perfection. His insinuations are subtle and perverse, and his opening words tend to exaggerate the limits God imposed, in order to put Him in a bad light: "You mean God told you not to eat any fruit!?"[16]

What substance could be in this tree's fruit, that makes it so poisonous? What is the source of the fruit's lethal power? Why is it so unique and prohibited? The Creator called the tree the "Tree of Knowledge." So it is not just any tree. It is a noble plant: the plant of Knowledge.

So now we can understand why it is forbidden to eat its fruit. Knowledge represents the "final ceiling" on all desires; it is not possible to build more floors above it, if you want to stay alive. The truth is that someone who "has knowledge," who possesses Wisdom and Discrimination, knows he can continue to eat many fruits. But if he ever wanted to free himself from the limit of that ceiling and give free rein to every desire, he would accelerate not only his physical death - which is natural for any human being - but he would no longer advance spiritually. His soul would remain tied to the mortal power of maya, the reptile that repeats his alluring refrain with a sweet voice.

At this point we can recognize the loving tactics of Sai Baba, who suggests that we not exceed a certain "ceiling on desires." Knowledge is the highest floor, and we cannot reach it unless we put ceilings on all the others. You cannot even begin to appreciate that last floor if you continue to live on the lower floors. You cannot reach it except by rising above the others.

The sum of all desires is like a building with a number of floors; for some people, it is a skyscraper. At the top there has to be a roof: if you do not close off the construction, it will collapse. This is what happened with the Tower of Babel, which was constructed without limits in order to challenge the power of God.[17] You reach the roof the moment you understand that enjoying the fruits of your own actions is like carrying a millstone, for anyone who wants to free himself from the cycle of birth and death. Then you begin to see ever

---

[16]The whole story is told in Genesis 3.1-7.
[17]See Genesis 11.1-9.

more clearly the urgency of running toward the roof, though not by skipping or avoiding the lower levels. From the roof the view is clearer, and everything seems small and relative, like a toy.

On the top floor, at the level of the roof, there is no longer such a thing as consuming fruit. On the floor of Knowledge, when you have understood how relative the fruits of all the other trees in the garden are, you no longer crave the enjoyment of the fruit of Knowledge. To eat that fruit, in fact, would amount to falling back into ignorance, that is, into death. The fruit of the tree is deadly for anyone who approaches it with the desire to eat it. And this shows that the serpent's invitation masks the supreme and primordial temptation: that of always enjoying the fruit of one's own actions. Of course, the desire to know is the most noble of desires, but if it is not checked by the awareness of being at the roof - in other words, if you want to know simply for the sake of knowing - all you will gain is a lot of mental turmoil.

The division among religions is due to desire (collective ego) which is precisely what religions are meant to overcome. Man has wanted to venture into an area of knowledge that, because of his love for the fruits of his own intelligence, has degenerated into diatribes and doctrinal controversies. This has betrayed the fundamental purpose of *religio*, which is to unite.

You cannot discover a truth like that of "being God" through mere speculation. Whether you are a prince is not determined through subtle arguments, but simply by being the son of a king! All that is needed to complete the reality of being the children of a king is having the awareness that that is what you are, and acting with the natural bearing that distinguishes people of that rank.

The craftiness of Maya does not stop here. The cunning serpent makes a move that is even more... diabolical. He succeeds in convincing the first couple to eat the mortal fruit by arguing that the Creator forbade it as a precaution, so that they would not rival His power. So the second illusion that maya perpetrates in man is to denigrate the objective of human life, the search for the divine Self. Maya does this by indicating, with its usual duplicity, that God would fear and punish any competition from a human who had the "knowledge of all things."

A father is anxious for his children to follow in his footsteps, in physical appearance, in temperament, in profession, etc... Could such a father be jealous if his children want to imitate him? And how could He who "created man in the image of Himself, in the image of God He created him" punish this "competition"?[18]

So the serpent Maya played the trump card of intellectual cunning with Eve: "Eat this fruit too," he said to her, "in order to be like God." If Eve had been on her toes, she could have answered: "But I already am like God! I do not need this fruit." Instead, that sophistic argument succeeded in convincing Adam, too. The dualistic conception of life had the upper hand in our first parents. They saw themselves so separate from the Creator, so different from Him, that they fell into the bondage of the senses, trapped by illusion.

There is One, not two. If one sees a second, then Maya is in operation. Maya is harmless to the devotee of God. That same Maya, so dangerous to the person who does not believe in God, protects the devotee from all harm. The cat carries the kitten in the mouth from here to there, and the kitten is unharmed. But a rat is killed by a cat. It is the same mouth in both cases. Maya brings trouble, yet it is the same Maya that tenderly protects the devotee of God. The devotee may do work for God and pay no attention to the powers of Maya."[19]

It is impossible to experience the spiritual through the sensual. What is beyond pleasure cannot be reached through physical, mental or intellectual enjoyment. The senses, which are the basis also for the intellect up to a certain point, cannot offer the experience of the Divine. The deception of the serpent consisted in persuading man to seek Divine Reality while still remaining at the level of the senses. In order to become what they already were, the first couple - to continue the Biblical image - decided not to heed the divine warning, and they ate of the fruit of desire, thus putting themselves under the power of death and its laws. In fact, a human who is not aware of his extremely noble state - that he is divine - is as good as dead.

---

[18]Genesis 1.27.

[19]*Conversations with Bhagavan Sri Sathya Sai Baba* (Hislop), pp. 63-64.

The consummation of desire made the first man fall from his primordial condition. It made our first parents feel "naked," as in fact anyone who lives in a house without a roof would feel naked. The ignorance behind that choice continued to be transmitted to successive generations as the "art of eating the fruits of one's own actions."

> *Do not waste precious time and life on impermanent pleasures.*
> *Have some control, a ceiling on your desires.*[20]

> *Desire makes man forget his real nature and reduces him to the*
> *status of a beast. It robs him of all his virtues and jeopardizes*
> *his honor and reputation.*[21]

---

[20] *We Devotees,* 1st edition (1983), p. 158.
[21] *Summer Showers in Brindavan,* 1979, p. 44.

CHAPTER TWELVE

The First and Final Reality that Permeates All Things

Be careful to avoid this error.
I may delude you
by singing with you,
by speaking with you,
and by performing certain actions with you.
But at a certain moment
My Divinity will be revealed to you;
you must be ready,
prepared for that moment.

Sai Baba

At first glance, Sai Baba's spoken message seems very simple, sometimes even obvious or banal. His moral teachings might seem like the pious advice of any good country priest: "Be good, do good, behave well, be kind to each other..." I have heard some people, for the most part intellectuals, express disappointment with this message, which is put forward in such an elementary way. Their criticisms are short-sighted. Certain factors have to be taken into account. Only close examination will reveal the profundity of Baba's discourses, and dissipate any hint of superficiality.

First of all, Sai Baba's audience is varied: His teaching is addressed as much to a simple housewife as to a physicist. What is extraordinary is that all types of people - with the exception of the usual superficial grumblers - are deeply satisfied by the answers that Sai Baba gives to the problems of life. However, there is a type of person who is so attached to the convictions he has accumulated over the years that he is unwilling to give up even an iota of his personal treasure of "knowledge."

In my own case, after having explored the austere doctrine of Krishnamurti, the stern aphorisms of Babaji in the Himalayas, having tasted the marvelous sweetness of Yogananda and the wisdom of Maharishi, I found a complete synthesis of all these teachings in the words of Sai Baba. Those words became the touchstone for my search.

Sai Baba is sometimes sweet, sometimes stern; on one occasion he will be clear even to a child, on another demanding and severe. He shows each person a different aspect of the same Truth, tailored for the person who reads or hears His words, and appropriate for him. Not only this: in my experience as an editor of His discourses, I have discovered that the same expression takes on different meanings in the various moments of my life. This is a sign that there has been a change in me, but above all it shows that the Master's words are capable of a wide range of effect.

A discourse which I may have read two or three months ago seems completely new to me today if I re-read it. After an interval, details which I missed or did not understand the first time seem perfectly clear. Even more surprising is the fact that the discourses are never obsolete or definitive. They seem to be intentionally open-ended, so that the same words, printed years ago in a book, can continue to impart new teachings.

Sai Baba passes easily from a moral exhortation that anyone can understand to a philosophical conversation at the highest level. He might speak to a scientist with examples and parables in order to make him understand a very simple concept, but He knows how to reveal, even to an unlettered person, the difficult path to non-dualism.

His Word is the image and emblem of the unchanging Reality which reveals Itself through multiple forms and figures, conquering the dimensions of space and time. It is in speaking of this Reality, incomprehensible to the human mind, that Sai Baba reveals all His glory and the mystery of His Being.

It is time to probe into His thought about this Truth, even though our treatment of it here must be limited. His "vision" of God, so to speak, is illuminating, and once again it is in full harmony with all Scriptures and with all religious traditions.

Man occupies a preeminent and privileged position in the search for this Divine Reality, because he is the only creature in the world capable of conceiving God. Above all, he is the only being "capable of understanding God who takes human form."[1]

But who is this God whom man has been seeking for millennia? What does He consist of? What idea of Divinity can man form, given the limits of his reason and intuition? In order to show how limited human powers are in trying to understand the Divine, Sai Baba gives a telling example:

Let us suppose an elephant had the desire to adore God. Being conditioned by his own nature, his concept of God might be of a powerful form of Elephant; nor would he be able to imagine Him any other way. If a mouse conceived some idea of God, he could imagine Him only as a gigantic Mouse. In the same way, man can only conceive God in human form, nor will he ever be able to conceive Him in a transcendent way as long as he continues to see himself as exclusively human.[2]

Not even the "specialists," such as doctors in theology and the interpreters of sacred scriptures, have been able to clarify the problem of God with all their knowledge. Sai Baba has some particularly stern words for them, because "all the speculations or various theories in regard to God are the product of pure fantasy."[3]

Here I feel personally called to account. As a scholar of theological science who specialized in moral theology, I have to admit that my studies did not bring to my spiritual life anything more than what was already there. In fact, you may remember that it was precisely during those years of study for my degree in Rome that I suffered a crisis in my spiritual life. Nor will I ever forget that among the very best professors in that theological heaven that was the seminary, among those eagles of acute intelligence and fervent pen, there were some who later suffered extremely painful crises of faith. Some of them ended up abandoning religious life altogether.

---

[1]*Discorsi* 88/89, vol. I, XIV, 1.
[2]*ibid., 4.*
[3]*ibid., 3.*

This showed me that theological study does not necessarily lead to faith in the Divine. What brings you to God is putting into practice what you have learned in theory. When you are engaged in study, even if you are already an adult, you become as small as any student at a school bench, and you worry about your exams, about impressing others, about your degree, about your future.

I do not mean to reject scholarship by saying this, but merely to rescale the importance we attribute to it, and in particular the importance of theological erudition. Some of the advantages of these studies are that you acquire a methodology and you learn to evaluate carefully the sources from which you draw your conclusions. I encountered some rare and fascinating sacred texts in my studies, but I now know, with some regret, that if your taste buds are not developed, even the sweetest fruit will seem bitter.

Besides, I have always noticed that it is the scholars, especially the theologians, who are most resistant and stubborn in face of the most evident and transparent truths, truths that even a child would understand. In order to approach truth, your intellect must be pure and free. What sort of purity and freedom can be in an intellect that is full of notions, full of pride when it recites them, full of the presumption that it possesses the truth, full of the arrogance that makes it decide that everyone else is ignorant? This is why Sai Baba goes so far as to say:

The concept of God offered by a lay person is better than all the descriptions of pundits and theologians, because the lay person prefers to remain silent, even if he can use the same terminology. And the result of that silence is general peace. In fact, the various interpretations produced by the theologians create divisions among people and wreak havoc in society, disturbing people's consciences. It would be better for these theologians to remain silent rather than create unrest and confusion.[4]

A learned scholar endowed with reasoning can give many descriptions of God. Some thinkers describe Him as Inscrutable,

------

[4]*ibid.,* 7.

Ineffable, Indescribable, Transcendent and Without-Attributes. However all these high-sounding terms are in the end nothing but chatter. If the meanings which are attributed to these words and the explanations which are deduced from them do not come from personal experience, they are worthless and treacherous, because they do not represent Reality.[5]

As far as approaching God through concepts and words, Baba repeatedly insists that that Reality cannot be described by those who have not experienced it. If asked, "Where is God?" He states:

Can you determine a location for Him who is in every place? He is immanent. It can be said decisively that God is everywhere. Further, in regard to time, it cannot be said that God exists in one era and not in another. How can He who has no beginning, no middle and no end, but who nonetheless exists in all three dimensions of time, be bound by time? Each word used to describe God is full of meaning. All the Scriptures have declared that God is found in all things.[6]

Love is God. See how everything in the world is full of love. Only with love can you experience love. There is no other means to understand the One who is the incarnation of love, except love itself. That love is not changeable, but resides stably as Spirit (atma) in every human being. The physical body is the temple of God, where love as Spirit is enshrined like a holy relic. Such a sacred and pure love can reside only in a pure heart.[7]

Ubi caritas et amor, Deus ibi est: "Where there is charity and love, there God is." This is a magnificent verse of Gregorian chant, one of the many masterpieces of music and prayer that have been almost entirely abandoned in the modern liturgy.

---

[5] *ibid.*, 5.
[6] *Discorsi* 88/89, XXX, 21.
[7] *ibid.*, 1-2.

The metaphysical essence of God is pure, self-subsistent being, beyond any attribute, outside the dimensions of space and time. This is exactly how He presents Himself to Moses in Exodus: "I Am who Am." This is what you must say to the sons of Israel: 'I Am has sent me to you.'"[8]

Jesus reiterated this "I Am" -- the vedantic tradition expresses it *aham* -- when the Jews were making fun of His claim to have come from God: "I tell you most solemnly, before Abraham ever was, I Am."[9]

It would be very interesting to do a study of what led the Catholic tradition to develop an image of God as transcendent, distant, beyond us, unapproachable. Psalm 139, on the contrary, renders homage to God as knowing the intimate secrets of men, penetrating men's thoughts from a distance:

Where could I go to escape your spirit?
Where could I flee from your presence?
If I climb the heavens, you are there,
There too, if I lie in the nether regions.

Many people see a kind of pantheistic doctrine in Sai Baba's statements. These are people who are used to the Christian polemics of the past, which tried to dig up anything that might show the weak spots in other religions. In fact, the West has always leveled the charge of pantheism against Eastern theology. In my opinion, the time has come to put an end to this misunderstanding, which has taken root as a prejudice in many Catholics.

As the word itself indicates, pantheism sees the world as made up of divine beings, each of which governs its own sphere of action. The source of the misunderstanding becomes obvious, when you hear expressions like "All is God." As always, it is language itself which unfortunately does not do justice to what it wishes to communicate.

If you go to the root of both Eastern and Western doctrine, you will see that both hold the same view: there is only one God who governs all, who gives life to all things, who moves all, and without whom

---

[8]Exodus 3.14.
[9]John 8.58.

nothing can exist. In order to make this divine omnipresence easier to conceive, the East chose to represent it as divinities inherent in various aspects of nature and of human activity. This in no way constitutes an attack on monotheism. In fact, Westerners too carry their colorful and varied divinities around in processions: all the various "Madonnas," from the Lady of Sorrows to the Immaculate Conception, and all the pantheon of saints who fill the Christian calendar, such as San Rocco, San Gennaro, and so on. Therefore, they have no reason to be scandalized when they see the same Reality expressed through different aspects and forms.

A Catholic entering a Hindu temple for the first time will probably be appalled to see that people worship something as monstrous as an obese human with an elephant head. For us such images are extravagant and perhaps even in bad taste. However, if he has the patience to study that image, called Ganesha, he will discover that it embodies a whole treatise on spirituality and mysticism. If he does not have the patience because he is too disgusted, then he should stop a minute and think what impression a Hindu might receive when he enters one of our Catholic churches. On one wall he will see a woman with twelve stars on her head and a serpent under her feet; on the other a shepherd showing a cut on his exposed thigh. Then there will be a holy apostle flayed alive, and another one nailed on a cross in an X. All the walls will be covered with children which look more like cupids than angels, and on every pilaster there will be a plaque showing, moment by moment in fourteen scenes, the torture, ridicule, and eventual crucifixion of a human being. To someone who is devoted to nonviolence, all this would have to seem scandalous and degrading. However, if he is really nonviolent, he will respect those who love such images, even if he cannot approve of them.

Besides, if we rummage around in the history of Western theology, we will discover that some of the declarations of the Councils are not so different after all from what Sai Baba teaches. The First Vatican Council went so far as to establish as a dogma that "God is alive."[10]

---

[10]Vatican Council I, Session 3, Chapter 1.   See Denzinger-Schoenmetzer, *Enchiridion symbolorum definitionum et declarationum de rebus fidei et morum*, Herder 1964, § 1782.

M. Schmauss's *Treatise on Dogma* explains this dogma by saying that God "is explicitly designated as He who lives, or rather as the fullness of life itself, self-subsistent life, the source of life. The living God speaks with a great voice through lightning and the clouds of the sky (Dt 5.23). .... God is also the creator of human life ..... The Spirit of God is the spirit which bestows life ..... Divine life is not a blind restlessness, or a formless flux, but rather it is holiness, light, love. Life, light, love are one in God (1 John 1.5; 4.15; John 1.4)."[11]

Today even science, especially physics, would not find the following sentence so surprising:

The Cosmos is permeated by God and all things are summed up in Him. There is not a single atom of the universe which is not full of God.[12]

All things are bound by one single Law. The noted scientist Leon M. Lederman has said: "As scientists, by now we are ready to accept some rather bizarre notions. The most precise theory that has ever been devised, quantum electrodynamics, begins by affirming indeterminacy as one of its fundamental premises. We have to deal with concepts such as curved space, voids full of physical properties, particles which are points with no radius but which nevertheless have spin, electrical charge, mass, and many other properties.

This is not all. Having lost any semblance of humility, the physicists of our time maintain, with considerable optimism, that these concepts are leading towards the final goal. This goal is a complete synthesis, in which a restricted number of objects governed by a unified force would succeed in explaining all the observations registered in all the laboratories of the world. It would even explain the evolution of the universe from the moment of the big bang up to the present, with projections into the infinite future."[13]

---

[11]M. Schmauss, *Dogmatica Cattolica*, Marietti, vol. I, p. 385ff.

[12]*Discorsi* 88/89, XL, 14.

[13]Leon M. Lederman, quoted by A. Zichichi in *L'Eco di Bergamo*, March 26, 1989, p. 3.

According to Stephen Hawking, another eminent scientist, the dream of modern physics and of science in general is to "provide a single theory that describes the whole universe."[14]

Sheldon Lee Glashow has said: "In looking for the ultimate building blocks of matter, we have come upon new objects which are not part of matter. These are strange particles which live for an instant, and then immediately turn into other better-known particles. There is no doubt that they exist, but to find out why has become the central mystery of modern physics. We have the key to the secrets of the Universe in our hands; now we have to figure out what door it opens."[15]

As is clear from all the declarations of Sai Baba, the nature of God is such that there is nothing unrelated to God. Therefore, nature too is seen as an expression of God, and the innumerable forms which make up the universe, from the smallest star to a galaxy or cluster of galaxies, all reveal the presence of the Divine.

At this point someone might object: How is it possible that God manifests Himself through the ugliness and the negative or evil traits which clearly exist in the world? It is true that nature is an expression of God, but it also reflects the decisions freely made by man. That the planet Earth is suffering from pollution and the threat of a nuclear holocaust certainly does not depend on a precise act of will or decision by God. God allowed man to make his own decisions, but He established a law for all things whereby every action determines an equal and opposite reaction, like a boomerang. It has been called the Law of Cause and Effect. In the East it is called *karma*; in the West it is better known as Nemesis, from the name of the Greek goddess responsible for meting out justice.

Although this law is easy to understand when you look into what causes the degradation of the environment, it is much harder to apply to earthquakes or floods. The law of reaction would suggest that natural disasters too are the Earth's response to human action. But in

---

[14]Stephen Hawking, *A Brief History of Time: From the Big Bang to Black Holes*, New York: Bantam, p.10.

[15]Sheldon Lee Glashow, quoted by A. Zichichi in *L'Eco di Bergamo,* July 30, 1989, p. 3.

this case it is hard to see how humans could be held responsible as the cause.

The reason that the interaction between the Earth's crust, meteorology, and man seems difficult to understand is that our philosophy does not account for a subtle, but real, aspect of reality. People normally think of the Earth or the sun as inert and lifeless elements, while in fact they are born, live and breathe like human beings, although through a different mechanism. There is life in them, and along with that life there is the supreme law which governs their behavior. It might seem a little extreme, but even the entities we call Earth or Sun or Moon have their own ethics, their *dharma*, through which divine life manifests itself in them. This applies also to all the systems of galaxies, to all the order which governs the universe. The "pagan" notions of all the civilizations that worshipped these heavenly bodies should be reevaluated in light of this truth.

Any interference in that order inevitably produces a "moral" disturbance in the life of every entity in the cosmos. Despite his own psychological strength, a boy can become morally unbalanced by associating with evil company, with the result that he ends up being drawn toward evil actions. In the same way, by being in the company of the cruelty and violence of humanity, the planet Earth loses its own "psychic equilibrium" and.... trembles or gets sick.

This is why Isaiah said: "The Earth is defiled under its inhabitants' feet, for they have transgressed the law, violated the precept, broken the everlasting covenant. So a curse consumes the Earth and its inhabitants suffer the penalty; that is why the inhabitants of the Earth are burned up and few men are left."[16]

The Holy Bible is full of instances in which calamities result from specific evil actions on the part of men. The idea that God repays men according to their behavior is a constant in it.[17] Our fundamental mistake is that we understand this literary motif of the Bible as a specific attribute of God, a God who is distant from man, who reigns

---

[16]Isaiah 24.5-6.

[17]See the following texts: Tobias 13.2; 13.5; 13.10; Wisdom 12.2; Jeremiah 30.11; Sirach 5.3-4; Psalms 7.12-17; 11.5-6; etc... These are only a few of the many passages that could be cited. In the chapter on reincarnation we will consider in greater detail how the words "punishment" and "retribution", so widely used in the Bible, should be understood.

on high, inculcates terror and delivers devastating verdicts. Instead of a God of love, He seems to be a highly anthropomorphic and vindictive Jove. By accepting the idea of a God who takes revenge, who punishes, who will not forgive a debt "down to the last cent," we end up with a God we cannot like, a God who is very far from the love which He promises and is supposed to inspire in us. If a cruel man forms an idea of God in his mind, that God can only be a reflection of his own cruelty.

If we replace this mistaken notion of God with the great Divine Law stamped onto the world from the very beginning, the law whereby all evil and all good is recorded and reflected, then we cannot blame God for being so cruel and vicious with man. We will have to accept our own responsibility. That Law is the first and final Reality, while all notions of God are simply the product of superconditioned human brains. They are ideas that have no substance, are completely changeable, and are therefore unreal. They are really adulterations of the one Eternal and Unchanging Truth.

Avatars descend to teach all these things to man. As I have told you many times, God does not come on Earth to solve all your little domestic problems and to give you a fleeting happiness. Every difficulty which you encounter and which you must face is the result of your own actions.[18]

In time, all your difficulties will automatically be resolved.... Good and evil depend on the kind of actions you have performed. Do good and you will encounter good results. If you do evil, the results will be bad. Why ask God? He will in any case give you anything you desire...

If you plant a lemon seed, you will not harvest a mango. If you plant a mango, a breadfruit tree will not grow instead. The fruits that will ripen depend on the seeds you plant. Therefore, do not give all your attention to the fruits of your actions,

---

[18]*Discorsi 88/89*, III, 8.

because it is obvious that you will gather according to what you have planted.[19]

Jesus too gave concise and extremely clear explanations of the law of karma. To one of his followers who had cut off the ear of the son of the High Priest with his sword, the Master said: "Put your sword back, for all who draw the sword will die by the sword."[20]

The law of karma needs to be examined in greater detail, because it is connected with the doctrine of reincarnation.

---

[19]*id.* IX, 22-23.
[20]Matthew 26.52.

CHAPTER THIRTEEN

The Apple of Discord

*The first thing to do
is to interrupt
the cycle of previous lives.*[1]

Saint Basil

When God sent Nathan to David to reprimand him for his sins, the holy prophet condemned the king for two things. David had committed a double sin: he had stolen the wife of his general Uriah, and in order to be able to marry her, he had sent Uriah to fight in the front lines of a battle, where he was killed.[2]

The prophet Nathan induced David to repent by skillfully telling him a parable that exposed his errors in no uncertain terms. He concluded his visit by prophesying the inevitable punishment to come: "Thus Yahweh speaks, 'I will stir up evil for you out of your own house. Before your very eyes I will take your wives and give them to your neighbor, and he shall lie with your wives in the sight of this sun. You worked in secret, I will work this in the face of all Israel and in the face of the sun.'" Then, when David had repented, Nathan went on: "Yahweh, for his part, forgives your sin; you are not to die. Yet because you have outraged Yahweh by doing this; the child that is born to you is to die."[3]

The double tragedy foretold by Nathan came to pass as prophesied. The son David had by Uriah's wife, Bathsheba, died, and Absalom, the son of David, "in the sight of all Israel went to his father's concubines."[4] Even though David had repented and had undertaken a harsh penance to make up for his sin, the boomerang of the evil

---

[1] *Primum quidem necesse est vitae prioris seriem interrumpi.*
[2] See 2 Samuel 11.
[3] 2 Samuel 12.11-14.
[4] See 2 Samuel 12.15-23 and 16.22.

action had been thrown. Having reached its target, it now had to find satisfaction in an equal return action.

The law of *karma* is inexorable. G. Von Rad says, "Through the law of eye for an eye, which is the hidden principle of the story, it is God himself who intervenes against the criminal. Theologians should begin at long last to give in to the occult power of this episode from secular history. This story has some truly spectacular aspects, showing that when men are left to their own devices they often bring on themselves a vicious cycle of errors and suffering."

It is not only bad actions that have a reaction. Fortunately good actions bring on positive consequences too. When the Egyptian Pharaoh, worried about the population growth of the Jews, ordered the nurses to suffocate all the male babies born to the Jews, they did not obey. God blessed the nurses, granting them children of their own.[5] The Pharaoh, on the other hand, paid for his cruel edict with the tenth plague, when all the first-born among the Egyptians died in one night.[6]

"Repent," says the prophet Ezekiel, "renounce all your sins, avoid all occasions of sin! Shake off all the sins you have committed against me, and make yourselves a new heart and a new spirit! Why are you so anxious to die, House of Israel? I take no pleasure in the death of anyone - it is the Lord Yahweh who speaks. Repent and live!"[7] In Isaiah we find: "Happy is the virtuous man, for he will feed on the fruit of his deeds; woe to the wicked, evil is on him, he will be treated as his actions deserve."[8]

In the desert land of Marah, where at the Lord's command Moses threw his staff into the undrinkable water and it became potable, the Lord made a pact with the people, "If you listen carefully to the voice of Yahweh your God and do what is right in his eyes, if you pay attention to his commandments and keep his statutes, I shall inflict on you none of the evils that I inflicted on the Egyptians, for it is I, Yahweh, who give you healing."[9]

---

[5]Exodus 1.17-21. "The man who is kind to the poor lends to Yahweh: he will repay him for what he has done" (Proverbs 19.17). See also Exodus 22.21ff.

[6]Exodus 12.29-30.

[7]Ezekiel 18.30b-32.

[8]Isaiah 3.10-11.

[9]Exodus 15.26.

The fourth of the commandments given on Mt. Sinai said, "Honor your father and your mother so that you may have a long life in the land that Yahweh your God has given to you."[10]

"The men whom Moses had sent out to reconnoiter the promised land disparaged the land, inciting the whole Israeli community to grumble against Yahweh. These men, who deprecated the land, were all struck dead before Him."[11] When the people protested to God about their hardships during the exodus from Egypt, poisonous snakes were sent.[12] It seems God has a particular aversion to grumbling, even when it is done in secret: "Whoever slanders his neighbor in secret, him will I destroy."[13]

Obviously the Bible does not speak of karma, but it is easy to find the equivalent of that sanskrit word in expressions such as: the law of retribution, the just vengeance of God, the punishments and threats of God, the corrections administered by God. All these expressions have served to make the merciful Father of all beings seem like a bloodthirsty and cruel stepfather, unyielding to any prayer for forgiveness. This is understandable if we conceive God only as a person, and we continue to imagine Him as distant from human beings, a father-master of our destinies. Such a God will reflect all the characteristics of the sinful human beings who conceive Him in their own image and likeness.

The holy writer of the Book of Wisdom seems worried about this distorted vision of God: "Do not court death by the errors of your ways, nor invite destruction through your own actions. Death was not God's doing, he takes no pleasure in the extinction of the living."[14]

In David's situation, the "just vengeance of God" executed its verdict in the space of a few months or years: in any case, during David's own lifetime. But this "justice" does not seem to work itself out always with the same rhythm and rapidity that it did in the case of David. Sometimes it seems that the trial-documents lie on the Judge's

---

[10]Exodus 20.12.

[11]Numbers 14.36-37.

[12]Numbers 21.5-7. As evidence for collective karma, see the following passages: Leviticus 26.3-5, 6-8, 9-10, 14-18, 19ff.

[13]Psalm 100.5

[14]Wisdom 1.12.

table (or is it the Executioner's?!) much too long, to the point that some crimes seem to go unpunished, perhaps forgotten by an inefficient bureaucracy... Some transgressions are punished too severely, and others not severely enough.

Why does a person who is very rich suddenly inherit millions of dollars? Why does some poor wretch, who is already burdened with a number of calamities, get prosecuted and jailed unjustly? Why does a lady who desired nothing but to have children, have to watch her beloved child die? Why are children born to incapable parents? Why does that 18-year-old, who is so full of virtues, die in a car accident, while his companion in the car, who is violent and aggressive, recovers fully in ten days?

In His teaching Jesus did not change any of the convictions that were rooted deep in the Judaic tradition. In the few sentences of His that have been handed down to us by the gospels, He makes us see that the justice of the Father is a reflection of human justice: "If you forgive others their failings, your heavenly Father will forgive you yours; but if you do not forgive others, your Father will not forgive your failings either." "Do not judge, and you will not be judged yourselves; do not condemn, and you will not be condemned yourselves; grant pardon, and you will be pardoned. Give, and there will be gifts for you... because the amount you measure out is the amount you will be given back."[15] In John 5.14, Jesus in the temple comes upon the paralytic He had cured a short time before - this was the healing that His contemporaries complained about because it had occurred on a Saturday - and He warns the man, "Be sure not to sin any more, or something worse may happen to you."

Are we really to believe that there is a God who weighs all our actions on a set of scales and re-distributes them as He wishes? Is it not more likely that the "human divinity," man himself, who is made "in the image and likeness of God," controls his own destiny, simply inheriting the results of his good and evil actions? In that case it is not that God forgives or takes revenge, but rather that there is a sacred and perfect law by which there is a corresponding reflection for every action humans commit. So there is no justification for blaming God; at most one can feel sorry for having cursed oneself. In the end, to

---

[15]Matthew 6.14; Luke 6.37.

denigrate God is to denigrate man himself, in whom God is manifest. If the blasphemers were aware of this, they would learn to love themselves more!

It is only natural that if you cling to the idea of a God who governs all the world's affairs from the outside, independently from human actions or at any rate not in direct connection with them, eventually your mind will feel a conflict. At the very least, it will rebel against such absurd and perverse behavior on the part of God. In this light, it is easy to sympathize with those who blaspheme God. If God does not know how to execute justice any better than men do, then all hope is lost, and when hope is lost, faith in God dies too.

It is difficult to total the credits and debits in all this divine accounting: only a Supreme Being can supervise it all. To understand the mechanism by which the books are balanced, we need to know something else: is there an installment plan? What is the deadline for paying off your mortgage? Many biblical passages imply that God judges according to how humans behave, and that "to the upright man his integrity will be credited, to the wicked his wickedness."[16] If this is true, then how is it that the wicked person often does not pay right away, and often not even in his lifetime, while the good person often does not receive his reward immediately?

The idea that there is a cycle of human lives enters precisely to deal with this postponement of debits and merits: it facilitates the paying off of debts, and the cashing in of credits, and makes the whole process more believable. Naturally here we are entering in an area which is, at least for now, at variance with the official doctrine of the Christian Church, except as a subject of research. It is clear therefore that what follows belongs to the arena of research and investigation: it is not how orthodox dogma is currently interpreted.

This is certainly the point of greatest division between Christianity and Eastern religions. I continue to believe that it is not worth getting worked up about a problem if it means causing dissension. Nonetheless it is worth considering it with serenity, without passions or partisanship, simply for the love of Truth. Most of humanity believes in reincarnation, and I am convinced that if we were to conduct

---

[16]Ezekiel 18.20.

anonymous polls to get statistics on how many Christians believe in it, we would get some surprising results.

The problem of reincarnation triggers some irrational reactions in people even before it is addressed directly. People who are very attached to life exult at the idea that they will be able to go through "new editions" of it, thinking that they will be able to enjoy it again as they do at present. Pessimists, those disappointed by life, prefer not to believe in reincarnation. They detest the idea, because for them it would simply mean prolonging the suffering and bitterness that their current life has already so generously showered on them.

In between these two immature attitudes, there is the Christian prejudice that it is preferable to be shipped to Heaven right away with a sacrament or two, rather than to have to continue a tiring and painstaking search, and evolve through many lives.

There are arguments both for and against reincarnation. In favor of the idea that lives repeat there is the fact that the entire rhythm of nature is based on cycles. There is nothing on earth or in the cosmos that is not subject to cycles: days, months, years, seasons all follow repeating cycles. Even the human body itself follows cycles. Each cell constitutes a cycle both in itself and in relation to the macrocosm. The atom follows a cycle of contraction and expansion, like the cosmos which expands and contracts from the big bang to a black hole, from creation to destruction. There is nothing in nature that does not begin with birth and end with death, to then be born and die again, and then again... without end.

There is no reason to think that everything that has come into being and then to an end cannot come back into existence again. Strictly speaking, even a body that decomposes or is cremated does not "disappear": all its mineral salts and carbohydrates are transformed into gases, ashes, liquids, which contain every single one of the molecules that made up the body, but now with a different structure. If it were possible to do what the Lilliputians of *Gulliver's Travels* did, that is preserve all organic wastes and everything that evaporates or decomposes, and if some genial mind were capable of weaving all the cells and atoms back together again, then what seemed to be lost would be back as it was before. Nature is very frugal: it does not waste anything that has been discarded. It re-integrates and recycles everything with a wisdom that man has not yet acquired.

What makes it hard for most people to believe that lives repeat is once again the illusory power of all this changing matter. It is indeed a dance of Shiva, which makes things re-appear, disappear, be born and die, but which always re-uses the same elements. Rabbits and turtles come out of the same hat. The hand which pulls them out is always the same. In the same way bodies are like the doves and rabbits, the top hat is the womb which nurtures them, and the Supreme Eternal Soul is the magician who puts on the show. What difference does it make if at the next show the white doves will be different ones? The show goes on, doves are always doves, white is always white. Not all doves die when **that** dove dies. The dove and rabbits survive their own deaths. Even though they die as the years pass, their manifestation as dove and rabbits does not stop. The essence survives individual existence.

But what worries the people who object to reincarnation is that they are afraid to lose their individuality. Anyone who is afraid to lose his "I" is already dead, because the "I" belongs to the world of illusion. It is destined to be extinguished, because it is not real. On the other hand, if by "I" we mean the Divine Essence which permeates all things and is eternal, then the fear of losing it is groundless. That Essence is the only Reality which survives all human experiences. In that Reality there is nothing which differentiates us or distinguishes us from one another. When you think about it, to be afraid of re-incarnation is to be afraid of no longer existing. It is a fear which derives from confusing a physical form with what endures beyond all forms, the Formless. It is to be afraid of taking on a new physical shape, which will annihilate the present form and condemn it to oblivion.

The greatest philosophers have demonstrated that the soul is eternal. On the other hand anyone who has any discrimination can see how brief the life of any body is. If the body dies and the soul survives, why should we not think that the soul resides in more than one body, one after another? Is it really so irrational to suppose that the Divine Spirit which lives in each of us, and which is pure in itself, needs more than one incarnation in order to complete what it has left unfinished in previous lives?

It is certainly not the divine soul which survives *post-mortem*: the divine soul lives in Itself and for Itself. But everything which accompanies that soul is part of a world which does not consist only in the body, or dense matter: it also includes a subtler world. That world is made of thoughts and desires, which certainly are not eternal, but which surely survive the physical body, and do not die until they are either satisfied or somehow fulfilled. Who can claim that he knows how to complete the difficult task of reaching God, and overcome all his bad tendencies and harshness of character, in only one lifetime?

Besides, are so-called "innate" tendencies really innate? Why is it that if you take four brothers, all children of the same parents, there will be one who loves music and is gentle, another who is devoted to sports and is active, another who is lazy and does not like to work, and a fourth who is an impulsive hedonist, all wrapped up in the pleasures of life? How can they be so different, to the point that if you took them individually, you would say they all belonged to different parents?

Genetic factors are said to be responsible for the psychic and physical characteristics of individuals. This is true, but only in part. Why is it that even two identical twins are different in both temperament and destiny? Is it so irrational to suppose that in addition to the factors science can determine, there are other subtler, hidden factors, which we cannot detect? Is it completely insane to think that when each person is born again in a new bodily form, he is followed by precise software, a program complete with applications and utilities, which had been put on hold at the end of his previous life? How many people leave their bodies, that is, die, thinking about projects they have not finished! People who have been present at death-beds know that in many cases, a few hours before dying, the patient inexplicably gains new energy out of thin air. When someone who is terminally ill shows a great interest in new ideas or new projects, and he gets up, or wants to, in order to get started, you can be sure he is on the verge of leaving his body.

Aside from our Divine Reality, each of us carries a treasure of thoughts, desires, longings and resolutions. Is it not quite realistic and logical to think that we are each like an unfinished work of art? Like Schubert's Unfinished Symphony, for example, waiting to be amended and retouched, in order to reach sublime simplicity and the highest stylistic purity.

Another consideration which supports reincarnation is the problem of Divine Justice. There is no doubt that this Justice could be presented more respectably if we pre-suppose reincarnation: all the social injustices, the wrongs, the sorrows, the suffering, the poverty, wars and all the other various mishaps which afflict man would simply be each person's just reward, without blaming anyone else. That way each person would carry his own burden, and he would have no reason to complain about it. Each person should carry his burden with dignity: he should pay off his own debt with joy and with diligence, like someone who is about to finish paying off a heavy obligation and does not want to fall into debt again. To which God should we complain about this imposition, then, if not to ourselves? It is up to us to solve our own problems, by means of the divine Grace which lives in all of us alike, with no preference for one person over another.

One objection to reincarnation is: if that is how things are, why is it we do not remember anything from all our supposed past lives?

Ancient mythology told of a river of Forgetfulness called Lethe. Upon drinking its waters, the souls of the departed forgot every previous joy and sorrow. In fact, our memory has a time-span that is considerably shorter than one life, much less many lives. Who is there who can remember, in a normal waking state, exactly what happened on one day a few years ago, picked at random from a thousand?

I refer the diligent reader to the studies on reincarnation conducted by such eminent researchers as Edgar Cayce, G.B. Rhine, and I. Stevenson. For my part, on the basis of indirect experiences of hypnosis, undertaken with discrimination and with the assistance of serious scholars, I would conclude that no experience is entirely lost within the ancestral memory of a human being. In essence, his entire preceding history could be recovered. I would not advise doing so, however: it would be painful, and it would probably re-awaken traumas which should at this point lie shelved in the archives.

To play some more with the image of the computer, I think it is a plausible hypothesis that in each of us there are all the files of our past lives, erased but still not entirely lost. Anyone who knows his way around computers knows that all you have to do is find the first letters of the file, and you can call up the entire file.

Our lives, then, are like ancient parchments from which the writing has been partially or entirely erased in order to make room for a new text. In the same way we have repeatedly cancelled and rewritten our lives on the same parchment. Each time an "author" forms his letters on the same material, he comes closer and closer to the Supreme Author. The final moment, in which the wandering I merges with the unchanging I, is the resolution of a long story, which has come to an end simply because it has run out of subject matter. That is to say, it has exhausted all the impulses and anxieties of the ego.

Even though many people say that there is no support for reincarnation in the Bible, there are some passages which seem to indicate a clear familiarity with it, and even faith in it. We will cite only a few.

Psalm 90, which is attributed to Moses, contains a poetic description of the ebb and flow of lives:

Before the mountains were born,
before the earth or the world came to birth,
you were God from all eternity and for ever.
You can turn man back into dust
by saying, "Back to what you were, you sons of men!"
To you, a thousand years are a single day,
a yesterday now over, an hour of the night.
You brush men away like waking dreams,
they are like grass
sprouting and flowering in the morning,
withered and dry before dusk.[17]

However in my opinion the passage which expresses the doctrine of reincarnation most clearly is chapter 8, verses 19-20 of the Book of Wisdom. Even though the commentators have hastened to demonstrate that this passage does not imply the pre-existence of souls, their reasons are not cogent. Solomon is reflecting on how Wisdom confers immortality, and wondering how to acquire it. Then he says: "I was a boy of happy disposition, I had received a good soul as my lot, or rather, being good, I had entered an undefiled body..."

---

[17]Psalm 90.2-6.

Verses 11-12 of Chapter 41 of the Book of Sirach speak of the destiny of the wicked: "A bad outlook for you, godless men, who have forsaken the Law of God Most High. When you were born, you were born to be accursed, and when you die, that curse will be your portion." Here the notion of reincarnation is fused with that of karma. One cannot exist without the other.

Certain passages of the New Testament seem to offer glimpses of reincarnation; in fact certain readings from the Gospels make no sense except in the light of reincarnation and karma.

Take for example Matthew 16.13-14. Jesus asks the disciples what people are saying about Him. The disciples tell Him that some people consider Him "John the Baptist, some Elijah, and others Jeremiah or one of the prophets." Of course you can always force the text, and conclude that this is a way of comparing the greatness of Jesus with the greatness of various prophets. However it would seem pretty clear that the disciples, who were certainly familiar with reincarnation, wanted to say: "People say that you are one of these prophets come back into the world." Mark's version is even clearer and leaves less doubt.[18] Luke's version emphasizes the idea of being born again: "Some say John the Baptist; others Elijah; and others say one of the ancient prophets come back to life."[19]

Descending from the mount of the Transfiguration, the disciples asked the Master why the scribes said that Elijah would have to come first. Jesus answered, "True, Elijah is to come to see that everything is once more as it should be; however, I tell you that Elijah has come already and they did not recognize him but treated him as they pleased.[20]

This excerpt from the Gospels sheds light on that other passage in which Jesus publicly praises John the Baptist: "I tell you solemnly, of all the children born of women, one greater than John the Baptist has never been seen... and he, if you will believe me, is the Elijah who was to return. If anyone has ears to hear, let him listen!"[21]

---

[18]Mark 8.27-28.
[19]Luke 9.18-19.
[20]Matthew 17.9-12.
[21]Matthew 11.7-15.

The episode in which Jesus restores sight to the man who had been born blind only makes sense if you assume reincarnation. "As he went along, he saw a man who had been blind from birth. His disciples asked him, "Rabbi, who sinned, this man or his parents, for him to have been born blind?"[22]

Why should the question of responsibility arise, in asking why someone is born blind? The question shows implicit belief in the law of karma. What the question is asking is: "Was this man born blind as a consequence of his own sins, or because of the sins of his parents?" In order to perform actions which could justify the painful consequence of being born blind, the man would have had to have a previous life. Without that presupposition, the disciples' question about the blind man makes no sense.

Jesus's answer skirts the question. This is what he often did, when it was a matter of not tarnishing someone's reputation or raising scandal, as in the case of the adulteress who was to be stoned. This is why Jesus does not attribute specific responsibility to either the blind man or his unfortunate parents, but says instead that he was born blind "so that the works of God might be displayed in him." In fact, He restored his sight, thus glorifying God's actions by performing a miracle.

On the whole, however, the Bible does not offer sufficient or conclusive proofs of reincarnation, if only because in interpreting the Bible people can always use subtle distinctions to dismiss the theory. This is one of the reasons that it is not very worthwhile to argue about reincarnation: humans can use reason either to destroy reason itself or to vindicate it, depending on what they want to do. In any case, if you look through the patristic writings, you will come across much more explicit musings on the subject.

In his *Dialogue with Triphon* St. Justin, who lived in the second century A.D., "says that the soul lives more than once in a human body, but it cannot remember its previous experiences. He says that souls which have become unworthy of contemplating God are united with the bodies of wild animals.[23]

---

[22]John 9.1-3.

[23]*Il libro della reincarnazione*, Armenia, p. 184. I refer freely to this book in presenting this summary of reincarnation.

Origen (third century A.D.) was a prolific author, and one of the principal proponents of reincarnation. I will quote only a small excerpt from his writings, which seems insightful to me: "Those who need bodies take them on, and when fallen souls have raised themselves to higher things, their bodies are again destroyed. In this way they disappear and reappear continuously."[24] It is strange that Origen was condemned in 553 during the Second Council in Constantinople, even though his writings are frequently included among the prayers of the Breviary.[25]

St. Gregory of Nazianzus (fourth century A.D.), who was the bishop of Constantinople, asserted that people who argue for reincarnation are in agreement with Catholics, who believe in the doctrine of the Resurrection. The saintly bishop said that the two sides are united in their conviction that "the body, whether now or in the future, is composed of the atoms of the universe."[26]

Through catechism, or rather through the ingenuousness of certain catechism teachers, we learned that at the Last Judgement every piece of our bodies would be recovered and put back together in order to form glorious and perfect bodies. If true, this "final" operation would require a colossal expenditure of natural and supernatural energy, which is contrary to the normal wise laws of Nature. Besides, we should wonder: *ad quid perditio haec*? Why all this waste?

I fear that for many people faith in the Resurrection has become a belief that the body, to which we are all so attached, will not in the very end go to waste. I also fear that the original meaning of resurrection, a catharsis from the material world through which one rises up to a spiritual-divine reality, has been lost. To nurture the hope of getting your body back at the end of time, perfected and with no physiological limits, is a pathetic blemish in the whole project of spiritual ascendancy. Not only is it opposed to every spiritual teaching of every age, which consistently urges us to transcend every material desire; it also would be a kind of second thought or joke in the divine

---

[24] *Ibid.*

[25] See Denzinger-Schoenmetzer, *Enchiridion symbolorum definitionum et declarationum de rebus fidei et morum*, Herder 1964, p. 149 (§ 223).

[26] *Il libro della reincarnazione*, p. 192.

plan. In the end we would all put on beautiful bodies, precisely when they are no longer of any use to us!

Would not the road to Truth be clearer if for the phrase "Resurrection of the flesh" we substitute the words "return into flesh," that is, "reincarnation"?

Eastern texts are much more expansive in explaining the idea of reincarnation. For example the Bhagavad Gita says: "The soul is never born and never dies; it was not born and will not be reborn; without birth, without end, eternal, ancient, it is not killed when the body in which it lives is killed. Just as one casts off old clothes in order to put on new clothes, so the soul casts off used bodies in order to take on new ones."[27]

Even those who walk towards the Spirit are not exempt from the law of eternal cycles. Without so much theorizing about reincarnation, Sai Baba brings the focus back to the fundamental purpose of every human being:

What is man's journey? Where is he going? Why is he continuously reborn? In order to seek the right path and the knowledge of truth. What road should one seek? You should return whence you have come. That is seeking. You have come from the Divine Essence, from God, and you must return to Him.[28]

Do not expect to find happiness in the other world; that world too is impermanent. Once you have exhausted your merits, you will again be cast out of it. Even in politics, candidates are elected for a term that expires after five years. Each year that passes shortens the right he earned through the election. In the same way, the duration of your "paradise" will depend upon your merits. When these are used up, you will have to return to the earth.[29]

---

[27]Bhagavad Gita II, 20.22.
[28]Discorsi 88/89, XIX, 36.
[29]*Ibid.*, XXXI, 21.

Why does the Church oppose or ignore the doctrine of reincarnation? It is a common opinion, held by various authors and supported by historical documentation, that in its first centuries the Church accepted a belief in reincarnation. The documents on which these opinions are based are the acts of the Fifth Ecumenical Council, also called the Second Council of Constantinople.

At that time, around the year 537, the Catholic Church was torn by a number of controversies, and the first priority for the men of the church was to uproot "heresies." It was not just that the important prelates of the time wanted to re-unite the faithful, who were dispersed among many ideologies; Justinian too, who was the reigning emperor, was looking for any means to avoid religious strife in the empire.

In all of his decisions Justinian would seek the advice of his wife Theodora, who was known to have a great influence on the emperor's actions. It is said that before becoming empress, Theodora, who was a woman of humble origins, had led a rather carefree life as a dancer, and in any case had had a rather turbulent and mysterious past. On the other hand Justinian, "convinced more than ever that he was vested with both theological learning and ecclesiastical authority, presumed to govern the Church. After arranging the condemnation of any writings or men who were obstacles to unity, he took it on himself to publish dogmatic edicts which defined orthodox belief. Once ratified by the ecclesiastical authorities, these were imposed on all without distinction."[30]

One of Justinian's most important interventions in church affairs was to eradicate doctrines like Origen's. These had already been condemned, but had spread again, especially in a Palestinian monastery founded by an ascetic named Saba, between Jerusalem and the Dead Sea. Having put aside Saint Saba's directives, this convent south of Bethlehem "became the principal center for origenistic propaganda. The doctrines of the pre-existence of the soul, of the migration of souls, and of palingenesis were particularly in favor there."[31] When the papal legate, Pelagius, was informed of these doctrines, Justinian was only too happy to seize the occasion to

---

[30]*Storia della Chiesa dalle origini ai giorni nostri*, S.A.I.E., Torino 1972, vol. IV, p. 577.

[31]*Ibid.*, pp. 579-580.

intervene in a question of dogma. So he wrote a treatise against Origen, which culminated in a violent condemnation of Origen and his followers. The treatise was brought into the council and it was rubber-stamped.

Whether the demise of the doctrine of reincarnation was due to these controversies, and whether it had been freely accepted in the Church during the previous centuries, are questions that I leave to historians to decide. I believe that it is no longer possible to keep so many secrets under lock and key, nor can we continue to sweep so much under the rug.

In any case, I am also convinced that from an ascetic's point of view, once someone has gone beyond the barrier of the body and turns all his interest towards the spiritual, the problem of reincarnation has no more meaning for him. For him to worry about it would be to fall back towards a level of consciousness that is bound by the limits of history and time.

In the suburbs of Bombay there was a tobacconist, Nisargadatta Maharaj by name, who was a great saint. He came from a Hindu background, lived in this century, and died only a few years ago. To a visitor who was asking him whether one should believe in previous lives, he answered: "Reincarnation presupposes a self which is capable of reincarnating. But this self does not exist. The bundle of memories and hopes which we call "I", imagines that it will last forever, and it invents time in order to make a place for its false eternity. In order to be, I have no need of past or future. Every experience, from birth to death, is a product of imagination. I do not imagine, therefore I was not born and shall not die. Only those who think they have been born, can think they will be born again."[32]

Once again, East and West can meet: the one encouraging a life which transcends time, the other pushing towards a "unique" existence. In the end, for both there is really only one life, either because thinking about other lives slows down your spiritual evolution, or because if you think you have only one life, you must live it fully, as if indeed there were no other lives.

---

[32]Nisargadatta Maharaj, *I Am That*, vol. II, Rizzoli-Milano 1982, pp. 7-8; American edition (Acorn Press 1982), p. 262.

CHAPTER FOURTEEN

Religion: Devotion to the One God

There is one Lord,
one faith,
one baptism,
and One God who is Father of all,
over all, through all
and within all.

Saint Paul to the Ephesians 4.5

Anyone who has had the good fortune to visit Sai Baba's ashram knows that the atmosphere there is saturated with peace and good thoughts. This is partly because there is a custom in the ashram of placing phrases from Sai Baba's teachings everywhere. Wherever you go, you come upon quotations which draw your attention back to spiritual values, and remind you that you are there only because you have resolved to develop your inner life. One of these quotations, which has made Sathya Sai Baba's mission famous throughout the world, is the following:

There is only one religion: the religion of love.
There is only one language: the language of the heart.
There is only one caste: the caste of humanity.
There is only one God, and He is omnipresent.

Some detractors think that this slogan implies a desire to unite all religions into one, making just one religion. They call this presumed aim "syncretism." In the past the Church had to undergo many struggles in order to avoid what at the time was properly regarded as the erosion of the "one true" religion.
Etymologically, "syncretism" derives from the Greek word *synkretismos*, which literally means "united in the Cretan way." It refers to the fusion of various mythological, cultural and doctrinal

elements taken from different religions. To attempt a sort of union by injecting into one religion rituals and symbols taken from other traditions would indeed create only confusion. This is why I think the Catholic Church acted wisely when it defended its own tradition from the intrusion of other forms of worship. As I said before, the liturgy should be clear and focussed, because its function is to inform and instruct. If you keep offering new bottles to a baby, it might come to reject the milk!

Once this principle is clear, it should be evident that there is no danger in dispensing the same "milk," even though it comes from different breasts. In other words, there is no basis for accusing a religion of "syncretism" just because it hears the same Truth in the teachings of different sages and saints. Truth does not need a trademark. It is not the *imprimatur* of some authority that makes a message credible. Truth is true in itself. You recognize it inside, in your heart. It is only a pure heart that can guarantee that a Truth is "kosher."

When the Hindus tell me that God pervades all things, I believe it, but not because it is the popular thing to do. I believe it because every time I look around, or open a book on physics or geology or astronomy, or stop to consider the miracles that surround me, I "see" with my own eyes that it is absolutely true! Why should I pay any attention to someone who tries to tell me that this truth cannot be true, simply because it was said by a sheep that belongs to a different flock?

Sai Baba has absolutely no intention of founding a new religion. He himself has said that there are plenty of religions already, indeed too many. The sacred task He has assumed is to lead all religions back to the one Truth which is God and Love. Any religion that fights or dismisses other religions in order to defend itself is not a true religion, because it is against Love, which is to be against God!

The etymological meaning of the word "religion" is not certain, but it seems to derive from the Latin *religare*, "to bind again." Sai Baba too leans toward this explanation:

The word "religion" contains the prefix re. Re means doing something again. The other part of the word connotes "unifying."

Religion may thus be interpreted as reunion, the reunification of two entities separated by time, or the restoration of their original organic unity. Jivatma and Paramatma, (the individual soul and the Universal Soul), have lost their fundamental Oneness... The restoration of the primal unity of Atma and Paramatma through self-realization is the primary function of religion.[1]

Religions have failed because mankind has lost sight of the primary function of religious institutions, which is to stimulate the search for God, to transform the devotion man has toward things into devotion toward God.

People from different nations and religions have dedicated themselves to seeking out the purpose of life. Because of all these searches, religions have taken various directions and paths.[2]

The first task of any religion should be to find out the reasons why humans repeatedly stray away from God. Every religion should make a great effort - and why not with the help of its sister religions? - to find out what prompts the turning away from God and the turning toward created things. Unfortunately, one of the principal and most ruinous concerns of religions is figuring out various ways to win converts. Going out to convert people serves no purpose except to inflate a collective ego; besides, before you convert anyone you have to have something to offer them.

If someone becomes interested in another religion, it is probably because he is dissatisfied with his own. If the new religion wants to make headway, however, it has to be "certified," and show that it can solve problems that other religions cannot.

Man has two eternal problems: a need for happiness that is never satisfied, and the fear of illness and death. If a religion does not succeed in resolving my doubts about these problems, and is not able to offer me something that keeps me from turning to mood-controlling drugs or a psychoanalyst, I have good reasons to believe that this religion has failed in its purpose. If I see a priest who is closed up

---

[1] *Summer Showers in Brindavan*, 1979, p. 55.
[2] *Discorsi* 88/89, XLI, 5.

like a porcupine in a black pessimism, just because he is afraid of dying soon, that is a bad advertisement for the religion he preaches. If I meet a sadhu (a wandering ascetic) who seems very serene, but who is filthy and ragged, I begin to seriously wonder if it is not necessary to give up cleanliness and hygiene in order to reach God. If to help me concentrate in prayer a community proposes beatings and concentration-camp austerities, I am not likely to join them. Even the Buddha left the community of monks he had started his spiritual life with, saying that excessive physical penances are harmful to the spirit.

Today it has become the fashion to go door-to-door to unload religious ideas the way people used to sell soap. You have to wonder whether what is motivating all these apostles is really the holy desire to expand the consciousness of nations, or rather the desire to expand their power.

Recently two young Jehovah's Witnesses came to my house. It was not the first time, but this time they came to ask me a specific question. It was Easter, so the subject of discussion seemed obvious.

One of them said to me: "Many families live without peace. What do you think is the most effective way to obtain peace?"

I stopped to reflect a moment: peace, I mused, is exactly what humans, all humans have been seeking for millennia. I thought it was an intelligent question, even though it was put forward as though the two young people already knew the answer, and were waiting for me to say exactly what they had in mind.

After a little while, they drew a Bible out of their bag and read me some passages. You know how Jehovah's witnesses use the Bible as the only possible resource for knowing the truth.

I tried to make them understand that any pre-established doctrine that does not allow freedom of inquiry or thought, any pre-established authority, any teaching delivered second-hand, ends up stifling the impulse toward seeking and turns religion into mere imitation. I said to them:

"I beg you, do not fall into the error that we Catholics fall into: I give you a dogmatic definition which you have to believe without asking any questions, and then you can do whatever you want. As far as the Bible goes, you have to keep in mind another crucial factor: who is interpreting it? who is reading it? do they have eyes to see? are their heads clear? do they have enough wisdom to be able to teach from those texts?"

The conversation got livelier.

I half-whispered, "God is in the silence of the mind."

One of them instantly answered, "But the devil can slip into your mind!"

"God never betrays anyone who seeks Him with a sincere heart! A person is sincerely religious when his mind seeks spontaneously, together with his whole heart, his whole soul, all his energy..."

To answer their initial question, I eventually said to them: "The reason that peace is always lacking in the world is that there is always someone who wants to impose his beliefs and ideas on someone else, in the name of a God whom he presumes to know. Please - I begged them - leave your bags outside, and let us speak like friends, hand in hand. If you use the Bible **against** anyone, this will only foster division! The way the Bible is interpreted varies according to the times, the place, and the level of consciousness. For any ten quotations you bring me, I can find a hundred others which will prove the opposite. Why argue? Do you not see that every religion is seeking precisely what you asked me about, peace? Why seek peace with drawn swords? The Bible too is sometimes used as a weapon. When you clothe your search in theories, no matter how noble, and you forget that true inquiry means putting into practice the teachings of the guide you have chosen, then you are on a road that soon leads to disaster and division. Why? While we are arguing we lose love, we get heated, everyone is set on defending his own opinion, which is after all just a point of view (of an ego, even if correct as a point of view). The next step is the loss of respect for one another. You can no longer accept the other person as he is, and you want to denigrate him, maybe even insult him...

"Through the conflict that arises from one's own positions, hearts become unfeeling. The most insensitive mind is the one that uses all its energies to fight the ideas of other people. Why, then, is there no peace in families? How can peace be brought back into them? It will happen when religions learn to respect one another, to accept one another, not to fight among themselves. When religions passionately seek everything that unites them instead of what divides them, then peace will descend on the great human family."

The two young people were a little sullen, and they did not seem very satisfied. They would have wanted to conquer a new convert. In fact they invited me to go to their meetings and rituals. I settled for reciting an Our Father together with them. Then I said good-bye.

The most important problem for anyone who is seeking God is to dominate all the impulses of the mind. It is these which are really responsible for the lack of peace. Only through peace of mind can man reach the Supreme Peace, God.

This is why the first objective of Sai Baba's message is to teach people to control their minds, by overcoming desires and passions. Of course Christianity teaches the same thing, but it has never given enough importance to the power of the mind. Though it teaches spiritual exercises as a way to evolve spiritually, it has never said that the mind is responsible for every aspect of a human being's life.

It is the mistaken conduct of the mind that is responsible for the alternation of joys and sorrows in daily life. With the sense of "mine" and "yours," dualism and discriminations arise in every experience.[3]

What can be done to correct the innate tendency of the mind to stray, its tendency to think always of the "I" and what gratifies the "I"? There are a number of recommended disciplines, but the first and most basic is to begin feeding your body food that is light and balanced, food that neither agitates it nor pollutes it.

On the material level, the foods man eats are expelled as excrement. On the subtle level, however, they are transformed into blood, and on a still subtler level, into man's mental substance. Therefore the mind depends on the type of foods that are eaten. The cause of the demonic passions that are evident in these times, is the food that is eaten. Patience, perseverance, love, and compassion are lacking: there are only devilish ideas. The principal cause of all this is to be found in food. This is why food should be pure and sacred. The human form itself is derived from food. The gross part of the water

---

[3]*Id.,* XII, 2.

we drink tones the body, and the subtle part gives it vital energy, the so-called prana. Thus by the foods he chooses man can manifest or suffocate his divinity.[4]

Sai Baba not only encourages people to eat properly: he has also developed a type of meditation whose purpose is to calm the mind and purify it from all the thoughts that upset it. As long as it is practiced regularly and without ambitions, this simple and pleasant technique confers great mental lucidity and the strength of will to confront life's difficulties. I think it is appropriate to include it here, because it is a key component of Sai Baba's teachings.

Despite the suspicions of the Catholic world, this way of establishing contact with your own Divine Consciousness in no way contradicts the teachings of Christ. Indeed perhaps it will restore a facet of the Christian tradition which even certain important men of the church have thought was lost forever.

The meditation on Light

1. - Preparation

1.1 - First set up a candle in front of you, and make sure that its flame is steady, not flickering.

1.2 - Sit comfortably, but with spine erect. Insulate yourself from the ground by sitting on something made of wood or wool.

To sit straight is important. Between the 9th and 12th vertebrae is the life-force. If the spine is injured at this point, paralysis occurs. If the body is in a straight position, as if it were wound around a straight pole, the life force may rise up through the straight body and give the quality of intense concentration to the mind. Moreover, just as a lightning rod attached to the roof of a building attracts lightning, in like fashion a perfectly straight body provides a conductor, so to speak, for divine power to enter the temple of your

---

[4]*Ibid.,* 17.

body and give you the strength to accomplish your task and reach your goal.

As another example, the divine power is always here, just as radio signals are here. But to hear the radio music there must be an antenna. Further, if the tuning device is not properly adjusted, there will just be some sound but no music. In like fashion, the divine power, which is always present, may flow into you if meditation is correct and the body straight.[5]

1.3 - Remember to say a prayer to God, asking Him to be your Guide and Sustainer in this voyage towards Him. It is good to prepare yourself by reciting Psalms or prayers, by repeating the Name of God, or by thinking about sacred stories.

1.4 - Take several deep breaths, without straining (your shoulders and chest should not rise and fall).

Note - This preparatory practice serves to slow down the flow of thoughts and still the body. This is because there is an interaction among bodily movement, the flow of thought, and breathing.

1.5 - Without trying to influence the rhythm of your breathing, accompany it by mentally forming the syllable JE as you inhale and SUS as you exhale. You could also use SO (inhaling) and HAM (exhaling). As you listen to the mantra JE-SUS, remain aware of its meaning. Continue this phase for 5-10 minutes.

Sohum - He am I. He with the in-breath, I with the out-breath. Or Sai Ram. Or the name of your choice, said with the movement of the breath. Breath is form, thus the name and the form go together. Breath is life. Life is God. Breath is God. The name of God and the form of God. Breathe God. See God. Eat God. Love God. The name of God will illumine every step of your life and take you to Him. The name must be said with love. God is love. If breath is said with love, then life is love. There is no shakti (power)

---

[5]*Conversations with Bhagavan Sri Sathya Sai Baba*, by Hislop, p. 187.

stronger than love. If it is said with love, the name of God, any name of God - Ram, Sai Ram, Krishna, Jesus, Sohum - that small name will open up and illuminate the whole of life. For the one who desires to realize God, only the Name is needed. The ocean is vast, but a huge steamship is not needed to go on the ocean. Just a small tire will take one on the ocean.[6]

2. - Omkara.

Now softly recite 21 OMs. Om is a more ancient contraction of the Latin AMEN. It is the sacred syllable which is the source and life of the Universe. The number 21 signifies the five external senses, the five internal senses, the five elements, the five bodily sheaths, and the individual Divine Spirit, the Soul.

The sound of OM is AUM. A starts softly from the throat. It is the earth. U comes from the mouth and the sound rises in volume. M is sounded with the lips, with decreasing volume. Like a plane, heard distantly, increasing in sound as it approaches and fading with distance. A is the world. U is heaven. M is divine, beyond all the senses.

OM is in every place, mind, tongue, heart, etc. First sound OM on the tongue and then in the mind. The sounding of OM 21 times is important: five outer senses, five inner senses, five lives (the five elements), five sheaths (the koshas), and the Jiva, the individual soul.[7]

Continue to be a witness to the ebb and flow of your breath.

3. - The Light.

Why a light? From the sand, if one takes, it will be depleted. From the water tank, if each one takes, the tank will go dry. But a thousand people can take the flame of one candle to light their

---

[6]*Id.,* p. 125.
[7]*Conversations,* p. 128.

candles and the flame is in no way diminished. Light a lamp or a
candle. Gaze straight ahead at the flame...[8]

3.1 - At this point you can open your eyes and calmly and steadily gaze at the candle flame. The candle should be at eye-level.

3.2 - After a few seconds of fixing your gaze on the light of the candle, close your eyes again. You will see a reflected image of the flame. If you do not see it, open your eyes and continue to focus on the flame.

3.3 - Diffuse this light through the inside of your head. Make sure it touches every cell of your brain.

Say to yourself mentally: *My intellect is illuminated.*

3.4 - Slowly and gently draw the flame into the region of the heart, and visualize the light in the heart as in the petals of a lotus flower. At the center of the light you can picture the Sacred Heart or your preferred image of God. Imagine the petals of the lotus opening one by one, illuminating the heart. Wash every thought, feeling and emotion in that light, dissolving all shadows. There is no corner where darkness can hide.

The light spreads ever more and becomes ever more intense: bad feelings cannot survive.

Now think: *I feel that love embraces all things.*
I am Truth.
I am Purity...
I am Peace...
I am Love...
I am Non-violence...
I am Compassion... Happiness...
Tolerance... Forbearance...
Forgiveness... Gentleness...

---

[8]*Conversations*, p. 186.

Prudence... Justice... Strength...
Equanimity... Patience... Beauty...

Note - Pause for a few seconds between each quality.

3.5 - Now allow the light to permeate every part of your body. It does not matter in what order.
The light reaches the navel, and from there it flows into the left thigh, leg, and foot, to the tips of the toes. Then the same for the right side. Then say: *My feet carry me only where God wills.*

The light rises through the body, inundating every organ and every space. Then it pervades the left shoulder, arm, and hand, to the tips of the fingers; then the right shoulder, arm, and hand.

Now say: *My hands can only do good work.*
Now no part of my body can undertake any activity that is evil, suspicious, or dark. Every part has become an instrument of light and love.

Let the light rise to the throat, and then to the head.
Say: *All falsehood is disappearing from my words and thoughts.*

The light reaches the eyes: *I can see only good in everyone and everything.*

It envelops the ears: *I can hear only good words.*

It floods the lips and tongue: *My lips wish to express only the praise of God; my tongue speaks only of the good; my palate tastes only foods beneficial to the body and spirit.*

The light rises to the nose: *I can smell and experience only God.*

Now the light rises to the top of the head: the entire head is full of light, and not a single bad thought remains in it. This light becomes a luminous crown that envelops and covers the head.

I AM IN THE LIGHT.
(There is a sense of separation between my body and the Light.)

THE LIGHT IS IN ME AND PERMEATES ALL MY BEING.
The light becomes ever more intense (from the top of the head). It shines all around and spreads in ever-widening circles, diffusing in every direction.

The light inside and the light outside are a single reality. The membrane of the body no longer separates me from everything else; the body too is all light.

I AM THE LIGHT.
I am not merely a Soul: I am the Image and Likeness of God.

The Light includes everything and everyone:
I am one with all the persons I love, relatives, friends, companions; I am one with all those whom I think are not friendly towards me, one with all those who seek to harm me, one with those who govern me, one with my superiors, one with all humanity (the sick, the poor, the derelict, the dying, etc.).
I am one with all animals, from the largest to the smallest, from the rhinoceros to the insect, from dolphins to mollusks...
I am one with all vegetables, flowers, grass, meadows, forests...
I am one also with the mineral kingdom, with crystals, rocks, mountains, lakes, seas, the planet, the solar system, the galaxy, the cosmos.
Everything and everyone is permeated by the same Light. My Light is the same Light of all the Universe. All is Light. All is Love.

3.6 - Now try to visualize the form of God that is most dear to you (Jesus, the Good Shepherd, the Sacred Heart, the Crucified, etc...) in the all-pervading Light. God is Light, Light is God.

I and the Father are one.
I am one with Jesus and with the Father.
I am Divine.
I am That: SO-HAM... SO-HAM... SO-HAM...

IE-SU... IE-SU... IE-SU...
JE-SUS... JE-SUS... JE-SUS...

3.7 - At this point you can formulate a prayer of praise, adoration and gratitude to God.

"Lord, my strength, my defense,
my refuge, my fortress, my bulwark..."
"You, Lord, know me, you see me,
you feel that my heart is with you..."
"My grace, my fortitude,
my refuge and my liberation,
my shield in whom I trust..."
"O God, my king, I want to exalt You
and bless Your Name
forever and always..."
"O Lord, how glorious is Your Name
throughout all the world."

Continue IE-SU or SO-HAM for a few minutes.
Savor the awareness or silence that fills your mind. Then bring the Light back into your heart, where you will guard it throughout the day and the night (in the form of Jesus or other form you have chosen).
Note - Rest for a little while, lying down if possible, before moving. Then gradually open your eyes and bring the blessing you have received into your activities.

Among the benefits this meditation brings is the power to control the senses and to channel them to constructive ends. Because it develops your power to concentrate and to contemplate the Divine, this practice can be of great help in your studies and other activities: it sharpens the memory and deepens intuition. Once you realize and experience that God is in all things, the "I" feeling, the sense of separation and egoism, vanishes. You love all creation. Through this universal love, your own character improves, and as a consequence so does the nation or community in which you live.
Since I have tried other forms of meditation, I can attest to the great efficacy (I am tempted to say superiority) of the Meditation on Light,

based on personal experience. I abandoned the other techniques for various reasons: either I did not approve of how they were taught, or the group that promoted them lacked a spiritual dimension, or sometimes I had doubts about the techniques themselves. As soon as I decided to adopt Sai Baba's method (after the careful consideration one should always give to such matters), I found that in a short time I had gained more benefits from it than I had from other techniques. Sai Baba's Meditation on Light has the great advantage of lessening the desire to acquire certain powers, or certain specific qualities useful to oneself or one's relation to society. It focuses attention exclusively on achieving union with the Divine, by contemplating and assimilating virtues that characterize Divinity.

In the end I believe that every technique can be good, if it is practiced with faith, with the right intentions, and with confidence in the Master who teaches it. The people who choose to practice a certain method do not all have the same goal. For each goal, there is a suitable technique.

In recent years, Sai Baba has constantly emphasized the spiritual disciplines essential for self-realization: the repetition of the Name of God, and the selfless service of others. In his address at Prashanti Nilayam on November 19, 1990, given on the occasion of the Fifth World Conference held in conjunction with His 65th Birthday, Sathya Sai Baba extolled these two practices, putting them even above meditation in importance:

Service is the highest spiritual discipline. Prayer and meditation, knowledge of Scripture and of the Vedanta, cannot help you reach the goal as quickly as service can. Service has a double effect: it extinguishes the ego and gives bliss.

The repetition of the Name is an ancient Eastern practice, which has its origin in the power of sound. The Eastern religious tradition is the homeland of the *mantra*. These are short powerful formulas connected with certain vibrations which great *Rishis* or sages knew could bring man to certain states of awareness, states which facilitated transcendence and union with God.

In our Christian tradition, ascetics and saints have always strongly recommended that one should whisper some sacred exclamation constantly to the mind. This is the same principle as the repetition of mantras or the Name of God. Perhaps our rich tradition of litanies derives from this awareness.

Unfortunately, in this age, when people are more interested in magic formulas than in reason or the heart, many people think that Eastern mantras have more power than Western mantras. They forget that the effectiveness of a prayer does not depend on how it is pronounced, or what language it is in, but on the quality of the heart that prays. As J. Blofeld says, "Where many people go wrong is in giving too much importance to how the syllables of the mantra are uttered. I am convinced that the sound, taken apart from everything else, normally counts for very little."[9] In this connection I will quote a little story Blofeld recounts, which makes the point very clearly.

"An Indian monk interrupted his annual retreat during the monsoon season in order to visit his mother, because he was afraid that she would be desperately short of food. He was surprised to find her in excellent health, and even more astonished when his mother told him that she had learned a special mantra, thanks to which, "through the power of the great Goddess," she was able to boil stones and turn them into nourishing food. However the monk was a very learned man, and as soon as he heard her recite the mantra, he began to correct numerous errors of pronunciation. Unfortunately, when the poor woman recited the mantra correctly, it had no result, so her son advised her to go back to her old way of saying it. In short order, thanks to her great faith, the woman again began to turn stones into food!"[10]

In the end the purpose of meditation, of the repetition of the Name, and of service is the same: to foster devotion. Sai Baba's most profound and moving discourses are on devotion to God. He reprimands us for the way we pray, asking for things we do not need, or for things "the Father already knows" we need:

---

[9] J. Blofeld, *I mantra sacre parole di potenza*, Ed. Mediterranee, p.119.
[10] *Id.*, 115-116.

The Love of God is the most precious gift. If you wish to ask something from God, pray to Him like this: "O Lord, I want only You." When you have Him, you have everything.[11]

When you pray, go to your private room and, when you have shut your door, pray to your Father who is in that secret place, and your Father who sees all that is done in secret will reward you.[12]

He always tells us not to think of God as some distant being, and not to keep Him away through rhetorical and flowery descriptions, but to hold Him close, like an intimate friend:

Whom do you praise? When you want to win someone as a new friend, and he comes to visit you, you shower him with formalities to make him feel at home and friendly toward you. You are very respectful, and you say to him very politely: "Come in, sir; please make yourself comfortable," all the while attending to him hand and foot. It is very different when you receive an old friend. There is no need to drown in rhetorical expressions or conventional attitudes. Every word you address to your friend shows your closeness and love. This is how you should address God: He is your closest and most intimate friend....Do not indulge in servile expressions toward the Lord. Consider Him your best friend. You will give Him immense joy if you treat Him as your soulmate, and allow your feelings of love and warmth to flow freely, rather than turning to Him with pretentious and affected images.[13]

I shall not call you servants any more, because a servant does not know his master's business; I call you friends, because I have made known to you everything I have learned from my Father.[14]

Devotion is the easiest road to reach God. This path has been compared to the attitude of a kitten who allows his mother to pick him

---

[11]*Discorsi* 88/89, XXXVIII, 4.
[12]Matthew 6.6.
[13]*Discorsi* 88/89, XXXVIII, 7.10.
[14]John 15.14.

up in her mouth to carry him about. When an avatar comes toward man, He cannot wait to gather devotees under His protection, "as a hen gathers her brood under her wings."[15]

This is the re-unification of all human beings in the Single Divine Being, the single Consciousness of being children of the same Father. This is the cause to which Great Beings have dedicated their lives: *ut unum sint*, "in order that all may be one." Devotion leads to union. The Mission of the Avatar Sai Baba too is summed up in that one sentence.

---

[15]Luke 13.34.

CHAPTER FIFTEEN

Schools and Education

*Education consists
in drawing forth the best
that is in the child,
body, mind, and spirit.*

Gandhi

I have already mentioned the system of education Baba uses in his schools, but now I would like to discuss it in greater detail. Sai Baba gives enormous importance to instruction and education: they are His most prominent social objective. When a Being like Sathya "descends" among men in order to awaken and improve them, where would He start if not from the beginning, by first educating the youngest children? Indeed it is the only way society will change: to inculcate the fundamental values which make human beings "human," that is creatures endowed with reason and intelligence, one must begin from the first years of life.

Sathya Sai's educational system is founded on five values, each accompanied by a technique. It is a sign of the high regard God has for his human creatures that these values, Truth, Right Action, Peace, Love, and Non-violence, are called "human values," values natural to man. The techniques through which these values are acquired are: meditation, prayer or reciting famous sayings, group singing or music, telling of stories, and group activities.

Each value is associated in particular with a specific technique, but all the techniques and values are inter-connected. For example, meditation is the most appropriate technique to pursue the value of Truth, but meditation should be accompanied by other activities like singing or working in groups in order to be most effective.

There have been studies and experiments and even conferences on this method. Two international conferences in particular should be mentioned: one in Odense (Denmark) on August 5-9, 1987, and one in Assisi on June 1-4, 1990. As a result of these conferences, full-fledged pedagogical treatises were developed which are of fundamental importance for learning the method. Renowned scientists and experts in psychology and pedagogy participated in the sessions. Among them I might mention Art-ong Jumsai, who is famous for having developed the landing system for the Viking modules which reached Mars in 1976.

Art-ong Jumsai is a person of high intellectual and moral stature. In the course of a lecture he gave at Odense, he asserted: "In all my years of research, I have never found a program as complete and as effective as the *Sathya Sai Education in Human Values*. It is a program which offers real results in transforming children. The person who created or invented this program must really be a genius!"

Wherever it has been adopted, the Program of Education in Human Values has surpassed all expectations. It has a systematic structure, and thus has interested prominent researchers. The program has already won acceptance in many countries, such as Thailand, India, Denmark, Germany, and now also Italy.

The results are evident in the sudden change that takes place in the children: better behavior, greater equilibrium, and a more harmonious development of personality. It has triggered deep changes and intense interest even in the teachers themselves.

Many people by now have become aware of the imbalance that has developed in the human psyche: on the one hand technology progresses at a breathtaking pace, and on the other society is tormented by anxiety and worry, and lives under the threat of nuclear holocaust, or at the very least, of a fatal deterioration of the environment. What has been lacking to prepare man to face these problems is an adequate formation of the human character, and the cultivation of values which make life more serene and harmonious.

In particular, one can see how critical the situation of humanity is from the following facts:

   a) racial, ideological, and religious discrimination continues;
   b) the power and integrity of the family is waning;
   c) there is less respect for parents, teachers, and leaders;
   d) violent and destructive behavior is on the rise;
   e) the young lack objectives and direction, and are generally dissatisfied with the schooling they receive;

f) species of animals and plants are rapidly being destroyed;

g) the environment is being irreversibly polluted.

The only effective remedy for all the ills of the world is a system of education based on values which have been forgotten. This is emphatically declared by the Universal Declaration on Human Values adopted by the United Nations:

"Instruction must aim at the full development of the human personality, and at the strengthening of respect for human rights and fundamental liberties. It must foster mutual understanding, tolerance, and friendship among all nations and all ethnic and religious groups, besides encouraging the measures taken by the United Nations to maintain peace."

The values taught must be universal, so as to completely transcend any superficial distinction of race or religious creed: they must represent the essence of human life or human values."

In practice, what does the Sathya Sai educational system entail?

It entails preparing parents (and in particular the most sensitive teachers among the parents) so that they can collaborate in a series of lessons given to their children. The *Sathya Sai Education in Human Values* program can last anywhere from a few days, as in a summer camp, to a number of weeks, as in a normal school year, during which it would use a few afternoons as an after-school activity.

It is geared for children from six to fifteen years of age, because these are the formative years in which one can successfully plant the seeds of values. Wherever the SSEHV system has been implemented, it has always achieved exceptional results. It represents the synthesis of a nine-year course, which was born about fifteen years ago as an extra-curricular program integrating moral, ideal and cultural concerns. Hundreds of thousands of children all over the world have followed the program with enormous success.

The ultimate purpose of the Sathya Sai method is to foster a healthy and well-balanced development of all aspects of the child's personality: physical, intellectual, emotional, psychic, and inquisitive. The present system of education is concerned only with the first two aspects, and to some extent the third, but it completely ignores the last two. The Sai system develops these five aspects of the personality by inculcating five fundamental values: Truth, Right Action, Peace, Love, and Non-violence. These five values correspond logically to the five ideals of education: knowledge, ability, equilibrium, power of introspection, and recognition of one's own true identity.

Studies conducted by scientists and psychologists have confirmed that humans are most receptive between the ages of 6 and 15. Sathya Sai's educational method focuses on this age span. It does not suggest or recommend changes or alterations in the current school program. It seeks only to reinforce it and enrich it, by giving it a new dimension of values.

Let us try to give an outline of the method. We will do this by briefly analyzing the five values through the words of the Master Himself. Each human value corresponds to a level of the human personality. Thus there are also five levels of man: the physical level, the emotional level, the level of the intellect, the level of love (not in the sense of sentimental attraction), and the spiritual level.

Truth

The human value of Truth corresponds to the level of the intellect. In fact it is the intellect which leads man to the discovery of Truth. It reaches this goal by determining what is not true, not real. What is true is immutable, eternal, imperishable, it does not change from one day to the next. When man begins to seek truth, he realizes that nothing he can analyze or examine is true. He realizes that everything he experiences through the senses is constantly changing. Through science he learns that everything is energy, that everything in the cosmos consists of vibratory fields. The vibration is constantly changing, and thus change characterizes the entire universe. Thirsty for permanent truths, and disappointed by the impermanence of everything that surrounds him, man thus learns to enter into himself, in order to discover what does not pass away, what is permanent.

Truth, in its real sense, is that which is forever changeless, which does not change at any time. It is Trikala Satya - Eternal

*Reality... All the material objects in this world which you see,
are in a continuous flux of change every moment, and they are
all subject to decay... But the Spiritual Truth of God is eternally
valid, valid under any circumstances and never changing.*[1]

Therefore the first goal of school is to lead students to discover that everything in the phenomenal world is relative, and to convince them that beyond the changing dogmas of science, there is an unchanging Reality that does exist. Unfortunately, the current schools fail in this objective, because their programs are based simply on teaching one notion or another. The true goal of school is to bring man to Truth. To lead children to discover the basic Law which governs all scientific laws is the fundamental and fascinating task of education.

As this inquiry proceeds, two human qualities should be developed in the child: memory and intuition. Memory is the useful capacity to preserve information and elements of knowledge. Intuition can be developed only by refining the intellect. We might say that intuition is the highest level of intellect. In fact it works in an area that ordinary intellect is powerless to explore. Intuition is the intellect of geniuses. The voice of conscience itself is intuition.

All five suggested teaching methods lead to stronger memory and intuition, but meditation in particular teaches one how to quiet the mind. This makes the intellect receptive to higher truths.

For each human value there are a number of corresponding sub-values. For example the human value Truth can be explored and expanded by considering Discrimination, Sincerity, the spirit of Inquiry.

Right Action

When Truth is translated into action it becomes right conduct. Its realm is the physical. Children come to behave according to a code of right conduct by learning to discipline their own bodies and to regulate all the inputs that they receive during the course of a day or a lifetime.

---

[1] *The True Flowers of Worship*, pp. 16-17.

Sai Baba has often emphasized the fact that you become what you think. Behind every action there is a thought. Thought is fed by the will, which is often in conflict with desire. In fact will and desire are not the same thing. We often desire what we do not will, or will what is not in itself desirable. Will is an impartial force which allows us to act according to truth. Desire too pushes us toward action, but it is often opposed to truth. The child must be trained to make this distinction, and thereby taught to put a ceiling on his desires.

It makes no sense to adore God as the incarnation of Truth, if then you neglect truth in your daily life. Right Action is born from Truth: it springs from the heart and infuses an inner satisfaction. It is an expression of knowing one's own condition. Trust what divine conscience prompts in you. No one should act against the dictates of his own conscience: this is the right path. True worship, therefore, consists in doing what is right according to one's own conscience. You think one thing and say another: this certainly will not bring you closer to Truth. There must be complete coherence among thought, word, and deed.[2]

One can strengthen a child's will, for example, by using every opportunity to give him autonomy. Thus he must become accustomed to wash his hands before eating, not to eat too much or too fast, to keep his clothes, teeth, nails, and hair neat and his belongings in order, to be on time, not to litter, and so on.

One must also work to refine the child's social qualities, his behavior at school and with his friends, and his obedience. His capacity to work with others and to be concerned about them should be encouraged.

One should promote all the ethical values which make him grow morally. In this way he will come to appreciate how pleasant it is to be at peace with oneself and with others, to speak quietly, to share things with others, and not to damage things, steal, lie and so on.

His motivation in all this must come from understanding that everyone is a link in the great chain of being, and the strength of the chain depends on every link. Young people instinctively understand

---

[2]*Discorsi* 88/89, XIV, 19.

the value of solidarity. If channeled in the right way, this instinct can produce exceptional results.

The teaching methods which are particularly suited to fostering right action are writing skits and taking part in performing them. Group activities are an excellent way to learn sociability and good behavior.

Among the subvalues of Right Action, one could emphasize courage, the sense of duty, gratitude, self-confidence, obedience, etc...

Peace

Surely peace is the ultimate goal everyone seeks. We all seek peace and happiness, in whatever way. You can only experience true peace when you have emotional balance. Thus peace is associated with the emotional level of man. It resides inside man: it is born from the realization that the source of fulfillment is not outside man.

No one is responsible for our peace except ourselves. You cannot improvise this capacity to find peace in yourself on the spur of the moment. It must be developed from the first years of childhood.

The dawn of peace can be brought about only by learning, practicing and teaching the art of living together in peace and amity in the home. Then peace in the world can be established without delay or travail.[3]

The teaching methods suited to fostering peace are meditation, through which the child learns how to create peace within himself, and creative activities, which accustom him to co-exist peacefully with his companions.

Among the subvalues of Peace we should mention calm, concentration, contentment, optimism, self-acceptance, etc...

Love

Love springs from the psychic sphere of man. Love is not simply an emotion: it is an energy which we receive and transmit every

---

[3]*Sathya Sai Speaks*, vol. VII, p. 183.

instant. It has the power to influence every form of life. Through an experiment he conducted with his university students, Art-ong Jumsai demonstrated that love is an energy which affects all living beings. Here is how he himself describes this unique experiment:

"I said to my students, in the university where I taught in Bangkok: "You must all radiate Love!" There was an uproar among the students, and they all called me *Acharya*, that is, Spiritual Guide.

"Professor," they said to me, "this is a university! Why are you asking us to radiate Love? You should be in a temple, not in a university!"

I answered them this way:

"All right. This is a university. We must be scientific. Well, then, if we can prove that there is an energy called Love, and that this energy can have a positive influence on living things, then will you promise to practice this Love?"

They all said yes. They agreed to accept the challenge. They said to me, "All right. If you think you can prove it to us, we will put it into practice."

I asked them to conduct an experiment on the power of Love. We asked another scientist to be an impartial observer (indeed he was skeptical about these matters), to oversee the procedures of the experiment.

Here is what the students did.

They took seeds of flowers, like daisies, and made them germinate and grow to the height of four centimeters. They thinned out the plants on the basis of height, so that all the flowers were exactly the same height. If any were defective, they were discarded. In this way they obtained a number of seedlings all identical in size and in health. Each one received an identical amount of water, which was carefully weighed out. Care was taken to make sure the conditions were the same for all, light, air and temperature. Everything was rigorously controlled. At this point the plants were split into two groups. Only half the plants were selected to receive loving attention. The students gathered and began to project nice thoughts on the group of plants designated to receive loving treatment. They thought of their love for their parents and their love for their plant. Then they would mentally pray that the plants would grow, be happy, and so on. In this way they transferred love to the plants, each in his own way.

This was the result: the plants which received love grew much higher and were full of flowers. They were covered with yellow flowers. The other group of plants did not grow as fast, and had still to flower. The experiment was ended so that measurements could be taken. We discovered that the plants which had received love had grown an average of 49.2% higher than the ones which had not. The students measured the thickness of the stems, and analyzed the results statistically, using variant-analysis and other statistical methods in order to determine the margin of error.

The plants which had been radiated with love were full of flowers, while the others did not have a single flower. We did a statistical study of the number of flowers, since some had more, some less. We discovered that the probability that the two groups should be so different was minimal.

There had to be a reason! The students therefore set themselves to finding out the causes which had produced such a great disparity in the two groups of plants. They found no possible reason except love.

In the end the students had to admit that the power of love really exists. They had to acknowledge that the radiation of psychic energy affects plants.

Afterwards I sent a report on this subject to a number of nations, where teachers attempted analogous experiments with the children in their classes. I received a large number of letters, which reported the same surprising results, and which taken together constituted a body of proof.

Love helps living beings, and especially plants, grow faster...

In the university where I taught, it was discovered that during these experiments with love, one plant had shrivelled up and died. I suspected that some student had cursed the plant. I asked all the students if this was true. At last, one student admitted that he had gone in on a Saturday in order to damn his plant. He had spent three hours inflicting this malediction. That was why the plant shrivelled up to the point of dying. The student also admitted that immediately afterward, he developed a terrible headache and nausea, and that he was sick for a long time.

This is a warning for all of us! - in case any of us gets the idea of cursing a plant, or worse, a human being. This is what happens when we transmit negative energy!"[4]

Love is the solution for suffering. As Mother Teresa of Calcutta says: "Humanity is suffering because it is hungry for love."
Love is expressed by giving and forgiving.
The first love that should be instilled in children is for their parents. Then they should be led to extend it to their families, their neighbors, their country, and finally to Him who permeates the entire universe.

Love is ananda, bliss; Love is power; Love is light; Love is God.[5]

The teaching methods most suited to fostering this value are, besides the example of a loving and tolerant teacher, telling appropriate stories, visiting places of worship, feeling and experiencing certain traditional holidays.
Among the subvalues to be stressed are caring for others, compassion, dedication, friendship, forgiveness, gentleness, sharing, tolerance, etc...

Non-violence

The meaning of ahimsa (non-violence) is that you should not cause harm to anybody in thought, word, or deed. [6]

The highest manifestation of human perfection is non-violence. It is a love which is not limited to friends or relatives; it extends to all creatures. Because of this, non-violence characterizes the spiritual level of man, his highest aspect. In practice, non-violence means: harming no one and being friendly, staying in harmony with nature and in mutual understanding with everyone, and refraining as much as possible from damaging anything.

---

[4]From the *Acts* of the Seminar in Odense, August 5-9, 1987.
[5]*Sathya Sai Speaks*, vol. VI, p. 197.
[6]*Summer Showers in Brindavan* 1977, p. 235.

Obviously absolute non-violence is impossible, because life is sustained only by other lives. However one must seek to cause the least possible offense, and only to the lowest forms of life.

One reaches Non-violence after understanding the motivations behind right action, after one has developed love, understood the ultimate Truth, and come to desire peace enough to be willing to sacrifice something in order to obtain it. The level of non-violence fosters the over-all growth of the child.

The child will acquire the value of non-violence by learning to love flowers, to raise plants, and to take care of pets. The subvalues to be emphasized are universal brotherhood, respect for other cultures and religions, citizenship, equanimity, respect for other people's property, causing minimum harm, etc...

Having understood the theoretical principles behind the human values, they must now be put into practice in particular lessons. Every subject studied in school provides ample opportunities to reflect on bigger issues, which make the subject more interesting. Simply studying a subject makes school heavy, and promotes competition. On the other hand a teaching approach that applies theoretical knowledge to practical life, and to the child's own problems as a developing human being, makes the hours spent at a school desk pleasant.

One of the objectives is to reveal the links which join mathematics to astronomy, astronomy to physics, physics to theology, and so on.

Another objective is to bring the scientific notion to the level and experience of the person learning it, and not vice versa. When teaching addition, you can reflect on the number one, which when added to itself grows to infinity, and you can compare this operation to God, who in His unity manifests Himself as many. You can play with a little numerology, showing how the digits of multiples of 9 always add up to 9. For example 27 or 72 or 6453 always come out to 9. From this observation, you can reflect on how the Divine is unchanging, even though it loves to express itself through various forms. Or else you can show how multiples of 8 diminish: $8 \times 1 = 8$; $8 \times 2 = 16 = 7$; $8 \times 3 = 24 = 6$, etc... From this game you can point out that if 8 represents desire, the more you multiply it, the less you get in final value.

Through imagination a good teacher can come up with any number of ways to enrich lessons based on human values.

Thus a typical lesson will have great variety: it could include a moment of silence in meditation, explanations with quotations, it could break out into a song on the given theme, absorb the children by telling them stories with moral lessons, involve them in making scenery or performing skits, and end with a debate in which they try to find solutions to problems of practical life.

In preparing the method based on the Five Human Values, Sai Baba has provided us with a highly scientific technique. Even though it might **seem** unoriginal - in fact the Human Values are as timeless as man. Its real novelty is the way the program is structured, which is absolutely effective. Children educated through this method grow up with a complete and balanced personality. They are even a stimulus to their parents, because they lead a more moral life. There is however one fundamental requirement, without which the whole system fails: **the Human Values must first of all be put into practice by the teachers**.

Sai Baba dedicates much of His time, and many of His discourses, to the problems of education, so there is a great wealth of material available to study Sai Baba's "pedagogy" in greater depth. Picking a few passages at random, here is what He says about modern schools and education:

The current methods of instruction do not offer an adequate education. Between ordinary people and scientists, there are very few intelligent people in the world. It is not easy to find a method which exploits the full intellectual potential and wisdom of a people. In fact it is precisely because of the improper use of scientific knowledge that people continue to suffer in the world.
Nowadays people believe that the ultimate goal of education should be the satisfaction of the senses. The current system of education serves only to develop a more active intelligence, but not to instill in people the qualities and virtues which are useful in life. The leaders of our country have kept themselves busy

introducing innovations and changes in the methodologies and systems of education. Many committees have been formed, but they end up meeting only to have tea, and not to conduct methodological studies which could provide models to imitate, in order to transform the current system of education. They have made progress on paper, but these advances have not been translated into practice.[7]

An existence based on truth transcends the three dimensions of time: it reconciles the past with the present and with the future. Unfortunately, however, this type of life has gone by the wayside. Today it is the common opinion that the proper mode of life is to do whatever one pleases. Students bear no love for their teachers, and do not regard them with due respect. They do not fear them: rather it is the teachers who fear the students. This is why, in the current school system, the teachers cannot wait to get away from the students.[8]

The teachers who have been introduced to Sai Baba's method have found it exciting and fascinating. Unfortunately, they are bound by routines which often hamper the implementation of the method. There is much to be done, and the work would be made easier if public institutions could unite the teachers in a common effort. It is my hope, therefore, that well-intentioned politicians and educators will soon be motivated to turn this project, which is so promising and full of possibilities, into reality.

---

[7]*Discorsi* 88/89, XIII, 3-4.
[8]*Ibid.*, 23.

Part III: Coming to Sai Baba

CHAPTER SIXTEEN

"Yes, Priest! Sì!"

Yes,
as a young man marries a virgin,
your Builder shall marry you;
and as a bridegroom rejoices in his bride
so shall your God rejoice in you.

Isaiah 62.5

There were about thirty of us, packed into a tiny room. He had called us during darshan. One of us had done what people often do at darshan: he had gotten up, and timidly asked, "Swami, please grant us an interview!" Sai Baba had replied as He always does: "How many are you?" After we answered, He paused a moment, as if considering how useful the interview would be, and then He said: "Go!"

This was the second interview I had received, at least in a waking state. I was trembling and anxious. I had acute laryngitis and had completely lost my voice. We sat down in a garden full of various animals, rabbits, roosters, deer. We were waiting for Sai Baba to return.

There He was! That small and infinite shape appeared in the doorway at Whitefield. He was walking with a tired step, holding up a fold of His robe, in order not to trip. His upturned hand moved gently in a circle, as if to say, "How happy I am to see you!" His gaze was full of bliss, directed toward some supernatural dimension, as if entranced. He was the One who seemed like the devotee, not the thousands of people at His feet with hands clasped in prayer. In fact, paradoxical as it may seem, He is indeed the real devotee: He is the one who pours joy on whoever asks for His grace, the one who gives you all of Himself, as long as you know how to wait patiently, the one who is concerned about your tiniest problems, and promises to take care of them personally. Who has more devotion, the mother or the child? The child who seeks protection and love, or the mother who gives all of herself without asking for anything in return?

The Divine Physician made a last visit, to a "ward" of other devotees and students from His college, and then He came up the ramp which leads to His private "emergency room," to look after still more patients. He opened wide the doors, and invited us to go in, receiving each one of us in turn at the entrance. We had left our belongings, with our money and documents, outside. It is right to go to Him with empty hands. Otherwise how could He fill them? One does not bring belongings to the Omnipotent, because everything is already His. We have to offer Him ourselves, our purified hearts, stripped of all superfluous baggage. This Doctor does not want our miserable parcels of possessions and banknotes. He asks us only for a pure heart: He is the one who dispenses not only cures, but even gifts, to His patients.

In the interview room, He called a student from one of His colleges, and with a stern air, reprimanded him for having a monkey mind. Then he turned to Antonietta, a true 20th-century *gopi*, and asked her to sing a stanza from the Vedas. The girl obeyed promptly and joyously, singing the verses with a musical voice. Swami interrupted her, and turning again to His student, said: "See how well a Westerner can sing the Vedas? You come from this tradition: shouldn't you be able to do it equally well?"

At this point He created some vibhuti, which He gave to each of the women, and made two rings, which He bestowed on two of them. Then He invited us into the next room, the tiny one. We were packed in like sardines. Sai Baba sat down, and I was crouched so close to Him I could touch Him. Paola, who was sitting across from me, broke the ice by telling Baba that there was a Catholic priest in our group. "I know, I know," answered Swami, and as if to confirm that He had picked me out, quickly turned His head toward me, fixing His eyes on me. At the time it did not occur to me that anyone else would have had to search a while to single me out among so many people. But He does not need clues: He knows everything about us. He does not need any suggestions in order to find what He is looking for. Thus He was able to pick me out instantly, without hesitation, even though I was dressed exactly like all the other men.

At this point He took the opportunity to give me some advice, and diagnose my spiritual condition. "At times you are prey to doubts about what is right and what is wrong, and so you torture yourself. Studying will give you stability. I will speak to you separately." He repeated this last promise three times, but as all long-time devotees know, when Swami promises something He never says exactly how the promise will be fulfilled, or when.

Suddenly, He fixed His gaze on me again and asked: "How is your wife?" That question turned me to ice. I was humiliated by the giggles of the other people. The fact that I had lost my voice distressed me, because I could not even ask for explanations, or try to justify myself. At that moment, in the space of a few seconds, I surveyed a number of episodes in my life, and understanding "wife" in its normal sense, I asked myself a lot of questions. Was it a warning to be on guard against certain earthly affections? Was it a warning to be careful about the future? Or was He challenging me about the present? I felt free from any emotional bond of that kind, and I would have wanted to tell Him that, if my voice would only come back.

I was looking at Him beseechingly, as if to say: "No, Swami. You know very well that it's not true. You know that I made all my decisions and vows with Your blessing, and with Your supervision. Why are You saying this to me? Is there still some emotional bond lingering in my heart? If so, I beg You, ... not here, ... not now!"

Instead He piled it on: "Sometimes you want a wife, other times you don't want her." I would have wanted to shout at Him, "But Swami, what on earth are you saying? You know very well that it is not true, you know very well that I have no desire for that type of relationship." In the meantime, in order to sweeten the pill, Swami playfully took me by the chin and gently pinched my cheeks. All the while He had kept His right hand a few inches from my nose, with the palm facing up. I could not resist the temptation of taking it. Actually it seemed as if His purpose in keeping it there was precisely to give me that consolation. I slipped my left hand timidly under His, and clasped it with my right hand, the way you do with an old and intimate friend. He left His hand in mine for several minutes, while He kept talking.

The girl who had sung the Vedas intervened, almost as if in my defense: "Swami, priests don't marry!" Sai Baba smiled at me and said: "No. You must not marry. Stay single!"

Meanwhile His advice kept coming: "Think only of God. Everything is God, and God is with you, in you, around you. Love is God. Live in love." He continued by correcting certain aspects of my thought and behavior. On the one hand I was flattered that He was giving me so much attention, on the other I was a little embarrassed because He was correcting my faults in front of everyone. I consoled myself by thinking of the passage from the Apocalypse:[1] "I chastise and punish those whom I love."

He asked if there were any questions. Despite my handicap I tried to ask a question, which came out in hoarse and pathetic English, "Swami, if God is always everywhere, where is He when men do evil actions?" He replied only, "I will answer your question in private, when I receive you individually." That means I have an appointment set, but I do not know the date. I have already received the answer to the question, but nevertheless I am still hoping the meeting will occur.

A lady who was seriously ill with a nervous breakdown got up to ask, "Master, please heal me!" Swami promised her that He would take care of her, and the lady now is fine.

To a friend of mine He said, "You are worried about your son. Don't be anxious. I will look after him." Everything that Swami said was accurate, and anticipated the future. That father was in fact worried about his son, and the events which came to pass showed how much the family was under the protection of Sai Baba. His son was in an extremely serious car accident, which occurred in the middle of the night. The car was completely destroyed, but his son suffered only a few superficial cuts on his head.

At the end of the interview in the little room, He invited us back into the previous room. I was still ruminating on all the things He had said to me. I still could not understand what His words meant, and I felt very depressed. Baba saw me crestfallen, and asked me,

"What is your name?"

---

[1] *Ego quos amo arguo et castigo.*

"Mario," I answered, hoarsely.

"What is your Church?"

"Catholic."

"There are many Churches... Catholics, Protestants, et cetera, but God is only one. Be alike and even-tempered with everyone. Jesus too said this."

We bowed at Swami's feet, and our interview was over. He accompanied us to the door and graciously said goodbye.

We were all silent and absorbed. When you come out of an interview with Swami, you feel a profound silence which touches not only the mind, but every region of the body. It is as if every cell suspends operation in order to observe a sacred silence. The mind no longer has anything to say. On this occasion, however, I was able to experience this state only for a few moments.

I took refuge under a shed. I could feel that many questions remained unanswered. Doubts began to surface. I felt blind, unable to understand, thick-headed. I kept asking myself, "Why did He talk to me in that way? Why can't I see how what He said connects with my current state of conscience, the real facts of my life?"

Seeing how worried I was, several women in the group said to me, "Look, you haven't understood what Baba meant when He referred to your 'wife.' He was certainly talking about the Church. It was perfectly clear. The proof is also that at the end He asked you what Church you belonged to." This interpretation was plausible: the fact that Swami had said "Sometimes you want a wife, other times you don't," would then refer to the crises brought on by the fact that the Church did not share my affection for the East. During those times I had considered withdrawing silently from the Church, and thus dissolving, so to speak, my "marriage" with her, in order to resolve the conflict. However the Church has always considered herself more as Mother, than as Wife. I felt therefore that my "family" had to have a different structure, not the one suggested by the ladies.

My thoughts gave no sign of becoming clearer, and I was getting more and more confused.

Wrapped in a white Indian shawl, with my head between my knees, I gave myself over to a healthy session of crying, all the while praying for help in my solitude.

"What do you want from me, O God? Tell me.
I want to give you all I have,
if, among the things I have,
there is anything that can be called mine.
Why do you speak through metaphors?
Why are your words obscure?
What use is Your coming here among us
if then we cannot understand You
or we need translators?
Tell me what You want; I beg You.
But tell me clearly.
You want me to speak to others about You,
but first You want me to live by Your example.
Without the perfection You demand,
words are useless.
Because of this I am always tempted to say nothing;
I do not feel worthy to speak.
If even the great Sages were silent,
why should I speak, who am not wise?
What do You want, O Lord? Tell me.
You want me all for Yourself, right?
You don't want left-overs.
You have no use for half-eaten apples.
You want whole, ripe fruits.
Now I understand:
You are the Wife
who sometimes I want to marry
and other times not.
You are the Bride
who must supplant every other bond.
And now I know that You are a jealous Wife.
Yes. You are a jealous God,
who notices even the tiniest infidelity
of a single thought,
even though You are ever ready to forgive.
But You are also a faithful God.
You do not want to share a heart with any other loves,
but in exchange you give everything to Your lover.

O God, this is how You steal the human heart!"

My prayer was interrupted by a young man who, seeing me so depressed, came over and said to me:
"Were you happy being with Swami?"
"Yes, but now I seem to have many more problems than I did before. Maybe God is not happy with me, and now I have to overhaul my life completely."
"You are very lucky. He treated you like one of His students. He corrected you lovingly. Many people would envy you the blessing you have received."
I was moved, and felt my spirits rise. Perhaps that sweet soul was Baba Himself coming to console me. Given that everything that happens in the ashram bears the mark of the divine, I did not hesitate to believe it. Immediately afterward, an Indian gentleman, around thirty years old, came over to offer me some vibhuti, which he had in a glass jar. He told me that Baba had materialized it for him, and invited me to take as much as I wanted. Then he stopped in front of a statue of Krishna, and started singing *Prema mudhita... Rama Rama Ram.* His voice was unbelievably like Swami's. If I had not seen who was singing, I would have sworn that it was Sai Baba.

That evening I returned to my hotel as usual (Whitefield does not have as much residential space as Prashanti Nilayam). My heart was still in torment. I had decided to write Him a letter. I shut myself in my room, and before sitting down to write, I lay down on the bed. I opened a book I had just bought in Bangalore: *The Brihadaranyaka Upanishad*, with a commentary by Shankaracharya. I read: "Every rite is connected with the wife. In the passage *Let me have a wife... This much indeed is desire* (I.iv.17), it is shown that all action is naturally prompted by desire... This (aggregate of desirable objects) was but the self in the beginning - the only entity. He desired, "Let me have a wife, so that I may be born (as a child), and let me have wealth, so that I may perform rites." This much indeed is (the range of) desire... The mind is his self, speech his wife, the vital force his child, the eye his human wealth, for he obtains it through the eye...

and the body is its (instrument of) rite, for he performs rites through the body."[2]

These aphorisms were quite mysterious, but taking them as a kind of prophecy, as if they were the *I Ching*, they seemed to shed some light on what the term "wife" meant: it meant desire, and exterior rites, which make the ego grow. If "words are the wife", and in the allegory the wife represents the totality of desires, my having lost my voice might mean: "This is how I want you: voiceless, without a single desire!"

I sat down at a table and wrote down all my feelings. The letter that emerged could be summarized as follows: "There is only one desire which overshadows all other desires, and that is the desire to be in perfect union with God. This is the true marriage I long for. If you used the word "wife" as a symbol of all my attachments, I beg You, give me the strength to end them once and for all. If instead it is a marriage proposal, inviting me to wed the divine, give me a sign by graciously accepting this letter."

The next day I went to darshan, with the fixed intent of making Him accept my letter. I thought, "God can refuse anything, but He cannot refuse to marry a soul." That is His only goal, and it is for that purpose that He incarnates from age to age, as the Bhagavad Gita says. I was anxious and over-excited. On the one hand I was sure that He would take my letter, but on the other I was afraid that if for some reason He did not, the sky would have fallen in on me.

From the distant gate, the brilliant flame of love was coming toward the clump of waiting humanity. I thought, "Swami, if You do not take my letter, I will pursue You, at the risk of being intrusive... I will torment You until I extract a **yes** from You." Swami was walking in a straight line, without any deviation. He was coming straight toward me. He slowed His step, looked at me with His loving eyes, took the letter, and whispered with a clear and decisive voice: "Yes, priest! Sì!" That **Sì** is not a translation: Baba himself said it in Italian.

I was the happiest man in the world. There was nothing on earth that I would have traded for that happiness. "Even if I never see You

---

[2]From *The Brihadaranyaka Upanishad*, with the commentary of Shankaracharya, Advaita Ashrama, Calcutta, p. 4, 132-133.

again, Your promise will gladden every day of my life. What else could I need?"

I understood His "Yes, priest" as another confirmation that I was to continue being a priest. I was not to change anything in my life as far as my vocation went. On the contrary, my duty was to live out my priesthood ever better and more fully. His **Yes** was the assurance that I would receive the grace that came through my vocation; His **Sì** afterward in Italian was His consent as a Bride. Naturally the marriage required another **Sì** from the groom, which could not be merely the simple monosyllable **sì**, all too easy to say. It was, and is, an obligation, a serious obligation, where it takes very little, even just a thought, to fall into adultery. When I think of this today, I feel a great responsibility, and I feel that I am always under the watchful eye of God, who is indeed loving, but also demanding. "Wretched and worthless servant, you knew that I reap where I did not sow, and that I harvest where I have not planted... Take the measure from him and give it to the one who has ten." In Christ's parable, that is what the master said to the servant to whom He had entrusted only one measure of grain.

I believe it is very reassuring to entrust oneself to Him who knows all things. In days of sunshine and love, we can say to Him: "If I simply tell You that I love You, You who are Time itself might see me falling into some future desire. Therefore, I will say to You: when you see me groping blindly on dark days, remember, I beg You, the love I feel for You now. If there are to be moments when I will abandon You, please, in your goodness and in name of my current love, do not abandon me, but stretch out Your hand and raise me."

Saint Bernard says, "The Fountain always gives much more water than the thirsty man needs." This is a great consolation for anyone who knows his own limitations. The following words of the saintly abbot are even more consoling: "Even if the creature loves less, because it is inferior, as long as it loves with its entire being, there is nothing it needs to add. Nothing is lacking where everything has been given. Therefore for the creature to love in this way is to have celebrated the wedding with the Divine, because it cannot love like this and not be greatly loved. Perfect and complete matrimony consists in the consent of both parties, and there is no doubt that the love of the Word for the soul is greater, and comes first."[3]

A simple "yes" more than makes up for all the days of sadness. That "yes" confirmed the Marriage I seek.

---

[3]From the *Discourses on the Song of Songs* by Saint Bernard.

CHAPTER SEVENTEEN

Doubt and Inquiry

Letters from a theologizing industrialist

*The love of Christ
is beyond all knowledge.*

St. Paul to the Ephesians 3.19

In my years of studying and seeing Sai Baba, I have had the opportunity to meet many people who had a great interest in this divine Being. The fact that I was a priest made many people curious about how I reconciled Sai Baba with Jesus Christ. The illusion generated by the different physical forms continues to claim many victims; the conviction that the one and eternal Divine Essence can only manifest itself through one physical body is deeply ingrained. To imagine that the Divine can appear through many forms strikes most people as irreconcilable with their faith. In fact for many timid seekers, this is the greatest obstacle, and it causes them to run aground or retreat in their inquiry.

Among the many interesting people I have encountered, two are particularly worth considering. The one approached the problem of the relation Christ-Sai Baba with a real spirit of inquiry, as a theologian; the other approached it in a spirit of love and devotion, tinged with anxiety about the apparent duality mentioned above. The first is an industrialist, Dr. Gianni Venier from Venice, who has dedicated himself to studying theology in his spare time, and has even attended schools of theology. The other is a nun, who even though tormented by doubt, as is understandable, nevertheless has intuitively recognized the Reality that presented itself to her as Sai Baba, and has been able to appreciate it for what it is. She has even experienced moments of profound union with that Reality.

I have asked their permission to publish excerpts from some of their letters, but I shall not reveal the identity of the nun, for reasons which will become clear presently. Next to the problems they express, I will place the answers I sent them.

The reason I am publishing this exchange of letters is that I hope it may be of use to the reader who has finished reading the preceding pages of this book. Perhaps he or she too has doubts similar to the ones expressed in these letters; if so, I hope that this exchange of letters will help to illuminate the astounding event they discuss.

Here is the first set of letters, with the "theologizing" industrialist Dr. Venier. I met him in India, and I learned that he had made several trips to see Sai Baba. His investigations always ran up against the Christ of the Catholic tradition, and he saw no way to reconcile that Christ with the divine Presence of Sai Baba. We had a long conversation about it, which we later continued in a series of letters. What follows are relevant passages from those letters.

December 19, 1989
Dear Don Mario,
... cloistered in my study, in that atmosphere of calm serenity that always precedes the Holy Birth of Christ, I would like to resume the long discussions we used to have, focussing in particular on some points you made in your talk (at the University of Padova).[1]

Let's begin with Christ - Sai Baba - us. I remember that your parish priest objected to you: "How does all this square with Christ, the Only-Begotten Son of the Father?" You know that I anxiously asked myself the same question in relation to Mary, who embodies the tension between the human and the divine that is typical of the Judaeo-Christian tradition.

In the case of Mary, I tried to re-formulate the problem of the identity between the divine and the human. As you know, for us Christians, that identity exists only in Christ, which leaves the problem

---

[1]The writer is referring to a Conference held on December 16, 1989 in the Main Lecture Hall of the University of Padova (Department of International Studies in the Faculty of Political Science). The topic of the conference was "The cross-cultural aspects of the modern religious person: The Case of Sai Baba."

of how Mary reveals the feminine face of God. In the Indian tradition, however, the avatar of our time is called Sai Baba, a name which denotes both the masculine and feminine face of God. Therefore the incarnation of God as Sai Baba indicates His becoming flesh both as man and as woman. Nevertheless, both in past and in recent times, various theologians of our tradition, such as Balthasar and Boff, have defended this same concept of the divine. In their works they emphasize this double embodiment, and they speak of a certain unity between Christ and Mary. It is therefore my intention to investigate the Indian tradition on this point, and I hope I can count on your help so that I can further my study.

Once we have resolved this problem, we will have made a considerable step forward in understanding the sense of divinity, understood as a relation of intimacy with God. We will also begin to overcome the antithesis between sanctity and divinity. It is evident in fact that saintliness shares in the divine precisely by having a privileged relationship with God, but this does not mean that saints see themselves as identical with God. For us, Christ is without discussion a divine person (one person with two natures); but Mary, and Sai Baba too if you will, are certainly not the divine essence itself in the sense of one of the Persons of the Trinity.

The great problem I always run up against is Paul:

"For there is only one God, and there is only one mediator between God and mankind, himself a man, Christ Jesus, who sacrificed himself as a ransom for them all." Christ is the only human manifestation of the Son; therefore He alone has a privileged and exclusive relation with the Trinity which for Christians is clearly the only expression of God (see I Timothy 2.1-8).

Your reflections over the "course of several days" have led you to correctly conclude that if it is true that Christ - the Son - is the Only-Begotten Son of the Father, then in Christ Sai Baba, Mary, the Saints, Avatars, and we ourselves are all participants in this extraordinary cosmic event which makes us all Children of the Father, Sons of God. Thus we all share in the divinity which makes us become God Himself (here we could cite Paul, John, and a number of other passages from the gospels). Your answer then brings everything back into orthodox Catholic doctrine. However I am not really sure that this is what Sai Baba means to say: your solution seems too simple to me.

Take the dogma of our Church: in my opinion some of it makes no sense, at least on the surface. On the one hand it asserts that Christ is the only possible incarnation of God; on the other it grants particular privileges to Mary (immaculate conception, perpetual virginity, assumption into heaven with both body and soul), and it gives similar privileges to certain Saints (omnipresence, omnipotence, and omniscience). Since sainthood cannot be a feature only of the West and of Christianity, it is obviously manifest in an extraordinary way in the Avatars of the East.

The relation God-man makes the identity of both man and God uncertain. In my opinion, this is where we need to seek the answer to our problem. Avatars present themselves as a much more complete manifestation of God than Christianity attributes to Saints, even if their relation with God and the powers they manifest are not very different from those of Saints. In any case the problem we have to resolve is the incarnation of God, which for us Christians seems to be indisputably and exclusively tied to Christ.

I completely agree with you about the extraordinary effect that Sai Baba has on whoever meets him, and I also accept your idea that there are three possible ways to approach him. I identify mostly with the first of your categories (an extraordinary influence which nurtures and strengthens faith), but also a little with the third (the search for other approaches to truth). You said that you identify most with this third category, though I was moved by your reference also to your spiritual path as a priest. You said many other things, and I assure you that I listened to everything with great interest. I still believe, however, that the relation Jesus-Sai Baba is an essential point for us Christians: does Sai Baba's relation to God necessarily pass through Christ?

December 29, 1989.

Dear Gianni,

I too was happy to see you in the audience at Padova. Because of your theological preparation, which since your encounter with Sai Baba is steadily turning from knowledge into wisdom, there was no one better equipped than you to appreciate what I had to say. Saint Paul used to say that "knowledge swells pride," and that Jesus was more concerned that justice be rendered to Wisdom.

I am grateful to you for the questions you ask me. They cause me to reflect, and as you well know, when you have to write, the things you want to say get filtered and re-filtered, making your thoughts clearer. I will discuss the main points of your thoughtful objections, and I hope to reach the goal, serving the cause of Truth.

The question of the Only-Begotten Son

As I said already in Padova, "Only-Begotten" is a divine attribute which refers not to a genetic descent, in the human-biological sense of the term, but rather to the oneness of the nature assumed by the "Word," which in the beginning was born from the womb of the Absolute. Language, alas!, is here too limited an instrument to express the Inexpressible, the Ineffable. Every word we take from our vocabulary can become a treacherous snare, but I will face that risk, because for now we have been given no other way to communicate. The Prologue to the gospel of John is without doubt a page of high, and I would venture to say, Vedic, wisdom. "In the Beginning was the Word, and the Word was God... and the Word was made flesh." The syntax of this passage has something timeless and dimensionless about it: it all continues to be true regardless of historical events. In this case the event is the incarnation of a being who took the name Jesus, and was said to be the Christ.

In our tradition we have become accustomed to saying His name without making distinctions: Jesus Christ. In recent years theology, and thus the liturgy as well, has favored the expression "The Christ" (i.e., The Anointed One). Even though this expression seems a little unnatural, it expresses better the Reality of one Divine Essence, Unique, Only-begotten (the Word of the Father has only one ultimate meaning, only one direction: it has no... brothers or sisters). It is that Reality which takes up residence in, and manifests Itself through, a human body, because it is only through a human body that it can establish contact with human beings. The human body selected for that purpose bore the name Jesus.

Now, whether in His family life Jesus had any blood-brothers or sisters, or whether they were only half-brothers and sisters, has no real importance. In order to defend a misconceived notion of Only-begotten, the Church has officially maintained that the "brothers" of

Jesus, mentioned frequently in the gospels, were really cousins. Having blood-brothers could in no way detract even a fragment of glory from the greatness of Jesus: the fact that He would share the same genetic lineage with them is irrelevant.

The same thing can be said in Sai Baba's case. The superhuman Reality took up residence in a historical body whose given family name was Sathyanarayana Raju. That Reality is God, a God which cannot communicate directly with modern man except by taking on the same physical shape, the same organism, the same physical requirements as other men. In taking over this body It adopted a new name, which indicates Its mission: Sathya Sai Baba, that is, the Truth which generates the real human being (in the sense that It is its Father and Mother).

In Sai Baba's case too, the Only-Begotten Son who "was born before all ages" manifests Itself through a form made of flesh and blood, subject to decay, aging, and death. However His spiritual, metaphysical, and ontological Reality is beyond all human comprehension!

The Essence of all beings pulsates in that little body, which is so tiny and powerful, on fire with Love, radiating light like the Sun. That is why His hand creates anything at all, with no limits: it is to show man the nature of the power that lives in that body. That is why, when He gives darshan, our hearts overflow with joy, and our whole being yearns to dissolve itself in Him. These are forces which cannot be seen, or measured in a laboratory, and which theology cannot grasp; they come from a heritage which is common to all beings, and whose source is in Him.

If the Ocean shifts, all the waves will follow It. There is heat both in the little flame and in the raging blaze of a gigantic fire. There is no fire without heat.

I would say, then, that the Only-Begotten is this unstoppable force which animates our lives. That force finds its most complete expression in the divine incarnations which from time to time, when it is necessary, are bestowed on man by the Infinite Goodness of Love. St. Athanasius understood this and explained it: "He is the One, the Only-Begotten, the good God, who proceeds from the Father as from the fountain of goodness, and who rules and contains the Universe."

In a few words of incredible clarity, the great St. Thomas Aquinas captures this Essence of the Only-Begotten which makes itself man: *Unigenitus Dei Filius, suae divinitatis volens nos esse participes, naturam nostram assumpsit, ut homines deos faceret factus homo.* The Only-Begotten Son of God, wishing that we might share in His divinity, took on our nature, in order that by becoming man, men might become gods. As you can see, therefore, the Only-Begotten is not the son of a carpenter in Nazareth, but that Essence which has existed from eternity, and which then filled the spirit of Jesus, allowing Him to identify Himself with It.

Mary, the Divine Mother.

I am glad that your studies have led you to the conclusion that Mary is much more than the rather simple-minded human and maternal image that she has become in our tradition. On the occasion of the last Feast of the Immaculate Conception, I had an intuition. At the risk of shaking up the nuns who were at the Mass I celebrated that day, I hastened to communicate it to them in my homily. It was only this year, after so many years spent in ignorance, that I understood that immaculate conception simply means "birth without sin," that is, without karma, with no debt left over from previous lives, birth in a state of absolute perfection.

So then I asked myself: isn't this just another way of saying that a human being has attained divinity? Does this mean that the Virgin Mary is really another Avatar? I rather liked this idea: it reconciled me to a sacred image which had become obsolete through so many pitiful sermons, which always aimed at exalting Mary's human virtues and Her "forced" maternity.

I thought: then Mary and Jesus reached the same goal, through two different roles. Mary reached it through silence, which is more fitting for women, who by nature are more contemplative than men; Jesus reached it through preaching and social action, which is more suited to men, or "Kshatriya".[2] In this way, a dogma which was hard to take (because it was imposed) ends up having a meaning deeper than what was intended by the minds who came up with it. I see the prompting

---

[2]This is the "Warrior Caste," one of the four castes of the Hindu tradition.

of the Holy Spirit in this: it often makes men utter Truths which they themselves cannot understand.

It cannot be denied that religion too has been conditioned by the fact that women were held in low regard for so many centuries. Mary, then, is not simply what she has been made to be, a poor mother who never knows what is going on, and who blindly obeys some hidden purpose. Instead she is the "Great Lady" who cracked the serpent's skull by saying "Yes." Mary deserves to sit beside Christ because they both came for the same purpose, and that purpose was to crush the head of Maya, the Goddess of Ignorance. In fact ignorance dies in front of humility.

Mary and Jesus are the feminine and masculine principles of creation, which today are united in the Person of Sai Baba. The sacred Hindu scriptures call these two principles Prakriti and Purusha. The early Christian tradition, before it was contaminated by later revisions, imagined Mary as a Queen, on a throne next to Christ. It even maintained that Mary's body was immune to the natural law of decomposition.

Both the Assumption of Mary and the Resurrection of Christ point to the same Reality. In the East God is often worshiped as the Divine Mother. The Indian respect for cows, which seems so ridiculous to Westerners, is simply the veneration for the divine attributes that are so evident in the cow: the cow eats from the meadow, and re-fertilizes it; with such modest food, it gives precious nourishment, the milk which is the basis of butter, cheese, etc... The cow asks for nothing in return; it is not aggressive, but is constantly attacked. This is the image of a true mother who loves with no expectation of reward.

The problem raised by the passage from 1 Timothy can be resolved if you pay attention to the phrase "*for Christians* it is the only manifestation of God." "For Christians" seems to imply, with noteworthy tolerance, that in other cultures there may be other ways in which the divine is expressed and explained. Paul seems to be saying: for us this is the way it is, and there is no reason to change the form of God. Others reach the same goal by other roads.

Dear Gianni, your inquiry will certainly yield a good result, because it is motivated by a genuine desire for truth. Do not forget that the human intellect, and therefore also theology, which depends on that intellect, has great limitations. The ideal is to fuse together what you can learn through study, with what humans who have pure hearts perceive.

The difference between theological study and Reality is the same difference that there is between a scientific manual, which analyzes a fruit down to the tiniest biological detail, and the experience of actually tasting the fruit. Sai Baba says, "Do not try to understand Me. Plunge yourselves into my Reality." Knowledge can be acquired through study, but the process is slow, difficult, and full of risks. Saints, however, often enjoyed an infused wisdom, the understanding that came from a total immersion in the divine. This is why, even without having studied, Saint Theresa, the Holy Abbot of Ars, and so many others could get to the heart of the problem when they spoke of God, and also... touch the hearts of those who are full of problems.

February 16, 1990.
Dear Don Mario,
...Today, I am going to begin my analysis of the concept of Revelation.

For all the religions which are based on it, Revelation means the self-manifestation of divinity.

For us Christians, God revealed Himself in Jesus of Nazareth. The Prologue to the Gospel of John says that in Him, "the Word was made flesh" (John 1.14).

Moreover, as the Revelation of God, Jesus of Nazareth is the true and only path which leads to the Father (John 14.6). Between the two, Jesus and the Father, the bond is so tight that it is impossible to distinguish them. Thus the Gospel says, "I and my Father are one" (John 10.30).

Therefore everything is focussed on Jesus of Nazareth. He and He alone is the fulfillment of Revelation, because it is only in the Risen Christ that believers will be resurrected, and will be allowed to share in divine life.

Therefore the divine and the human were completely united in the person of Christ, as the Fathers of the Church, and all the great ancient Church councils from the first to the second Nicene Council, declared. The way of salvation has thus been indicated and traced once for all.

From what we have said it might seem that everything has been resolved, that every question has been answered. Instead a whole series of questions keeps arising again, two thousand years after the fact. Actually, it had to be this way, given that the basis of the Christian religion is constituted by a mystery, the dogma of the Trinity. This mystery deals with the very essence of God; it is the key to the interpretation of every other aspect of Christianity.

Now, according to this dogma, the one God, as He gradually revealed Himself through the Old and New Testaments, exists and lives as Father, Son, and Holy Spirit.

...For Christians, God is Father, Son and Holy Spirit, in an eternal and mutual relationship, interpenetration, and love. This is the unfathomable mystery, which Origen conceived as energy and communication, and Augustine conceived as the expression of love ("If you see charity, you see the Trinity").

Now the Trinity is a single nature or substance in three persons. In the Christ, however, there is a single person and two natures, the human and the divine. What is one in Christ, is multiple in the Trinity; what is multiple in Christ, is one in the Trinity. For us Christians the incarnation is a unique and unrepeatable event, because there is only one hypostasis of God as the Only-begotten. But has God communicated with His creatures only through the Son?

I often get the feeling that it would be easier to accept everything as an impenetrable mystery, but then the questions keep coming up again: who is Jesus? Who is Mary? And then who is Sai Baba? Who are we?

So we somehow have to clarify these reciprocal relationships which in the end concern God, the Absolute Itself. It cannot be meaningless to believe that Christ is the only way, as well as being truth and life, as John writes (14.6). We Christians consider these three concepts essential even in defining the Church: our community in Christ is itself based on our sharing in one way, truth, and life.

Let me go back again to the conclusion of your letter. It is clear that the Only-Begotten is not the son of a Nazarene carpenter, but rather the pre-existing Word. But it is also true that the Son, the Only-Begotten, is the incarnation. He incarnated, taking on human nature without giving up His divine nature, and He incarnated in Christ, and only in Christ. We're back to where we were before: there can be only one incarnation because there is only one Person, or hypostasis of the Trinity, which incarnates.

Maybe it would be better to come to the conclusion that you stated in your introduction: "language is an inadequate instrument for expressing the inexpressible, the ineffable." By seeking answers we inevitably run some risks, but how can we keep from seeking answers?

PS. - I listened again to the recording of your lecture on Sai Baba at Padova. Two concepts are not entirely clear to me.

In the first part of your talk, when you speak about Sai Baba's miracles and the intimate knowledge of the structure of matter that they entail, you make the following analogy: as a computer is known perfectly only by the person who made it, so matter is wholly known only by its creator. From what you say it seems that for you knowledge is the same as creation. Is this what you meant, or did I misunderstand you?

My other question regards your conception of the relation between God and the categories of good and evil. In order to defend Sai Baba against the accusation of being a devil, a personification of evil, you end up denying that the distinction between good and evil is grounded in God, that it can be attributed to God. To quote your exact words, "The phenomenal world has a dualistic structure. Since everything comes from God, God is above, or rather beyond, the purely human categories of good and evil." God therefore is the Supreme Witness, indifferent to either side in the struggles of life.

Just after that, however, when you are explaining the concept of avatar, you say: "When justice declines, God incarnates." How can you reconcile this statement with the previous one? What *justice* are you talking about? What concepts of good and evil does this justice refer to?

February 27, 1990.
Dear Gianni,

...I agree with everything you say, except for one point, which I know might be considered one of the pillars of Catholic doctrine: "for us Christians the incarnation is a unique and unrepeatable event, because there is only one hypostasis of the divine as the Only-Begotten." And then, later: "It is the Only-Begotten which incarnated, taking on human nature without giving up His divine nature, and He incarnated in Christ, and only in Christ."

To the first point I will respond by saying: how is it possible to limit the supreme power of God when He decides to take on a form (any form, at this point!)? Just as He has taken the form of an amoeba or of a fawn or of the star Sirius, penetrating into each of these forms as a level of consciousness suitable to them, so He takes His "maximum form" (maximum in terms of the evolution of forms) in man. That is why man is blessed with a supreme consciousness, even though he limits it by misusing his free will. Beyond the level of human-man, God takes the form of God-man, who is a man who surrenders his own free will (i.e., drowns his ego in the Divine), and who thus reaches the highest level of consciousness possible for a human being.

Why on earth would this God have only one possibility, only one chance, to take on a "special form" in order to fulfill a "special mission"? Even if this were the correct understanding of the whole Christian tradition (a view I find rather doubtful and self-contradictory), our power of reason, on which all science, and theology too, is based, will compel us insistently to revise our views, insofar as they are flawed and lead to philosophical and theological absurdities.

God resists any limit imposed on Him by our lame logic. If He wills it, He can send a Christ, or several Christs, for each century, whether or not humans insist on bowing before the conclusions they have come up with in their own minds by misinterpreting, or over-interpreting, the meaning of the Scriptures. Human interpretations can degenerate into mental theories, which can then become the idols of a fossilized cult, turning men into mummies. But the Divine Economy is frugal and wise: It has placed the treasure of Eternal Wisdom, which reveals the why of all things, in each human heart. "The Truth will set you free." The Truth cannot be reached if we stand on a stool we think is sound, but which in fact is shaky.

As for the second point, I will observe that a healthy theology has to pay close attention to its choice of words. There is a reason that today even the liturgy has replaced the expression "Christ" with "the Christ," which means "the Anointed One," that is the Consecrated One, the Chosen One, the Only-begotten Himself. The Only-begotten cannot incarnate in the Only-begotten. The Only-begotten incarnates in a human being. Two thousand years ago, that human being was Jesus of Nazareth, who through a genuine hypostasis, identified himself with That, and gradually became One with Him.

It was the consciousness of the son of Mary, the man Jesus, which became one with the Consciousness of the Only-begotten, Christ. The mind of the yogi who was born in Bethlehem and who grew up in Galilee expanded until it merged with the mind of the universal Planner. The best actor is always in on the director's plans, because he understands him. So like the director himself, he too observes the play of creation. Perceiving that men have forgotten their true nature, and need the helping hand of the Divine, it is that yogi/actor who presents His plan of salvation to the Father, and not vice-versa.

Now for your P.S.

1. - Yes, knowledge is a power to create. When the engineer has worked out the design of his computer, all he has to do is build it. When Leonardo da Vinci dreamed of a mysterious woman, the Mona Lisa was born. The gap between thinking and creating depends on the individual will and on necessity. Sometimes a subtle or esoteric contact is established, so that the moment you conceive a desire (that fosters your spiritual evolution), it is instantaneously fulfilled in physical reality. The instant the calf moves towards its mother, her milk begins to flow... This is a superb metaphor that comes from the Upanishads. Our knowledge is limited. That is why we have to work so hard to fuse metals, produce chemical reactions, make discoveries. We know only a tiny fragment of the whole history of matter. But nothing of all that the human intellect does not know escapes divine wisdom. For a man established in full divine consciousness, the mysterious latticework of molecular structure is like an open book. To modify that structure any way he wishes, all he has to do is inject into it the shakti (energy) he has in a finger... A miracle!

2. - When I spoke of good and evil, I said, exactly: "In this game, we can see the dualistic nature of the phenomenal world, in which good and evil are simply human categories, and in which everything has a precise purpose. The Supreme Existence does not participate in this game by rooting for the good: It is simply a witness, the Supreme Witness. Everything comes from Him: how could He take sides?

"The distinction between good and evil, ethics, moral codes, all come from man, and vary according to the time, the place, the era, and the nation. The only unchanging code is what is defined as the Eternal Law (*Dharma*). The Divine Energy leads all things to the supreme sublimation of Love."

If God rooted for the good, he would be limited by it. If He were to grieve for evil, evil would be His master. God, the Absolute, cannot descend to the level of the game itself, except when he disguises Himself as a player: the Avatar. Some time ago Baba said something like that: I have come to fight against evil... life is a game, play it... etc....

There is only one God, and He is unaffected by all things. However when He takes on a form, He goes on stage playing a role to perfection: He cries, laughs, suffers, gets sick, but - beware! - not as humans do. He does it only and always in order to teach. In order to reach Him, the path that is recommended is the path of goodness, of Justice or Dharma. Once you have reached Him, however, there is only Bliss, self-fulfillment, and complete immunity from all good and evil actions. Justice, which leads to transcending the categories of good and evil, is itself conditioned by good and evil. Remember Arjuna: Fight, Arjuna! These relatives of yours are nothing but a glimmer of illusion, and your duty is to fight... "Who is my mother? Who are my brothers?... My mother and brothers are all those who do the will of the Father!"

I hope I have been thorough. Never forget the golden rule suggested by Swami: "Pray in order to obtain God; when you have Him you will have all the rest..." "Seek the Kingdom of God, and all else will be added unto you."

April 2, 1990.
Dear Don Mario,

When I returned from my long trip I found your letter of February 27, and I promised myself that I would answer it before Easter.

So here I am writing, happy to continue this stimulating and challenging correspondence.

In regard to your first answer, I confess that I do not agree with your assertions. God did not take form, one form out of many, in

Christ. By saying this it seems to me that you risk confusing God with creation.

Creation is something distinct from God: the amoeba, the fawn, the star Sirius, and lastly the summit of creation, man himself, are not forms of God. If you do not keep this point clear, you inevitably fall into pantheism. God is the agent, not the immanent, cause of the world. God transcends creation, He is the totally other.

God however reveals Himself to man, He chooses to speak to man using his language. The Word made itself flesh. God, who had already spoken to man through the prophets (and He continued and continues to speak through prophets even today), nevertheless spoke with man *directly* only one time, when he became man. This event is unique, nor could it be otherwise, if we want to save God's transcendence. This is the Christic mystery, rooted in the mystery of the Trinity. All our Christian faith rests on this point.

But what part do the saints, avatars, Swami, and above all, Mary, have in our faith?

Allow me to leave this question open for the moment.

In regard to your second answer, on the other hand, I agree with you: I too see it as you do. Like you, I too am convinced that all language is inadequate. Therefore let us try to express with infinite caution how Christ "became" the Son, as a single Person with him, in the unity of the Father: that is, how Christ became conscious of this. At first Jesus speaks and acts under the authority of the Father; later, however, "the word of God", "the word of the Lord", "word of the Christ" become interchangeable expressions. Finally Jesus "becomes" the very Word of God: Jesus Christ, the Word made flesh, sent as a man to men. He speaks the word of God (John 3.34), and brings to fulfillment the work of salvation entrusted to Him by the Father (see John 5.36; 17.4); whoever sees Him sees the Father (see John 14.9)...

Sometimes I get the feeling that we really do understand each other, and that we are gradually coming to speak the same language. What you wrote in answer to my P.S. helped me, and I am truly grateful to you for it. The way you expressed your thought reminded me of some pages of St. Augustine, which are very dear to me. They read: "God is always present in the core of our being; give yourself to Him, and with Him, by rediscovering yourself, you will have everything." "Do you wish to be truly free? Your supreme freedom is to serve Christ."

Many of Swami's sayings re-echo in Augustine's thought, and even more in the words of Christ as they are reported in the Gospels...

May 7, 1990.
Dear Gianni,

Forgive my delay in answering. I have no excuses, except my overwhelming passion for editing Sathya's discourses, which make me forget all the rest of the world.

I will try to clarify the point I made before, which triggered your disagreement. God is not to be confused with Creation, even though in the phenomenal world there is not a single speck of subatomic matter that does not bear His divine copyright.

When we say that the created world is God, it is only an error in words, because we know that if for the word "God" we substitute the Absolute, That Which Is, the Indescribable, the Unnameable, the Eternal, the Formless, etc..., the assertion does not make sense. However, to say it again, "there is nothing that exists in the world that was not made by Him, that does not receive energy, existence, and life from Him,"[3] that is not dissolved by Him. Because of this, we say that He is everywhere, even though that statement is imprecise (because our vocabulary for saying such things is imperfect). This does not mean that He has been confused with the world.

Let's take an example. An automobile is made up of various parts, of which the engine is surely the essential component. Without an engine, in fact, the car will not go, unless you push it... The motor is as essential to the car as DNA is to cells. But the Really Essential entity is the human mind which conceived and drives the car. The engineer and the driver are intimately related to the car, but they cannot be equated with the mechanism itself. When you finish your trip, you get out of the car and go home. The car continues to live, to be efficient and capable of movement, but you are resting peacefully in bed or in a chair thinking of your exams. This is how it is with

---

[3]From the Preface to the Catholic Liturgy.

every component of existence, from the amoeba to the elephant, or rather, from the cilia of a protozoan to the seams in its stomach which allow it to absorb cells. The Supreme Driver, who is also the Supreme Engineer, travels in all these, to drive creation according to laws He knows, because He is also the Law-giver.

If, therefore, I say that God is in all things, I am not at all making the error of pantheism or immanentism. That Engineer accompanies every detail of His works, but He can also withdraw from all of them, when He decides to end the play and return the cosmos to its initial state, as the Unmanifest. Note that I did not say that He withdraws from a portion of creation when things die, because He continues to direct every operation even in "death" or in the dissolution of matter, from salts, carbohydrates, vitamins, etc... to the calcium phosphates in ashes or fertilizers. *Vita mutatur, non tollitur* (Life changes, but is never destroyed). Is this what you meant by your expression "agent cause"?

In other words, what you say is true: God is something distinct from creation. We have said that He is the One, but everything depends on clarifying what lies behind that one monosyllable, "God." Is it the Absolute, or is it a Creator, a something that works and acts, and that therefore cannot be called simply the Absolute? In distinguishing these aspects the Hindus are clearer than we are. Brahman, the Absolute, the Paramatma; and Brahma, the God who creates, the Engineer, the Adorable, the Atma. But if we read our Scriptures carefully, they reveal the same truth: the unnameable God of the Israelites, the Eternal, the Supreme Spirit which also resides in each heart; and Wisdom, the God of the fathers, the God who makes men win or lose...

In my opinion it is difficult to imagine any unshakable basis for the belief that God spoke "directly" to man only once. Let us go back to what we have already said: God does what He wills and pleases, and no theology of ours can stand in His way.

So then Mary, the saints, the avatars, Jesus, Swami,... What are they all doing here? What corner can we find for them in our faith, which is already so well-set and jelled? They are the Divine Road signs for man, who through the labyrinth of time, has strayed from the splendor of his initial faith. Of course, as many people keep reminding me, why do we need a Swami, when Jesus already said everything?

The reason people need tutoring after school, private lessons, is that they do not learn their lessons well during the normal school year. It is not the message that needs to be stated again: it is the students, who are a little undisciplined, who have missed the point of the lessons because they were not paying attention.

That is why the Divine Teacher still finds time, will and energy to walk among our school-desks and point out the Way again with a caress or a gentle slap. That Teacher is no mercenary: the private lessons he gives are always free (the only price he asks is serious effort). The fact that this Grace is given again and again in history is no indication that It is lacking in some way, but rather that we are. Should we not be grateful for this Love which is lavished on us?

Moreover, we should not forget that the Actor changes, but the Spirit which moves Him is always the same.

The Christ in past, present, and future, Beginning and End, Alpha and Omega...: all Glory is His, now and forever. Amen.

A warm hug to you and Marisa. Om Jesu admirabilis. Om Maria, Mater Divinae Gratiae. Om Sri Sathya Sai Babaye Namah.

CHAPTER EIGHTEEN

Anguish and Ecstasy

Letters of a nun devoted to Sai

I do not envy or favor anyone.
I am impartial towards all.
But whoever serves Me with devotion
lives in Me;
he is a friend to Me,
as I am a friend to him.

Bhagavad Gita IX.29

After hearing about Sai Baba's message and understanding its principal points, Sister W. wrote enthusiastically to her confessor, in order to tell him about her new discovery. Her confessor was skeptical, so the nun felt she had to explain to him that knowing about Sai Baba would not harm her. It would not make her stray away from her Christian faith; she was receiving nothing but great spiritual benefits from Sai Baba. She wrote to him, "Knowing about Sai Baba has given me an overall sense of well-being. The principal theme of Baba's teachings is love."

August 15, 1989. Om Sai Sri Jesu namah.
Dearest Don Mario,...

I am nearly at the end of my stay in the ashram of the Atma. Baba foresaw and prepared everything with care and love, even what to our eyes seemed completely coincidental.

Yes, I really believe that Prashanti Nilayam is in the heart of all those who love Sai Baba's message, and who have experienced the sweetness of the Abode of Peace. I too have had a glimmer of this. Indeed at any time I can close my eyes and see Sai Baba's sweet and graceful Form walking among the devotees crowded in the ashram.

I can turn on my tape recorder and hear His melodious voice singing. I can adorn myself with the 46 jewels that I was given just today. This was a gift I was expecting, and that Baba bestowed on me without my having to ask for it. In fact I had been thinking of asking you for a set of guidelines for behavior. I realize that Baba knows our thoughts, He watches over us, and that life with Him is a constant succession of wonderful things, of small and great miracles. I see His hand in everything... What else can I say to you, Don Mario? My heart is full to the brim with joy, and it wants to join the Gopis, who addressed God saying:

"If You were a tree,
we would want to be vines to cling to You;
If you were a flower,
we would want to be bees, to fly to You in swarms;
If you were the ocean,
we would want to be rivers, to lose ourselves in You;
If you were the infinite sky,
we would want to be tiny stars, to gleam in You;
God, omnipotent God,
we do not live, we cannot live, away from You.
We wish to play with You.
To live with You.
To breathe our souls into You."

Because of her "interest" in Sai Baba, Sister W. experienced tensions with her fellow-sisters, who warned her about her "heterodox" beliefs. When later, in order to convince them, she gave them some things to read about Sai Baba, the situation got worse: they viewed her as gullible, ingenuous, and a traitor to her faith. In a moment of bitter pain she wrote to me, confiding an extraordinary "interview" she had had with Sai Baba:

October 8, 1989.
I will go on to tell you what Baba revealed to me on the 13th of September. That day I was quite downcast (I miss having friends to talk to about Sai Baba), and I was also angry with Him. I was asking Him why He had made Himself known to me... When I was through

expressing my bitterness to Him, I continued to look at Him in silence. From the silence a dialogue emerged, which left me rather perplexed when I re-read it:

"You do not know who you have been, but this life is your last hand to play. That is why I have made Myself known to you, in order to help you. Dear daughter, I know that you struggle very hard, and that your will is weak. It is no use to you to know what you have been: it is enough for you to know what you are now: divine. At the point you have reached you can no longer go back, because the road is no longer there; I have erased it. You can only go forward. It is a difficult stretch of road ahead, but if you only knew how close you are to seeing the snow shining in the sun! Believe this, because it is the truth. I love you, dearest daughter, and I cannot wait for you to be with me. Your journey, your search for Me, has been long and tiring... Whether you loved Me during the journey does not matter; what counts is your love now. Understand what I am telling you, my child! You are not alone. I am with you. Trust Me. Do not search for doubts that are not there. You know that I am your God, why do you wish to deny it? Always feel My presence in your heart, and call Me in every circumstance, ask Me and I will always answer you. I look on you with joy, and I love you so much."

January 11, 1990.
Dearest Don Mario,

The astounding history of Babaji, that great Master who is immune to death, who appears always as a young man, and who they say is in intimate contact with Christ, makes me think of Christ's words: "What concern is it to you if I wish him to remain here until I return?"

If I remember correctly, I think you told me that you had been to see Babaji. You were very lucky, given that according to the book he lives on the northern peaks of the Himalayas, and his body is visible only to a small group of people on this earth. Since you saw him, what do you think about him? Sometimes I wonder if India isn't all science-fiction.

Do you consider the presence of a guru essential in one's life? Can Sai Baba be my guru even if I am not near Him physically?

Dear Don Mario, I feel like I am entering ever deeper into another world, a world which is raised above earthly problems and anxieties, a world which quivers only with the Divine. Your words upset me: God is everything, God is nothing. Can't God be conceived as something definite? Where on earth is India leading me? Towards God, I am sure of it; and Baba, who is surer than I am, says that I am not made to live in this human world. He encourages me to live in God, for God and only for God, with my heart and mind always turned toward God, immersed in God.

One morning, gazing at the living Image that you gave me, I said to Baba:

"Dear Master, don't you think that as your disciple I should at least see you?"

Baba answered: "Why? Aren't you seeing Me this very moment? Remember that every time you look at Me in this picture, I am really present."

I said: "But what is the sign that this is really true?"

"The sign is the peace which enters your heart, the fact that your breath and mind fill to the brim, and you are lost in sweet silence."

I exclaimed: "Does that mean I can have Your darshan whenever I wish?"

"Whenever you wish."

I told Him that this seemed too good to be true; and He said: "If you don't believe these simple things, how will you believe greater things?"

"Baba, what do I have to do?"

"Dear child, you do not have to do anything except love God. You are now in My school, and I want you to spend all your free time with Me."

Dear Don Mario, I have realized that I have spent enough time learning, and now the time has come to Love, the time in which I have to strengthen and intensify my love for God.

On New Year's Eve, at 10 p.m., I couldn't decide whether to go to my room, or to go to a hall where some guests were celebrating and waiting for the new year. I asked Baba, and He answered: "Stay with Me, W., spend this time in My company; you have guests every day and all day." These words moved me, because they are like the words of Jesus: "You will always have the poor with you."

January 20, 1990.
Dearest Sister W.,

India is the country where what we poor Westerners consider extraordinary is ordinary, almost normal. Miracles in India are not news, because spiritual giants who perform such miracles have lived in India for centuries, for millennia. Of course, along with them, there are also hoaxes: weeds always grow together with the good grain.

I will respond briefly to your shower of questions.

The guru who guides your life is your conscience, shaped by the word of the Lord. Follow the teachings of the Lord Jesus, and also, if it gives you joy, those of Baba, and you will never need to ask what to do, because it will become apparent to you. Sai Baba says: "You should always ask yourself: Is what I am doing pleasing or displeasing to God?" Naturally Sai Baba also knows how to be a guru... The sum of what He tells you through His words and His mystic Presence is all the instruction you need.

How can you sum up God as some determinate thing? The moment you try to define the Absolute, It "dies," and is therefore not Absolute. You can experience It, however, in stages. In the same way only you can experience the love you feel for someone: you cannot transfer your act-of-love to other people so they can feel it in the first person the way you do. When you yourself feel it, it is immense; when you try to give someone else a description of it, it ends up sounding like a scene from "Grand Hotel."

Where is India leading you? Of course you know. India will give the final touch to all your religious education. This does not mean that you should become Hindu or Buddhist. That would be really foolish! But it means completing what you have learned with a depth of thought that has survived "intact" through thousands of years. The Vedas are holy scriptures which at first were handed down orally, and then transcribed by Vyasa. They date to extremely ancient times, and are lost in the origins of the world itself. In written form alone they date from 5000 years before Christ. Truth is one. It is man who makes it cloudy, in order to hide it from the eyes of his brothers, and in order to gain material advantages. This work of confusion is the accomplishment of the "devil," that is, Maya. This Illusion is itself part of the divine Plan: it slows, but deepens, the search for the Ultimate Good.

Fall in love with God, under whatever form or name you wish to see Him and call upon Him. Call on Him every moment of the day. When you are tempted by your senses, abandon yourself to Him with all the passion you have. When you are discouraged, wet His Image with your tears. When you feel distant from Him, rest your heart on His, make them beat as one, cover His face with kisses, and tell Him that you are His and His alone. A torrent of Bliss will flood your soul, and your life will pick up again with renewed vigor.

All Glory and Honor to Him who never tires of running after us in order to save us.

April 10, 1990.
Dearest Don Mario,

I am alone, with Baba. Or rather, I cannot talk about Baba with anyone, and when I do, I only cause trouble. The other day, when we were all gathered together, a sister made some insinuations for the nth time. It irritated me: I answered back that enough was enough, and that if she had something to say, she should say it openly. I added that everyone is free to follow and love Christ as she pleases, and with whatever aids she feels are necessary. With this last remark I raised a real hornet's nest. For a while I tried to face up to the attacks, but then I followed the advice of an inner voice which was saying: why are you getting so upset? Let them talk!

What they said was basically this: it is obvious that a Muslim cannot help you in seeking Christ... people like that do everything for money; we have to proclaim Christ and His Gospel, and not other things...

I spoke to my confessor about the Conference on Human Values at Assisi. He was pleased until he learned that even though the program was open to all, the participants would be mostly lay people involved in an organization which was started in India, and headed moreover by a man named Sai Baba. At this point he started saying that even Human Values can be distorted if they are presented by people who espouse non-Christian, and particularly non-Catholic, doctrines. This triggered a lively discussion... When he left he said that I would be doing him a favor if I would take some time to speak with him about this subject. He cares for me, and he is convinced that I am on the wrong path.

What do I do now? Should I go? Should I stop going?... It is clear that he will never accept the Sai Baba question.

Speaking of "never," one day I said to Baba: "The Catholic Church will never accept You, just as they will never accept Your theories, or rather Your truths." I got this answer:

"In the fullness of time, God sent His Son. In the fullness of time, the Father began moving towards His children. There will be a particular fullness of time for each child, because it will not happen at the same moment and in the same way for everyone... I love you so much, dear daughter. God does not worry about how things will go, because in the end they will in any case go according to His Will."

Thinking about the imminent visit by the Mother Superior of our Province, and about the fact that she can go anywhere, I had the idea of hiding Baba's picture. Then I felt that I would be acting inconsistently with my faith, so I left it where it was, telling Baba not to get me into trouble. So the Mother Superior (who had certainly been informed about everything) said to me: "I went into your room, and I saw another Jesus Christ." I said: "You mean Sai Baba!" She answered: "Be careful, because many ideologies which define themselves as religious are considered sects. Sects cause you to lose your faith; if you care for your faith, I repeat, be careful."

April 19, 1990.
Dearest Sister W.,

I see that you know how to establish a dialogue with God in order to face the problems of daily life. This is the only way to overcome them. Don't lose heart when tests come: they serve to draw God's love ever more fully to us. It is too easy and comfortable to love Him when everything is going well. The greatness of a person's love shows when everything seems to be caving in on him, and he nevertheless remains true to his word. Don't worry if you can't talk to anyone about Sai Baba. First of all, confirm your faith in Christ, whose power of manifestation is unlimited. Resolve to love Him with all your heart and in all your actions. When you come to feel that it is not you who is living, but rather that He is living through you, you will attract many people to you. They will come not because it gratifies you, but because they need to understand. Perhaps this is what Jesus meant when He said: "When I am raised from the earth,

I will draw everyone to Me." To lose yourself in Him means to extinguish your ego, to merge your will with His, no longer to distinguish "I" from "you," to experience yourself only as "we."

The fact that you are irritated by your sister nuns shows you still have some way to go. Their provocations were commissioned by Him, in order to foster your spiritual evolution. This charming story will make it clearer to you:

After many austerities, a disciple decided that the moment had come to receive the last set of teachings from his master, the teachings given to the most evolved aspirants. But his teacher decided to test him before granting his wish. He told him to come to him only after washing himself very carefully in the river. The disciple did so. However the master arranged for someone to come by the moment his disciple came out of the river, and to dump a container of garbage on him. Infuriated, the disciple ran after the person and beat him up. The master let his student know that he was not yet ready for the new teachings, and that he would only be worthy of them after another three years of spiritual discipline.

After three years went by, the master asked his disciple again to come to him, after carefully washing himself. The same thing happened again. After the disciple's bath, the master's accomplice came by and emptied a pail of putrid filth on the wretch. The disciple erupted in curses and insults, but this time he kept his hands to himself. Two more years, said the master.

After those two long years, the disciple was told again to bathe in the river and come to the master. This time, when the bath was over, a basket of manure was emptied on him. The disciple finally absorbed the lesson: he controlled himself, and turning to the person who had discharged such an unpleasant task, said to him, "Thank you for having been the instrument of such a great lesson!"

At that point, and only then, he was ready to go to his master.

I had told you that it was not yet the time to speak to your confessor about Sai Baba. People who have not seriously investigated the subject are easily deceived by stereotypes and misconceptions. Why provoke such things? Is it not more important to live Baba's teaching, than to talk about it?

When the proper moment comes, it will be possible to talk about Baba's teaching openly. Do not scorch the earth around you: your sister nuns, your confessor, your Mother Superior. Maintain good relations with everyone. **Demonstrate** with your behavior that something has changed in you. Then that image on your dresser will become familiar to everyone by itself, and not because you wanted to impose it on them by getting angry or holding up your end of an argument. Speak with God constantly, as if you were talking to Jesus in person, Jesus in front of you in flesh and blood. Take walks with Him. Tell Him everything. You can even lose patience with Him for His reluctance to show Himself. Put all your problems at His feet, at those sacred Feet, which are fresh and perfumed like two flowers. Go read the last discourse, in issue 2/10 of Mother Sai,[1] called "The Best Friend." Fall in love with God, in whatever form you like to visualize Him. Abandon yourself to Him. When we have Him, we have everything. What else do we need?

April 1990.
Dearest Don Mario,

Some time ago, I was living my days in a state of confusion, and I could no longer see my way clearly on anything. I did not know where I was going, what I was looking for, who I was following. I felt like I had gone back to being the person I was before I knew about Sai Baba, with the same negative qualities I had then. One Thursday morning, I decided firmly to let Baba go and to retrace my steps. He doesn't help me. Why should I listen to Him? I sent Him away: "you can go now, and the sooner the better!"

After that, I started to pray, looking first at a picture of Jesus, and then, as usual, I addressed the Father. At the very thought of Him I was immersed, submerged in a sea of peace, serenity, Love. I prayed like this: "Daddy, please forgive me if I called someone 'daddy' who isn't, if I gave my heart to someone I shouldn't have; if I made a mistake, I am ready to undo it. I do not want to lose your Love, I want to believe in you, in Jesus and in Mary, His mother."

Then I went on to ask Him this question: "Tell me, Daddy, who is Sai Baba?" There was no answer except a sentence of Sai Baba's, which crossed the sky: "Do everything with love in your heart." I

---

[1]An Italian periodical containing Sai Baba's recent discourses. [Translator's note.]

paid it no mind: I had resolved to remain in prayer until He gave me a clear answer. I asked the same question to Jesus too, but it seemed as if He did not want to interfere in things that pertained to His Father. After a while, I gave up. I felt that I was squandering Love with that silly stubbornness, and I said to Him: "It doesn't matter if You don't want to tell me who He is; but allow me to remain in this adorable presence of Yours."

It was at that moment, when I no longer was expecting anything, that other thoughts crossed the sky: "I am He, Baba is I. Dear daughter, it is not easy for you to understand it, but it is really true."

Now I will tell you a dream I had. I was confessing my sins to Baba, in a strange way. I was holding a little book in my hands, and I was reading it aloud, while Baba listened. At the end of a page, Baba explained to me in His words the meaning of what I had read. Then I began to read again, as the dream dissolved. When I was awake, I could no longer remember anything of what I had read or what Baba had said, so my first reaction was: why do You allow me to dream about You if then I can't remember any of it? But then, thinking about it carefully, I remembered a detail which explained everything, that is, explained the "lesson" Baba wanted to teach me. During the dream I was preoccupied with asking Baba a question, and I was waiting for the right moment to ask it. The question was: Are You really God?

"As long as you worry, as long as you ask yourself these questions which should by now be obvious, you do not penetrate into the depth of My message, of My teachings, of My Love, but you remain just on the surface! As long as you have these misgivings in you, how will you be able to understand my discourses, even if I were to explain them to you through your inner senses?"

May 3, 1990.
Dearest Sister W.,

"Guru" is a Sanskrit word. It does not mean simply "teacher," but rather "he who dissipates the shadows of ignorance." A Guru never gives advice, he never lays down rules: he simply indicates the path. Sometimes we priests are the ones who need light the most, and when that is the case we certainly cannot presume to shed light for other people.

At the moment I too am grappling with the fundamental order I received from the Divine Teacher: practice what you preach. Therefore my building project is underway, and my construction site, like all construction sites, is in disarray, and will be until the building is completed.

In your case, you should treasure all the clear suggestions you receive in your innermost heart: that is where He speaks to you. You know very well it is not your mind talking, when the instructions you receive come in meditation. That is your true Guru! In fact Baba says to act according to your own conscience, because that is where He expresses His will.

If doubts about Sai Baba's physical manifestation cross your mind, invoke the Holy Spirit. Tell Him all your torment, the misunderstandings with your sister nuns, entrust yourself entirely to Him, without any reservations, without any conditions, without expectations. Abandon everything to Him, **no matter what happens**. In fact, in any circumstance, no matter what happens, even if it is an unpleasant incident, as long as you have the Holy Spirit, which is the Spirit of Truth, you will have lost nothing. If you place your trust in humans, you will end up with what they can give you, that is, nothing. Ask insistently for Him: with Him you will have everything, everything, absolutely everything!

Haven't you seen two lovers walking together? They pay no attention to the world that surrounds them. Even if the sky were to fall in, they would continue to look in each other's eyes and lose themselves in each other. When they say that love is blind, it does not mean only that passion is blinding; it also means that by offering yourself totally to another person you drown in him. That is what our love of God should be like. What reason could we have to fear or to worry, when we are certain of His Love? What else could we look for, when with Him we have received everything?

The dreams you have had are very reassuring. You know it: it was not your mind that dreamed, it was He who deigned to come to you. He has affirmed this a number of times. Dreams are His ordinary way of reaching all the devotees of God. In His efficiency, this way of being in many places at once is more convenient, and less wasteful of precious energies... It does not matter if you do not remember these dreams: the instructions that were given were impressed upon your astral body, and will never leave it. In fact sometimes it is necessary that the conscious mind **not** see them, because it would mar them with all its silly rationalizations, like the elaborate mental investigations you still conduct on Sai Baba's physical manifestation. His teaching is a divine mine: the more you dig, the more diamonds you find. It is inexhaustible, and it has stratifications that correspond to every level of our consciousness. That is why His discourses are always new, and we seem to forget them even after we have read them ten times. Every time we read them, His Word digs deeper, and reveals a new layer.

So let your project at the moment be to understand ever more deeply the spiritual discourses that come your way. Do not forget that if you have these opportunities, it is He who is bestowing them on you. Be grateful to Him for this. Sometimes I think how many obstacles you could have in receiving that Word! Do not waste this opportunity. Great opportunities are never repeated. Read and re-read those teachings, and make yourself a little program, a simple one, not an ambitious one, for putting them into practice. In essence, His word is quite simple, even though very challenging: do not waste time, do not waste food, do not waste money, do not waste energy, do not waste knowledge. If we began just with these things, it would be more than enough.

We live for His Love, with His Love, in His Love. Let us never forget it, not even for a minute in a day. Let us ask His forgiveness when we allow ourselves to be distracted by worldly concerns. Let us say to Him: my soul is Yours. What can I give You, if everything is Yours? I'd like to hear from you if you know of anything that we can give Him that is not already His. Let me know.

With Him life is splendid, an infinite joy. Sometimes our body cannot bear the intensity of this light...

In the Bliss of Sai, in the Light of Christ, and in Their divine Friendship, I bless you.

July, 1990.
Dearest Don Mario,

Your letter reached me in a period of non-love, so it is hard for me to know what I can give to God that is not already His: sin, bad qualities. The latter are, as Baba says, the first things we should surrender to God. I too am convinced that everything is His, and that in the end the powers of evil will be transformed into good. I do not think however that this means we should say that sin, evil, bad qualities are already His: they will be once they are transformed. You might answer that God is the Eternal Present, and because of this He already possesses the ultimate and final reality. If that is true, then even my sin is His, and so I have nothing to give Him. I have come from Him in purity, and in purity I must return to Him. But does having come from God at one time imply having had a beginning? Have we not rather always existed in God, so that we are always eternal as He is? I think it is wrong to say we have come from God: we probably have never left Him. We have simply taken on a certain mode of life and of relation with Him. However, we distance ourselves from God, or draw closer to Him, through our free will. But even this idea seems incorrect to me. As if I could distance myself from myself! So how could I possibly move farther or closer to God if I am God?! I think I understand that only one Reality exists: God, and only one Soul, His. That explains why I am others, and others are me, and why all together we are God, we are one thing.

This sheds light on something that bothered me every time I thought about it: the fact that Baba is, as they say in India, the reincarnation of Sai Baba of Shirdi. Just in these days, between one ocean-wave and the next, I was asking myself: if Baba is God, He has His own Soul. So if He is the reincarnation of Shirdi Sai Baba, as He says, then where did Shirdi Sai Baba's soul go? Sai Baba of Shirdi is someone like us, and like us he went through his cycle of rebirths. With his last physical death he was ready to merge with God, that is his soul was ready to fuse into God's. By reincarnating in Baba, the soul of Shirdi Sai Baba is gone, and has become that of God, or at least of both joined together. I asked Baba why He did not incarnate in a body directly, "from scratch." I think the answer was that all creation came into being at once, including man. The births there are now, and those there will be tomorrow and after tomorrow, are all re-births. When in my depression I was telling you that we are all a fixed number of persons, always the same ones, constantly reincarnating, I really think that's how it is. A fixed number of persons, or rather of souls, some of which are in a physical body, some in an astral body, some in a causal body, without counting the ones who have permanently reached Beatitude...

An experience I had in these days: who can describe the sublimity of what he has experienced in prayer? I found myself in the presence, on the conscious level, of the Formless God. He told me that God goes way beyond the form of Jesus or of Baba. Nevertheless, He told me that since I wish to love Him in a precise form, I should love Him and see Him in the form He has taken at the present time, that is Baba's. Concerning Jesus, He told me that Jesus will be the Teacher, the Model I must follow. My life must conform to His, must be a copy of the Most Lovable Redeemer. There is always only one Lord and only one faith.

Just when I thought that Baba had answered the fundamental question, the catastrophe occurred. Yesterday, a day which commemorated the ascension of Jesus, during my morning prayers, I heard these terrible words, "Baba is a serpent, an incarnate snake." I cried as I have never cried in my life, saying that it was not true, it was not possible.

This morning, after praying futilely to Baba, and also to a priest who died recently in an aura of sainthood, I withdrew alone on a little hill... I felt rather happy because Baba had expressed the desire to come with me. I was alone, and everything was very beautiful. I was looking at the flowers, and eating the cherries I could reach. It seemed as if Baba were saying: Taste Me and admire Me in each thing. Meanwhile I was still reprimanding Him for yesterday's experience; at least I was asking Him for an explanation. At a certain moment, my attention fixed, horrified, on a reptile, a long black snake which was a few steps above me. I immediately thought that if it was poisonous, I would have no possibility of escape. So panic-stricken, I yelled, "Baba, no!" The snake changed direction and disappeared in the grass.

I am tormented by two thoughts, because I doubt that this event was a coincidence. Either the priest wanted to confirm that Baba is indeed a serpent, or else Baba wanted to tell me that He will protect me in any difficulty, however painful or frightening...

Dear Don Mario, could you give me an explanation?... I am waiting for Baba to show me the road I have to take. In these days I wrote to Him, telling Him that I cannot go on any longer with these doubts and uncertainties, and without being able to reconcile His physical form with that of Jesus - and by Jesus I mean my entire life as a believer and as a nun...

June 5, 1990.
Dear Sister W.,

In your long and heartfelt letter I did not find a single point which was contrary to love. I don't think it is possible for you ever to be in a moment of "non-love." How can honey be bitter? Human beings are nothing but Consciousness-Being-Bliss; we are nothing but Love. The only thing that can change is our sense of taste, which varies according to our health and what we have eaten before...

You gave a good answer to my question: we really cannot offer Him anything which is not already His. Nonetheless, our weaknesses are not His in the sense that He prompted them, but in the sense that it is up to Him to destroy them. Give Him room to conduct this therapy. Perhaps your current painful state, this current test, is the beginning of the cure. Kill the desire to find an explanation for everything. We cannot understand Him! We can only attempt to imitate Him. When we have reached Him completely, when our hearts have fused completely with His, everything will be clear to us; His plan will no longer be so mysterious. Now "we see Him as in a mirror, but then - in Samadhi - we shall see Him face to face."

What you say is very beautiful, that God takes what is His, a sanctified body...

Your karma, that is the heredity of actions and effects you have accumulated, and which no one can escape, compels you to live among blind people. Accept it with the right attitude, resigned, but full of hope and certainty that the blind will see, thanks also to your sweetness, the breath of your love, your patience. Sick people are often nervous, impatient, and aggressive. You, who have seen, and who can no longer "not see," you lead the blind by the hand along the road of tolerance and goodness. Excuse all their aggressiveness, and have compassion for them, as you do for a blind man who gets mad because you helped him cross the street. That intense love will destroy the apathy which surrounds you, and it will protect you as a case protects jewels.

Sometimes, instead of the Divine Voice, your brain picks up the stray voices of the negative thoughts which surround you. If you do not repeat the Name of God, if you do not meditate, if you do not pray from the heart, that case can break, and anything can invade your inner sanctuary. Even the phrase "... he is a serpent."

Baba has an infinite and fathomless love. At the moment when you thought He was a snake, He wanted to give you darshan in that form, and He went away only because of your foolish fear. Besides, the snake you describe is poisonless, harmless, and contributes great good to nature by maintaining the equilibrium of insects and harmful small animals. Baba has asserted, "All forms are Mine." It is extraordinary that you should have come upon Him right at that moment, in that form, as if to tell you: "If you believe I am a serpent, then I will show Myself to you in the form you expect." Reflect on this: don't you feel fortunate?

What other proofs of God's love do you want? Why always make demands on Him who has already given all? All we can do is to surrender ourselves, and to leave our heart with Him, just as it is. If it is bleeding, He will heal it, if it is swollen with tears, He will draw them out and flavor them with love, if it is crippled, He will rehabilitate it, if it is stony, He will replace it with one of flesh.

Do not reinforce the passing clouds of turmoil, of anxiety, of ups and downs. Stabilize yourself by reading His discourses, by re-reading the Gospels, but above all by putting into practice even a speck of what you read. Begin slowly, little by little, proceed safely, and you will arrive at the goal healthy and sound. Accept your loneliness in this inquiry: the moment you accept it, it will no longer pain you. He who perseveres to the end will be safe!

Dear Mother...

An Open Letter to the Catholic Church

My dear Mother,

I have been wanting to write to you for a long time, but I did not know how to go about it. You always seem so busy. Since you take on the problems of the whole world, you end up not having the time or capacity to listen to a small voice like mine.

I write these lines to tell you that I am still very fond of you, even though sometimes I feel that you are preoccupied with other things. I would have wanted to feel your presence when I went through difficult moments. Instead, it was precisely in those moments that I felt abandoned by you. There are saints in your ranks, but sometimes, the actions of those who do not serve you with selflessness and self-sacrifice stand out even more. I am certain that this was nothing but human error, or maybe one of your profound lessons, so that I might learn to live without external supports.

Unfortunately, many people hurl harsh criticisms at you, not realizing that you are simply the distillation of their own tendencies. The cheese-curds will be good only if the milk is good; they will be salty if made from goat milk, sweet and rich if made from buffalo milk... Those who criticize you harshly do not realize that they are condemning themselves.

I often have my hands full trying to defend you against those who are most angry at you, those who see you as "stepmother," those who can remember only the most unpleasant events in their lives. Some received some wrong from some priest or nun while they were at boarding-school, and based on that they condemn you unconditionally, and reject everything you do, even when it is full of wisdom. Many people have not understood your teaching-methods, and they see your teachings as a trick, as if you wanted to hide the truth in order to make people believe things that are to your advantage.

Many men and women, whom you washed with your water of baptism while they were still in diapers, now have rebelled against your care, deeming it at best obsolete. Often they accuse you of trying to enslave people, as if your care was a plot designed to subjugate their individual conscience to your will.

Thus they have lost faith in the doctrine you teach, and seeing your dogma as a mere imposition, they have shaken it off their backs. In the past, to be honest, you did occasionally give in to an impulse to dominate others; but these people have not understood that all you are doing by affirming those axioms so strongly is firmly pointing out a road that does not lose its veracity even after millennia.

Dear Mother, I would like you not to become resentful if I tell you these things. Do not bristle. These voices do not normally reach you, in the high walls of your palaces. It is easier for those of us who live on the street to hear them. Do not delude yourself, Mother. For the millions of people who acclaim you, there are as many millions who demand greater clarity from you, and who would like you to shed some light on many questions. I am certain that if you were to change your attitude, and give up trying to be a domineering mother who wants to be always right and never admits a mistake, you would draw into your fold all those children who have wandered away from you in search of other shores, where they can find compassion and not condemnation.

In this letter of mine, I would like to lay before you what I consider to be the fundamental causes of this decline in your prestige, among both Catholics and non-Catholics. I merely hope that this might be of some use to you. Consider me like a son of yours, who wants to see you always young, and spotting a wrinkle or a grey hair, wants to give you a cosmetic hint so you can improve your look.

One of the reasons you draw hostility on yourself is because of your tendency to lord it over others. I know. You are extremely beautiful: you have a history, a tradition, you have given birth to great saints, you have raised up many people from wretched poverty, you have given refuge to orphans, and beds to the sick, you possess magnificent temples, which are the expression of the combined devotion of the humble and the mighty. You have swayed important men in governments, and have reached the top of the world. But if you want to be the Mother of the whole world, accept all creatures as if they were yours, and do not give too much weight to differences in forms and politics. If you wish to be alone and unrivalled, give up being a prima donna: then everyone will love you for your simplicity and humility, and they will recognize that they are your children. Do not get lost in marginal questions of morality, because ethics vary from nation to nation. Focus on the substance, which is what every man and every nation has been seeking for millennia. In the Truth of Love, all men will recognize their brotherhood. Only there is there Peace.

You want a single flock under a single shepherd. Well then, expand the scope of these metaphors. Think of the flock of the world, with all its faiths, its religions; think of the Good Shepherd who reigns alone over all men. He does not concern Himself with intrigues and political tangles: He goes to the house of the poor and of those who seek Him and thirst for truth. As you know, this was the Flock Christ was aiming for: do not let your workers confuse this Flock with the object of their own greed and desires.

Do not worry if everyone likes to maintain their own rites, their own forms. There is no reason for you to be discouraged just because among 6 billion human beings, 5 billion believe in their own divinities and have their own exotic ceremonies. They are not different Gods, and those who worship them are not pagans, I can assure you. Those divinities are simply exterior forms, disguises of the same God whose love is so inexhaustible that He constantly comes up with new ways, new tricks up His sleeve, in order to relieve the human condition, which is so often sad and painful.

Dearest mother, embrace all, without barring anyone and without any hidden conditions, and do not be afraid to kneel in front of the divine "forms" worshipped by others. They too are perfect, just like the one you adore, and behind their masks, there is the one, highest, ineffable God that you, in your mother's zeal, would like to inculcate in all nations. If you admit that it is not the form that should be worshipped, but rather the Essence enclosed in it, it will be clear to you that there is no reason for division among these 6 billion people, and you will not hesitate even to pray in front of a statue of Ganesha or in a pagoda.

Most adorable Mother, believe me, one form has the same worth as another. And this is true above all in the realm of intellect. How many useless arguments and controversies there have been, simply to say the same thing in different words! Moreover, when the Lord assigned you the task of spreading His message, He did not prohibit you from thinking that He would come again. "If of old He had already spoken many times and in different ways to the fathers," why should He suddenly have gotten tired of bestowing His Word on us? In fact, He even forewarned you that He would come again, but He did not reveal to you the form in which He would appear. I beseech you, Mother, do not commit the same error that a sister of yours made about two thousand years ago, who thought that all revelation was finished with Abraham, Moses, and the Prophets. God never tires of running after us, because His love is inexhaustible, and He is always ready to do what He did through Jesus, as He had done it before and... as He is doing it again today!

O Mother, you don't know how I dream of some day being at your side, accompanying you on a magic journey to discover a living Treasure: He whom you have presented to millions of human beings, and who has come again, playing a different part, to reveal all the Love of the Father... Come, dearest mother, do not be stubborn, don't say "Quiet, you!" to your child, who is pointing out to you a true Fortune, one that is not even far from home. Do not pretend to scorn that Treasure, for fear of losing your age-old dignity. You cannot even imagine the welcome that is waiting for you in that sacred Abode, where that Treasure glows. I assure you that you will receive honors that in two thousand years you have never enjoyed from any nation of the earth.

The Lord of that Abode has been waiting for you for millennia. Don't be afraid, Mother, He does not want to de-throne you. Not at all. He definitely does not want to do that. He is waiting for you only so that He can crown you personally. On that day He will give a great feast to celebrate your meeting with Him, and even the angels in heaven will exult. The whole world in unison will vibrate with the primordial prayer, Amen, and hymns will be sung to celebrate the triumph of the Christ!

There is also another reason that many people distance themselves from you, and that is the type of truths you teach and how you go about teaching them. Societies change, your children have grown up. You mothers always have the tendency to see your children as toddlers, even when they have reached 30, have a family, and children of their own! We have grown older, over the last two thousand years. We no longer want the same food you gave us as babies. We have reached the age where we want to personally examine and understand the truths you taught us when we were small.

At that time, in order to keep us in line, you presented us with a God who was severe and quick to punish. That depiction no longer fulfills our needs. We want to study, to investigate this Reality which is so simple and at the same time so complex, and we want to do it without the constant terror of being declared heretics, or of being thrown out of the house just because on some point we agreed with some friend. What children appreciate most in their parents is the freedom to conduct their own investigations. If then, in that same spirit of freedom, the parents too join in the child's inquiries, his respect for them reaches the stars.

Dear Mother, what I would like to see in you is precisely this: let your children search where they want. If the efforts are prompted by sincerity and honesty, the results will be excellent, and the seekers will return to you with a renewed and everlasting affection. Don't be frightened by our theories, don't cry scandal if someone tells you that Jesus lived and "died again" in Kashmir, or that we are re-born as many times as it takes to return to the House of the Father. Let us search... or are you trying to hide something from us? You consider us still young and immature? The most precious thing in all this is that there are still some people in the world who want to search through God's archives. You should be proud to have such courageous and enterprising children. These are precisely the children who should be dearest to you.

You cannot deny that in the course of so many centuries you too have occasionally had to change course, and that you have occasionally gotten a little cramped up on certain theological and scientific questions... But you are always our dear mother, even when you hit a few bad notes while playing your music. Actually, that makes you even dearer to us: it makes you seem closer to us, more ours, less haughty. And, as long as you don't try to deny your mistakes, we smile at them, and are willing to forgive you instantly.

Another reason people are unhappy with you is that you suddenly change your forms and your content. We were all anxious for an overall renewal, a kind of revision that would touch both the "dress" and the "heart" of your existence. Instead, the sudden elimination of our customary rituals not only disoriented us, but above all, it greatly diminished your credibility. I know very well that you were trying to adapt your disciplines to modern man, because you saw that in practice almost all your children ignored them. But Mother, permit me to observe that it would have been better to keep the standards high, in order to raise the general level of conscience. It is better to have three good sheep in the flock, than a hundred who are lazy and spoiled. The highest peak grabs the attention of the good climber, while only the lazy climb little hills.

Let me explain what I mean with a few practical examples, touching on only a few points, out of many. The fast required for taking Communion at Mass used to be rigid: not even a drop of water after the midnight preceding the Mass. Now we are allowed to eat a normal meal, including alcoholic beverages, up to an hour before Communion...

Previously, meat was not allowed on any of the 52 Fridays of the year; this has been reduced to only the 5 Fridays of Lent. Moreover, by changing the rule, nothing has been gained, because from what I can observe most Catholics eat meat during Lent too. In fact the supermarkets have sales on all types of meat just at that time. All this in an age when even doctors recognize the benefits of a vegetarian diet!

The powerful and moving "High Mass," which used to set Sunday apart as the Day of the Lord, was rich with Gregorian chant sung by the whole congregation. It has been replaced by a drab mass, celebrated with one eye on the clock, and with music that is generally uninspired. The High Mass used to fill the church with incense. That perfume not only fostered transcendent states in the faithful, but for the whole week following it left a trace of that solemn ritual.

Mother, I can imagine what you are thinking now. You think that I am like a follower of Lefevre,[1] nostalgic for the old ways. No, Mother. If you really want to know, I do not like rituals all that much, but I do believe that for many people they are a useful instrument, which help people to grow, and help them to approach the Incomprehensible.

I once came upon a book by a certain Leadbeater, a bishop of extraordinary sensitivity in a church that is a cousin of yours, the Liberal Church. In the book, called "The Sacraments," this high prelate describes things he has "seen" during the celebrations of the Mass. His experience is something really extraordinary. You cannot imagine what happens, on a subtle level, in a church while a High Mass is being celebrated. If you could "see" the energies that develop at that time, and how everything, even the smallest gesture, the simplest vestment, has an extremely profound esoteric significance, and a great charismatic power, you would have already issued a proclamation to revive the ancient way of celebrating the sacraments. I would only like to tell you that after reading that book, I experienced again the old passion of the sung Mass; but now we can only mourn the loss of a language we have forgotten.

In any case, these are simply a few matters which touch only the skin of religion, that is, the rituals and disciplines it promotes to help man reach the Divine. What should we say, on the other hand, about all the points that concern the doctrinal aspect? For many of the truths you present to us, such as Paradise, Hell, Purgatory, Limbo, the Resurrection of the flesh, the Ascension of Jesus, the existence of God, etc..., you no longer give us any plausible explanation. In catechism classes, these subjects are taboo. The children are told stories about various biblical episodes, which they act out in skits, but none of it is put together into a system, as the saintly Pius X had done. It is obvious that simply memorizing formulas is of no use. Instead, for example, a definition like "God is in heaven, on earth, and in every place," can generate an infinite series of lessons, which can range from cosmology to nuclear physics, and eventually reach theology.

An entire year of catechism instruction could be based on studying and explaining the *Works of Bodily and Spiritual Charity*. In any case,

---

[1]Lefevre resisted the changes of Vatican II and defended the traditional liturgy.

it wouldn't be a bad idea to change the stilted Victorian language, and call the book *Selfless Service of the Physical and Spiritual Needs of Others.*

In short, Mother, if you want me to say it straight out, I have found, among your so-called faithful, a shameful and crass ignorance of your teachings. When I cite even the most famous passages in the Gospel, I see blank faces, as if I were speaking of some recently-discovered scroll. I feel ashamed of this ignorance every time I meet a Hindu or Buddhist: with them I can always have conversations at a high theological level, even when the people seem anything but religious. Indeed I have met people who call themselves "atheists" or "non-observant," but who are thirsty for God, and attentive to anything spiritual. Others give up their own comforts in order to dedicate all their time and energy to helping the weak and downtrodden, seeing them as God.

A few days ago, I was on a plane headed for India. Next to me there was a young man who was paralyzed with fear. He was pale, in a cold sweat. On my right there was an Indian. He was obviously wealthy, and was wearing a lot of gold. He was a jeweler. He was talking to me about money, his career, the pleasures of life. Then, noticing the psychic and physical condition of the young man on my left, he asked me: "What's wrong with your friend?" I told him, "He is suffering, because he is terrified of flying." Hearing this the Indian broke into a hearty laugh; then he leaned over to speak to the young man. Still suppressing his laughter, he said to him: "You are afraid to die? Your life does not belong to you, it belongs to God. Why are you afraid of losing something that is not yours? Let Him care for what is His!" Descending into the midst of all his previous worldly chatter, those sentences seemed like a diamond among so much gravel. They made me correct the judgement I had formed on my wise travel-companion.

Mother, this is how I would like your men to be. I would like to hear them speak of God, without false piety, and yet without becoming disembodied essences who have no practical sense. They should be in the world, not of the world, with their minds always in God. In order to bring this about, you should, in my opinion, do something which might make you unpopular, and which might cost you a couple of influential friends: you should put all your emphasis on spiritual values, undervaluing material and worldly concerns. And you should begin by setting the example.

You are often preoccupied with trying to solve certain urgent problems, like abortion, divorce, drug abuse, and many other evils that afflict the modern world. But these are nothing but the symptoms of maladies that are rooted deeper, in a lack of religious and spiritual education. Right conduct arises spontaneously in anyone who has a deeply-rooted faith in God. If men have no idea why they need to obey moral laws, they will have no conviction, and even their good behavior will not last long. In order to reach the goal, man must regain his self-confidence, he must stop considering himself worthless, a sinner, a poor wretch. He must realize that he is the son and co-heir of the Father Himself, and capable of attaining the same goals that Christ set by His example. Men are behaving like devils, because deep inside they are convinced that that is what they are.

Mother, it is time for me to end this long letter. I would have many other things to say to you, but I prefer to limit myself to the points I have set out. I am sure you will be understanding, and I am confident that you will not misinterpret this book. Indeed it is because of the love I feel for you that I have dedicated it to you.

"If you yearn for Peace, respect each person's conscience." When I heard that your Pope uttered these wise and consoling words, as the theme for the new year 1991, I felt that the time was ripe for me to speak.

No one among us knows how much time he has to accomplish the mission for which he has come into the world. No matter how much time I have left, I wanted to finish this book as if it were the last project of my life, as if it were my testament. There was no longer enough space in my heart to hold such a secret; I had to confide this Love to you and share It with you. I should like the contents of this book to help shed light on the journey toward the Divine. I could say with Lactantius, *Quo perfecto satis me vixisse arbitrabor, et officium hominis implesse, si labor meus aliquos homines ad erroribus liberans, ad iter caelestis direxerit*: having accomplished the goal of indicating a heavenly path to others, I feel that I have put my life to good use.

That Love has no limits: it is so over-abundant that no one need fear not having enough of it. Let no one try to monopolize that Mine, because our hands and hearts are too small to fully appreciate its Treasure, which flows out in such copious quantities, a limitless bounty.

Dear Mother, know that
I believe in you, knowing that you are
one, because when you love Peace you do not wish to divide;
holy, because when you preach Love, you are with God,
catholic, because when you are righteous, you are understood by all;
apostolic, because if you know Truth, you cannot conceal it, but you spread it to the four winds, without however expecting any reward from your efforts.

With all the love of a son, I tenderly embrace you,

always yours,
don Mario

My Beloved is fresh and ruddy,
to be known among ten thousand.
His head is golden, purest gold,
his locks are palm fronds
and black as the raven.
His eyes are doves
at a pool of water,
bathed in milk,
at rest on a pool.
His cheeks are beds of spices,
banks sweetly scented.
His lips are lilies,
distilling pure myrrh.
His hands are golden, rounded,
set with jewels of Tarshish.
His belly a block of ivory
covered with sapphires.
His legs are alabaster columns
set in sockets of pure gold.
His appearance is that of Lebanon,
unrivaled as the cedars.
His conversation is sweetness itself,
he is altogether lovable.
Such is my Beloved, such is my friend,
O daughters of Jerusalem.

Song of Songs, 5.10-16.

Farewell, Mother!

The History of an Excommunication

One certainly did not have to be a seer to predict that when this book was published, there would be a reaction on the part of the church hierarchy. The author's aim was in fact to awaken some interest, of whatever kind, in a great Voice from the East, which is announcing a time of redemption for our ailing human race. To tell the truth, I did not imagine that the Church would have recourse to such anachronistic measures. Those measures led me to wonder seriously (in other words, it was not pure fantasy) what my reaction would be if, instead of an excommunication delivered by registered express mail, guards had come to my door, with orders to burn me at the stake in the public square...

A few days ago I saw again a very beautiful, but rather bitter film by Lilian Cavani, called "Galileo." I tried to put myself in the place of Giordano Bruno, when he was condemned and burned alive. The chilling screams of that monk, enveloped in flames, moved me deeply. I was asking myself: would you too be capable of facing the stake? The fear of losing one's body is instinctive, and I trembled at the very thought that I might give in, if even only mentally. But I also reflected: a fire kills you in a few minutes - terrible minutes, but brief. What would happen to me, on the other hand, if to escape being burned by those flames, I consumed myself in the fire of betraying the Truth? That would indeed be the most disgraceful death sentence: no remedy, not even Time, could ever lessen it or even ease its pain.

The Italian press gave a lot of attention to the fact that I was excommunicated. Some journalists showed that they understood what happened; others, with the usual superficiality, confused the issue by mixing up the Divine with the so-called Indian "gurus." Obviously from the Catholic press there was a unanimous condemnation, and an encouragement to morally lynch the sinner.

The Vatican was careful to avoid giving me a regular trial. I had dealings with only Cardinal Camillo Ruini, the Vicar of the Diocese of Rome. Cardinal Ratzinger, the head of the Holy Congregation for the Doctrine of Faith, the only body with the qualifications to judge my case, was evidently not even consulted. Of course the Pope, who I know is inflexibly reluctant to allow anyone to leave the priesthood, was not even asked. The sentence which declared me to be a "heretic," and the subsequent condemnation, were issued with surprising rapidity, as the facts I am about to narrate attest. No legal defense was allowed, or even suggested, for the "defendant" (who in Canon Law is termed *delinquens*, that is, a "delinquent" or "culprit"). I still do not understand why it was decided to avoid a legal procedure, though a judge in an ecclesiastical court told me that this way I was spared many humiliations and psychological pressures.

I have decided therefore to do as my editor suggested: to give an account of the events that occurred, for three reasons: 1) to give the public - whether Catholic or not, it does not matter - an opportunity to judge the matter; 2) because I have available all the communications and authentic documents which concern the case; 3) because I think it is always better to hear the news "first hand." The newspapers always have some vested interest: they have to please whoever keeps them in business. The present writer, on the other hand, no longer has anything to lose. His intention is to bequeath to history a brief documentation of the case, without any literary embellishments or personal judgements, so that the reader can judge with complete liberty, without having to give up his own opinions. Above all I do not wish to condition the reader's response with this account, and that is the reason that I have wanted it to appear at the end of the book, as an afterword.

Although the Church has excommunicated me, I continue to love Her as my Mother, even without the return love that any son, no matter how degenerate, should be able to expect from his mother. However in entrusting to the reader, and to posterity, the circumstances of how I was excommunicated, I must state my conviction that every human judgement is empty. The only judgement that I love with awe and respect is God's. I know that I have acted in His presence with a pure conscience, and that everything that I have written and said flowed from a great love for Truth. Even this afterword is an opportunity for me to shed light on a truth, a more contingent, not absolute, truth, one rarely touched on by journalistic accounts. I am also happy to offer this account to America first,[1] because I know it is a free country, where there is respect for the freedom of opinion and freedom of the press, and where the people are not subject to a caste of priests.

When the Pontifex of the Roman Church rehabilitated Galileo a few months ago, and apologized to scientists for the errors of the past, I thought about all the documents, all the trial-transcripts, all the condemnations that were issued against that eminent astronomer. I was musing: who knows when the world will ever see first-hand what was actually written and said, not only about Galileo, but also about all the other people who ended up burned or tortured or exiled? Thinking about this, I decided it was proper to write some historical notes about my case, so that anyone interested can know what actually happened. Besides, too many people, Catholics among them, do not know how the mechanism of the Church-organization works, and resign themselves to masking their ignorance with a facade of propriety.

I declare that what follows, concerning the events surrounding my excommunication, is the whole truth and nothing but the truth. As for the interviews I had with various prelates, who were then my superiors, I took care to transcribe them immediately after the meetings, so that the accounts would be as accurate as possible. The letters are obviously both in my possession and in the archives of the Vatican. On the prompting of church authorities, excerpts from them were used also by the press in spreading the news of my excommunication. Those authorities were so concerned with spreading the news that after four months they spread it again, as if it was brand-new, through all the national press, and even in Switzerland. I think it would be ingenuous to imagine that this happened unintentionally through some office-worker's mistake.

Now then, I will describe what happened.

---

[1]This *Afterword* was not included in the Italian edition and appears here for the first time in the English translation. (Editor's note.)

During the months when my first book came out - in September-October of 1991 - the episcopal see of Bergamo was virtually vacant. The Ordinary of the diocese was resigning: he was seriously ill, and had reached the age of retirement. Some time before, I had tried to contact that bishop, Monsignor Giulio Oggioni, and even wrote him a letter, but I never received an answer.

His place was taken by the current bishop, Monsignor Roberto Amadei. He had been my professor of Church history when I was studying theology (1965-1969). I thought it was appropriate to go and pay my respects, thus taking the opportunity to start a dialogue which I had never been able to have since 1978. Before going I received a telephone call, in which I was informed that the new bishop would like to meet me. Even though I suspected that that call might be a prelude to disciplinary action, I was happy that the invitation reflected my own desire for a meeting.

I made an appointment with the secretary, and I waited anxiously for the day to come: March 16, 1992.

He greeted me cordially and asked me to sit down. After a few initial pleasantries, he spoke to me about the book. (I will abbreviate Bishop as B and my own answers or interjections as M.)

B - They have telephoned me from Rome to tell me about this book of yours. You uphold some ideas which are not in line with those of the Church. For example, the Christ, for us, is Jesus Christ, and there cannot be anyone else. You make a distinction between Jesus and the Christ.
M - Yes, but I mean to say that there is a difference between the human and the divine nature of Jesus Christ: the first is the container, the other is the content; the first is illusory, the second is real.
B - This is precisely the point of real divergence between what you say and the official doctrine of the Church, the Magisterium. I cannot agree with your opinion. You end up putting Christ and Baba on the same plane!
M - Not exactly in those terms, but I understand that it would be easy to interpret it that way. I know that it is difficult to explain it, especially with centuries of interpretations behind us, but, Monsignor, who can deny God permission to take whatever form He wishes whenever He wishes?

B - Mario, God cannot contradict Himself. If He has revealed to us that He has come as savior only in Jesus Christ, He cannot break His word.

The conversation continued a long time on this theme. We touched upon various subjects, such as the Only-Begotten, the Truth which - according to the bishop - "was revealed *in toto* and once and for all, by Christ, etc... Nor did Jesus disappear as man: he is as eternal as the Christ, to the point that the two go together." I looked at him, puzzled; then I asked him:

M - Are you maintaining that the body of Jesus still exists? But where, Monsignor?

B - For example, in the Eucharist.

M - Tell that to any child, and he will tell you that he sees nothing but a piece of bread. I ask you please to tell me where the true body of Jesus, in flesh and blood, could be hidden or manifest.

B - See, Mario, here too you are not in agreement with the Church...

M - But why, Monsignor? Has the Church never made mistakes in its thought?

B - Let's not get into that; it is beside the point.

M - Why do we have to come to a point where I am told, "Let's not get into that"? (it wasn't the first time that phrase had come up). Monsignor, permit me to ask you a provocative question. Our Scriptures tell us that the Christ will come again. How will we recognize Him?

B - (after a moment of hesitation and confusion) That will happen at the end of history, when humanity will have finished its existence.

M - Even the astronomers say that this Universe is unbelievably vast and in continuous expansion; do you really believe that only the history of our tiny human race is marked by a single, definitive close?

B - There are no other worlds. Therefore, that is how it is.

M - There is no need to posit the existence of other worlds... Besides, if humanity ends for good all at once, what would be the purpose of Christ returning in the flesh, in all His glory? To show Himself to whom?

I was starting to get passionate in these discussions. The tone was familiar, given our previous teacher-student relationship, but I was

also aware that I was getting into some mine-fields. I saw him as a
retired professor of history, and he saw me, I think, as a student. I
returned to the battle-zone once again, but my questions were aimed
at asking him to be understanding about my spiritual search.

M - There is no possibility of ever revising any opinion, which
necessarily depends on the human intellect? Those positions can
never contain errors?

B - But of course not, Mario! Otherwise we would negate the
principle of contradiction...

M - The principle of contradiction...! I realize that for you I am a
heretic.

I used that word, "heretic," almost positive that my interlocutor
would, as an historian, feel how anachronistic it was. I thought that
would soften the discussion, that he would say something dismissive
about past events that are now gone for good. Instead, the Bishop
remained silent, he lowered his head, he did not say a word.

I smiled at him, and said:

M - So now, what will you do with me?

B - I have no idea.

A long silence froze the room. Then, I tried again on another tack:

M - There is to be no consideration for the theologians whom I quote
in the book, who support the same ideas I do? The Church is always
made of men, and it has always made use of the thought of
theologians and renunciates.

B - The Church is good, and not at all a "prima donna" as you assert
in the letter of your book, because it is Jesus Christ who guides her...
In order to know God, nothing is necessary except the official
teaching of the Church, which gives us the correct explanation of the
sacred Scriptures. Theologians do not supply official teaching (sic!).

M - And yet, all of our theology is enriched by theologians, for
example, by the thought of St. Thomas, whom I cite a number of
times in the book.

B - St. Thomas does not constitute the Magisterium, the Official
Teaching!

M - Then why do you make us study him so much in the seminary,
why do you give him so much importance, almost as much as the

Bible? Are you perhaps implying that one can reach God only through the Teaching of the Catholic Church?

B - Exactly! There is no salvation outside the Church!

My spirits fell.

Here I have transcribed only a few fundamental points of the conversation. The bishop touched on a number of other themes, in the effort to convince me that I was wrong. It was not really an interrogation; rather he was sounding me out to see if I really thought as I wrote; and it became evident that indeed I did. My position seemed irredeemable, and all vestige of hope was lost when he subtly suggested that I change my mind, and I assured him that I would never, never at any time, betray what I felt and continue to feel in my conscience.

Every once in a while my interlocutor would take the book and pick out some critical phrase in order to comment on it and contest it, then he would put it back down with the cover facing down. He had entrenched himself in a doctrinal position. Sometimes he would listen to my words, but I would realize then that he was simply using my own words to show me that I was in error.

Nevertheless, he did not have an inquisitorial attitude. Listening to me, he was even gentle, and he corrected me without rancor. At least that is how I saw it. It was as if he was constantly repeating, and he even did say it, with the air of someone taking note of an incontestable fact, "You are wrong, given that we are right."

Most of the time I had no opportunity to give adequate answers, or to take the time to supply subtle explanations: you cannot do that chatting in a living room. Obviously, any speech I made to defend the truths set out in the book was soon dismissed as superfluous. I did not neglect to speak to him about Sai Baba, about His message, and about the great transformation that He brings about in the human heart.

M - I would like to tell you (and I meant it in the plural) one last thing, before we end this conversation - this conversation which demonstrates how what divides is always how the truth is interpreted, not the Truth itself, which is pure. Why don't you take into consideration the fact that many people who have gone to Sai Baba have felt an impulse to renew their own Catholic religious faith, which is what Sai Baba himself suggests?

B - I will make a comparison which, of course, is perhaps inappropriate for your position: even an assassin can be the instrument of salvation for someone. This does not make him any less an assassin.

M - To be honest, your example seems to me ill-chosen...

Recognizing the impertinence of what he had said, the Bishop apologized for the example, but then reaffirmed it a number of times in the same terms.

At the end, he graciously offered me a coffee, which I courteously refused; he asked me for my telephone number, and then he accompanied me politely to the door. At the door, as I was about to leave, he looked me in the eyes intensely and asked me to remember him to the Lord. "And I depend on your prayers also," I answered slightly facetiously, "given that I think I shall need them more."

The general impression of the conversation was that it was serene. The truth is that it was the serene contemplation of an impenetrable wall, behind which was hidden the absolute certainty that Catholics are better than other people. The events that followed made it clear.

A few weeks later, in the Catholic daily *L'Eco di Bergamo* (everyone knows that it is supported by the Curia), two articles appeared one after the other, which refuted various points made in my book. They were written by a priest who taught at the diocesan Seminary. It was the first official response on the part of the clergy. In full compliance with clerical etiquette, this colleague of mine did not think to contact me before writing against me, and therefore I did not think it appropriate to answer the heavy accusations that he leveled against me in public. Some friends showed me the articles, and I was consoled by the large number of telephone calls I received supporting my position, and lamenting that an unknown priest should want to execute his brother by filling paper with ink. Many people were in fact astonished that a priest should attack another priest so relentlessly.

On the 24th of May I received a registered letter by express mail from the Vicariate of Rome. No particular paragnostic powers were necessary to guess what it contained. I here transcribe it:

Rome, May 18, 1992. Prot. N. 447/92.

The Cardinal Camillo Ruini, Vicar-General of His Holiness John Paul II for the Diocese of Rome,

seeing that

- the Bishop of Bergamo has informed the Vicariate of Rome, in a note of December 17, 1991, that the writings, the public declarations and the - to say the least - disconcerting ideas upheld by the Priest don Mario Mazzoleni in regard to the Indian teacher Sai Baba, whose convinced follower he declares himself to be, excite significant astonishment and scandal among the faithful;

- the priest, on November 23, 1990, dedicated the book entitled *A Priest Meets Sai Baba* to "the Catholic Church," a book which, though it begins with the praiseworthy intent of seeking the action of the Spirit of God in every man and in every religious experience, ends up disavowing the truths of the Catholic faith;

- an attentive reading of the book reveals that the author has lost his Catholic faith in the Holy Trinity and in Christ as the Only Savior, and, especially in the letters addressed to a friend (pp. 210-213 and 216-217), the unicity of Christ the Savior is expressly denied;

- the assertions moreover that accept Sai Baba's claim to be a divine incarnation, that defend his works, miracles, sayings and doctrines, are grave affirmations against the faith;

- the public declarations of don Mario Mazzoleni have caused confusion and scandal because of the fact that they come from a priest who continues to exercise his ministry in the name of the Catholic Church;

- since the good faith of the writer shows clearly from the tenor of the book's dedication, it is all the more necessary to call the priest back from error with an urgent request to cease causing scandal and to return to the doctrine of the Church, invites

the Priest Mario Mazzoleni to retreat from his heretical doctrinal positions, to cease causing scandal, to explicitly retract his errors within the suitable time of three months; with the warning that if the retraction is not forthcoming the Cardinal will have to proceed to declare excommunication latae sententiae [in the broad sense] for heresy according to Canon law 1364, and subsequently to bar the priest from the exercise of the power of his office, until he returns to the Catholic doctrine.

He further invites the same priest to a personal interview on the subject in his office at the Vicariate of Rome on the day June 3, 1992 at 10 a.m., or else on June 6, 1992, at 12 noon.

Camillo Card. Ruini
Vicar-General

I took stock of the gravity of my situation, but I was not excessively upset by it. On the contrary, the cardinal's invitation to a meeting seemed like a good opportunity to speak to him about my experience, and to make Sai Baba known to these men. This has always been my only dream as a Catholic priest. I called to make an appointment, which was set for June 3, the anniversary of the death of Pope John XXIII.

Fortunately I had some friends who lent me their small apartment in Rome, given that my transportation and lodging expenses were completely on my shoulders. I was received at 11:15, after spending two hours in the waiting-room. The cardinal did not speak much, but he listened to me, examining me from behind his glasses, which rested on a thin and impenetrable face.

I felt very much at ease; I had no fear, and inside me, I constantly brought my thought to Him who holds all the threads of history. I thought about what Sai Baba often says: "See God in everyone. I disguise myself in the forms of all beings." So while the cardinal was gathering the papers of my dossier, I enjoyed picturing Sai Baba's form inside those vestments. "Your stage-directions are stupendous," I was saying to myself, and so are You! What are you doing to me now?" I felt like the spectator at a movie, in which both the cardinal and I were playing our respective roles.

On the prelate's writing desk there were a few papers, some letters from various bishops who had written to protest against me (and whom I obviously did not have the pleasure of either meeting or contacting), and my book, this time with the cover facing up. I noticed that the cardinal looked at Swami's picture for a few instants.

We spoke of many things. In order to be polite, and for fear that I would forget important points, I had transcribed in a letter to him the various things that I wanted to say when I met him. I ended up saying exactly what I had written. Here is the text of the letter:

Most Reverend Eminence,

In the present letter, I intend to entrust to writing what perhaps will come out less clearly in our meeting.

First of all I would like to express my gratitude for the attention that has been bestowed on me, and for allowing me to clarify in person the reasons for what I have done. One might say that I was anxiously awaiting this call, because, regardless of the decisions that my Superiors may make in my case, I wished to communicate to them an experience which continues to leave a beneficial mark in everyday life.

Sri Sathya Sai Baba's message is based on an unlimited ecumenism, where ecumenism does not mean the suppression of the different religions in order to make one chaotic hodge-podge religion, but rather the constant search for the points that different religions have in common. The goal of this search, as the great Master says, is that there be only one Religion, the Religion of Love.

When one studies Sai Baba's teachings, as I have been doing for 12 years, one constantly sees that his goal is not to found another religion, but rather to elevate the level of human consciousness. He does this by directing everyone who comes to him toward a life full of truth, righteousness, peace, love and non-violence. He tells the devotees who come to his ashram to put into practice intensely the fundamental principles of their respective religions. Often the people who have turned to him are not practicing any religion, or else they have strayed away from their own church. The real miracle that I see constantly repeated is the desire those people experience to return to practicing their faith.

I beg you, Eminence, let us not shut the door on these people: they are living through a rather delicate moment, and for our Church it would surely be a gesture of noble outreach, as well as practical evangelism, to include them in our fold. Sai Baba does not want new churches, he wants to fill the ones that already exist!

I know that the Church is seriously worried about the formation of new sects. But I can unconditionally guarantee that Sai Baba has given clear directives that new religious communities should not be created in opposition to the official ones. If groups of devotees gather in centers, this is to be only in order to carry out charitable works and to study Sacred Scriptures. Let me point out that a Hare Krishna or Jehovah's Witness or a Seventh-Day Adventist will never set foot in a Catholic church to participate in Sunday worship, but I assure you that there are many devotees of Sai Baba who are praying in our parish churches with renewed fervor, and that they take communion with a mystical zeal rarely found among normal Christians. Sai Baba's devotees gather once a week in order to pray and to sing, but their worship is directed toward the same God that is worshiped in the churches.

I am acquainted with all the Sathya Sai Baba Centers in Italy. Many times I have exhorted their members to simplify their exterior rituals, which derive from their sympathy for the exotic world of India, and to ask their parish priests for permission to meet in the parish church to pray and sing the praises of the Lord. Unfortunately, misunderstandings and prejudices keep them away. Nevertheless there are now many priests who contact me in order to find out more about Sai Baba and his teachings. In these last months I have received innumerable letters of appreciation, most of them from Catholics. The dissenting voices (which as always, are the noisiest) make up a tiny minority.

What grieves me most, in this whole experience that I am going through, is to see the extreme superficiality with which Sai Baba and his message are being addressed by the Church. Meanwhile millions of people of every nation, race, and religion are continually overwhelmed by his astounding greatness, and I see the most erudite and intellectual people surrender one after the other to what they have seen with their eyes and felt in their hearts.

Eminence, I do not want to get involved in defending the theological positions I have expressed in my book. I realize that they are open to discussion, and that they may be "disconcerting." Believe me, it was not at all my intention to create scandal. If this has happened, it is due to my ingenuous zeal, and I shall try to make amends.

I promise that if I am allowed to continue my ministry as a priest, I shall hold no more public lectures, nor will I give interviews to the media about Sai Baba. In all these years I have never contaminated my ministry with any theories foreign to our doctrine.

Given that the only thing that really matters to me is that our Church come to know Sai Baba in a serious way, without divisions, I declare myself available to take part in any committee that might be set up to study Sai Baba thoroughly. I am willing also to take part in any trips to visit him, as long as they are undertaken with a scientific attitude and without prejudices. It may be useful to say that I am in contact with doctors, physicists and scientists who have been studying the Sai Baba "phenomenon" for years.

Whatever measures are taken in my regard, I declare that I shall always be happy to serve the Church in any other way, through consultations or studies, because I shall always feel that I am united with Her.

> Devotedly, in the Lord.
>
> Don Mario Mazzoleni
> Rome, June 3, 1992.

When I spoke to the cardinal about Sai Baba and His Mission of Ecumenism, he interrupted me, almost worried, in order to say: "There can be no ecumenism, because the whole truth has been revealed only to Catholicism."

These words wounded me more than the threat of excommunication.

From the whole meeting I realized that my superior had not read my book, but, as he confirmed to me later, he had given it to a subordinate to read. This person had written a summary of it, which was entirely negative. Before ending our interview, I ventured to interrogate the cardinal. I asked him: "Eminence, if you had had the same experience I had, if you had encountered a being with unlimited powers, who astounds the world of science, who brings exalted figures from every branch of learning and spirituality to their knees, who performs every kind of miracle, whose very sight gives infinite peace: you, Eminence, what would you do?"

The cardinal did not answer immediately, he took some time, and then he said to me: "I would leave the position I occupy." I could not understand whether that was a suggestion directed to me, or whether it reflected an honest need to withdraw in order to think.

Towards the end of our meeting, which lasted about an hour, the prince of the church praised my intention to keep quiet; he also took note of a letter that the parish priest of my little town had written, praising me vigorously. I was to give this letter to the cardinal. Then, taking up a typewritten sheet from among his papers, he told me that it was a declaration that I could sign, and he began to read: "I, the undersigned, Mario Mazzoleni, etc..., declare that..." The cardinal stopped; he went no further in reading that text. He put the sheet back under the other papers, and he asked me to give him an answer stating my intentions, within two months exactly from the date I received the registered letter. Since I was not given the text of that abjuration, I cannot transcribe it, but I know very well how they go.

He accompanied me to the door of his study. I remembered that same study well from the days when I was living in Rome, when it was occupied by Cardinal Poletti. I kissed his hand and took the first train for Milan, immersed in many thoughts, but deep down full of peace in my heart. I was about to take another trip to India, where the Master was waiting for me, to give me the consolations that no other human being knows how to give. I decided to mail the answer before leaving, well within the time-limit set by my superiors.

Before writing, I collected myself in prayer, and asked Sai Baba to prompt me with the right words, to avoid any word that betrayed bitterness or resentment, which so easily creep in under such circumstances. Here it is:

Most Reverend Eminence,

In answer to your letter on the same subject, I hereby affirm the following:

The criticisms leveled against the book *A Priest Meets Sai Baba*, a book which that letter summarizes from a not-impartial account written by a reviewer, are stated in such a way that I am exonerated from having to present any counter-arguments, or any defense of my doctrinal positions, which are categorically declared "heretical." Such counter-arguments would, however, be necessary in any regular disciplinary process.

I take the liberty of humbly reminding you what is written in the encyclical *Dignitatis humanae*, which asserts that "everyone has the duty, and therefore the right, to seek the truth in religious matters... with a freely-conducted inquiry"; that "man receives and recognizes the commands of the divine law through his own conscience"; that "therefore he must not be compelled to act against his conscience, nor must he be prevented from acting in accordance with it, especially in religious matters." I bring to your attention, therefore, that the request to "retract explicitly" - under the pain of excommunication - is at the very least contrary to the official teaching of the Church.

As the author of the book in question, I re-affirm that I have not lost my Catholic faith. On the contrary, after my encounter with the great "Indian Master" Sri Sathya Sai Baba, I feel that I live it with greater intensity, in a spirit of real communion with all other religions. These all share the one goal of reaching the same and only God, who transcends all changing names and forms.

Between the two alternatives I am offered, either being exiled from the Institution of the Church, or else being exiled from my Conscience, I cannot and will not select the latter. Institutions do not accompany anyone beyond the grave, while the only reality that one can present to God is one's conscience. The Lord who "examines the heart" is our Judge: if in my case I have committed, or am about to commit, an error [by refusing to retract], I beg His forgiveness and the light to rectify it; if I am acting in accordance with truth, may He forgive those who condemn me.

Eternal praise be to the Christ, to Him "who was born from the Father before all ages," Him who outlives all the good and wicked actions of men, and who will never die.

AUM Shanti Shanti Shanti!

Santa Croce, July 14, 1992.
The priest Mario Mazzoleni

The date of the letter coincided with the holy day of Gurupoornima, the day devoted to one's Teacher. Sai Baba has often explained that that Master is inside the heart of each of us. I was gratified by the coincidence, and left with serenity for the East.

Although no one had told Sai Baba about my situation, He bestowed many attentions and particular favors on me. He also created a ring for me, as if to consolidate our relationship, and He put it on my left hand. Obviously He knows everything, as He demonstrated to me on numerous occasions.

Upon returning to Italy, I expected to find the decision from the Vatican, but there was no registered letter from Rome in my mail. That silence amazed me, and, I must confess, it unnerved me a little. If you must be beheaded, better today than tomorrow. Anyway, I thought, if grace is ever forthcoming from that law-court, it arrives with considerable delay, usually a matter of centuries.

Thursday, September 24, the fateful letter arrived. This time, it was a fully formal decree, printed on a sheet twice as large as the protocol, and on a yellowish parchment. At the top, in the center, there was the coat of arms of cardinal Ruini in orange ink. In accordance with tradition, it was composed of the classic cardinal's hat, red with red cords and fifteen tassels of red silk on either side. Under the hat, the personal heraldic emblem: a shield with a cross resting on an open book. At the base, there was a banner with an inscription that I thought was particularly eloquent, given my case: *Veritas liberabit nos*, "The Truth shall set us free"!

With its ribbons and tassels, the decree repeated exactly the text of the preceding letter, with only a few additions. For example, it mentioned a decision "not to postpone the matter any longer" and "to proceed to an extra-judicial decree in accordance with Canon law 1342." This was meant to excuse the writer for not having granted any possibility of a normal trial, with defense lawyers (either chosen or appointed), which is the normal procedure in ecclesiastical law. It was the procedure followed for example in the case of P. Leonard Boff, and others.

The condemnation is: excommunication *latae sententiae* for heresy, in accordance with Canon law 1364, with the penalties established in Canon law 1331. The decree concludes with the following declaration: "The above-mentioned disciplinary actions shall be in effect until the priest, with the grace of the Lord, retreats from his obstinacy and insubordination in accordance with Canon law 1347, section 2." This final explanation clarifies what is meant by *latae sententiae*, "in the broader sense."

In order that the reader may form a complete picture of the position that someone who has been excommunicated occupies, I shall give a few essential details. In fact many people who heard about what happened showed that they were not at all aware of what it meant: they confused it with a suspension "a divinis," from the divine offices, which is more common in the case of both monastic and secular clergy. I confess however that I too was unaware of many details, which I shall now present to the reader.

The *suspensio a divinis* bars one from performing any of the rites or acts he is authorized to perform through having been consecrated by his religious order. That means that a "suspended" priest can never celebrate mass, hear confessions, or administer any sacrament. He can however receive them. He is forbidden to celebrate the rites, but he can be present at them and even take part in them, as by taking communion, going to confession, etc...

Excommunication, on the other hand, is a formal action by which the superior authorities forbid a person "1) to take part in any way as a minister in celebrating the Eucharistic Sacrifice or any other ceremony of public worship; 2) to celebrate sacraments or holy rites or to receive sacraments; 3) to exercise any function in any ecclesiastical offices or ministries or duties whatsoever." In the event that the "guilty party" should not obey the aforesaid measures, "he must be driven away, or else the liturgy must be interrupted, unless some grave situation prevents it" (Canon law 1331).

It is evident, therefore, that excommunication (which can be imposed on any Catholic) excludes the condemned person from the community of the church and of the faithful. This measure can be imposed for various motives, in my case for "heresy," and the person excommunicated is considered an outcast in every sense. At one time, it (not "he") was forbidden even to enter a church, and it was forbidden to bury his remains in a Christian cemetery. Of course, until just a few centuries ago, he would end his earthly existence inside a spectacular bonfire in the town's main square.

I will pass over the financial aspects: an excommunicated priest loses any right to any kind of financial support. He is, so to speak, fired without any severance pay, any compensation or benefits, and he therefore finds himself suddenly deprived of any income.

Certain currents of thought in the Church have declared that excommunication is simply a "medicine" with which the Church seeks to "heal" the sick person, in the hope that he will return to the fold. However the question arises: if the Church has always considered the sacraments medicines through which one draws nearer to God and overcomes one's infirmities, how is this "healing" ever to take place? Is it not rather a punishment, and would it not be better to say so openly, without pretenses?

Here we have come to the end of my history as a priest. This is a chapter of my life which will now be filed away. I felt that I owed this explanation to the reader, even though the affair is no longer of any concern to me: to be suspended from certain ceremonies, said to be divine, certainly does not preclude access to the Divine. I can no longer go to Mass, no longer lose myself in the warm atmosphere of a Midnight Mass, to be moved by the sweetness of Christmas carols, but I can always speak heart-to-heart with the Lord, pray to Him, love Him, meet Him. Everyone can. Because of this, even "atheists" know how to pray. This is the real consolation, which no one will ever be able to take from me: there is not a single person in the whole world who can pry you away from God.

To belong to a religious institution does not automatically mean that one belongs to God. To be in harmony with the Divine, one must respect the conscience of every person, and listen to one's own. At that point one can say: If God is with us, who shall be against us?

"Why fear when I am here?"

Mario Mazzoleni

ESSENTIAL BIBLIOGRAPHY
FOR LEARNING ABOUT SAI BABA

A) Primary Sources

Baba's discourses are published in English and in various other languages by the *Sri Sathya Sai Books and Publications Trust,* Prashanti Nilayam P.O., Anantapur Dist., Andhra Pradesh PIN 515134. They are grouped into various series. The *Vahini* series are all written by Sathya Sai Baba himself, while the *Sathya Sai Speaks* series are a collection of His discourses held over the course of a number of years.

Bhagavatha Vahini
Dharma Vahini
Dhyana Vahini
Gita Vahini
Jnana Vahini
Prashanti Vahini
Prasnothara Vahini
Prema Vahini
Ramakatha Rasa Vahini
Sathya Sai Vahini
Upanishad Vahini
Vidya Vahini

Sandeha Nivarini - Dialogues Dissolving Doubts.
Summer Showers in Brindavan 1972
Summer Showers in Brindavan 1973
Summer Showers in Brindavan 1974
Summer Showers in Brindavan 1977
Summer Showers in Brindavan 1978
Summer Showers in Brindavan 1979
Summer Roses on the Blue Mountains 1976
Indian Culture and Spirituality, Summer Course 1990

Discourses on the Bhagavad Gita

Sathya Sai Speaks, Volumes I-XI
Voice of the Avatar - 2 volumes
Conversations with Bhagavan Sri Sathya Sai Baba
SANATHANA SARATHI, a monthly publication containing Sai Baba's recent discourses.

Note: The publication dates are variable, because these publications are constantly reprinted or re-published in new editions.

B) Biographies and Books about Sai Baba

For details of Sai Baba's life the fundamental reference is the biography written by N. Kasturi, *Sathyam Shivam Sundaram*, in 4 volumes.

Sandweiss, Samuel. *Sai Baba: The Holyman... and the Psychiatrist*. San Diego, CA: Birth Day Publishing, 1975.
Hislop, John. *Conversations with Sathya Sai Baba*. San Diego, CA: Birth Day Publishing, 1978.
_____. *My Baba and I*. San Diego, CA: Birth Day Publishing, 1985.
Murphet, Howard. *Sai Baba Avatar*. San Diego, CA: Birth Day Publishing, 1980.
_____. *Sai Baba - Man of Miracles*. York Beach, ME: Samuel Weiser, 1973.
Roof, Jonathan. *Pathways to God*. Faber, VA: Leela Press, 1991.
Krystal, Phyllis. *Sai Baba - The Ultimate Experience*. Dorset, England: Element Books, 1985.
Warner, Judy. *Transformation of the Heart*. York Beach, ME: Samuel Weiser, 1990.
Baskin, Diana. *Divine Memories*. San Diego, CA: Birth Day Publishing, 1990.

These publications may be purchased at local Sai Baba centers, in certain well-stocked bookstores, or by writing to:

Sathya Sai Book Center of America
305 West First Street
Tustin, California 92680

Sai Baba Books

ISBN 1-887906-00-2
$12.00

Sai Inner Views and Insights *by Howard Murphet.* A compelling book by one of the world's greatest storytellers. Murphet traces his experiences with Sathya Sai Baba over the past 30 years. Not only does he describe miracles vividly, but he shares his experiences and insights into Sai Baba's teachings.

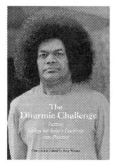

ISBN 0-9629835-6-X
$12.00

The Dharmic Challenge *by Judy Warner.* A provocative collection of stories that illustrate the difficulties of living a dharmic life. 14 Sai devotees explore different facets of dharma, such as Truth, Right Conduct, Duty and the need to be guided by conscience.

ISBN 0-9629835-8-6
$9.00

Song of My Life *by Jeannette Caruth.* A joyous and triumphant prose poem that gives the reader a vivid glimpse of the author's devotion and powerful insights into the nature of God. V.K. Narasimhan says, *No one can go through this poetic saga without feeling the thrill of a journey to God in the company of a devotee immersed in Divine Bliss.*

Sai Baba Books

ISBN 0-9629835-4-3
$12.00

Sai Baba's Mahavakya on Leadership by *Lieut Gen (Retd) Dr. M. L. Chibber* provides a blueprint for society on how to re-establish leadership inspired by idealism. A model for leadership appealing to everyone from corporate planners to government policy makers, to youth, parents and teachers.

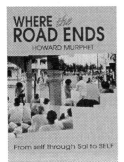

ISBN 0-9629835-3-5
$12.50

Where the Road Ends *by Howard Murphet.* Murphet's personal search for the meaning of life from childhood to old age. *After I came to Sai Baba, He gradually revealed Himself to me as God. This book attempts to show how He brings greater and deeper understanding of life's purpose and a higher degree of happiness to the individual and thereby to the life of mankind.*

ISBN 0-9629835-2-7
$7.00

Journey to Sathya Sai Baba, A Visitor's Guide *by Valmai Worthington.* A definitive guide for first time travelers to Prasanthi Nilayam. Written by an experienced Sai Baba group leader who shares the knowledge she has gained from helping hundreds of people over the last twelve years. This guidebook goes beyond providing answers to practical questions such as accommodations, food, dress and passports. It covers customs, behavior, and the subtle issues of readiness and spiritual awakening.